TICKING BOMBS
Defusing Violence in the Workplace

TICKING BOMBS
Defusing Violence in the Workplace

Michael Mantell

with Steve Albrecht

IRWIN
Professional Publishing
Burr Ridge, Illinois
New York, New York

Cover photo: Ed Pritchard/Tony Stone Images

© RICHARD D. IRWIN, INC., 1994

Senior sponsoring editor: Cynthia A. Zigmund
Project editor: Waivah Clement
Production manager: Irene H. Sotiroff
Interior designer: Mercedes Santos
Cover designer: Tim Kaage
Art coordinator: Mark Malloy
Art Studio: Electronic Publishing Services, Inc.
Compositor: TCSystems, Inc.
Typeface: 11/13 Palatino
Printer: Arcata Graphics/Kingsport

Library of Congress Cataloging-in-Publication Data

Mantell, Michael R., 1949–
   Ticking bombs : defusing violence in the workplace / Michael Mantell with Steve Albrecht.
      p.   cm.
   Includes bibliographical references and index.
   ISBN 0-7863-0189-9
   1. Violence in the workplace—United States.   2. Employee crimes—Prevention.   I. Albrecht, Steve, 1963–   .   II. Title.
HF5549.5.E43M36   1994
658.3—dc20   93–44770

Printed in the United States of America
1 2 3 4 5 6 7 8 9 0 AGK 1 0 9 8 7 6 5 4

For the victims and their families

Foreword

Violence in the workplace is one of the most complex, vexing, and frustrating problems facing American managers today. It is a recurring nightmare in companies throughout this country and around the globe. Recent statistics show that what was practically unheard of a quarter of a century ago, violence in the workplace, is now one of the fastest-growing crimes in the United States. Last year, 25 million people were victimized by fear and violence in the workplace.

No company or organization should think it is immune to having a tragedy in its workplace. It can happen. There's no excuse, nor is there any rationalization for this type of conduct.

Starting at the top, every chief executive officer, every manager, every employee must be committed to and involved with helping to find solutions to this devastating problem. The necessity for CEO involvement in this issue, in particular, was driven home vividly to me when I found myself with two workplace tragedies in Dearborn, Michigan, and Dana Point, California, last May. I will never forget the feelings I experienced after meeting the employees and family members of the victims at both locations. No one ever should have to experience such tragedies.

So what causes irrational behavior by irrational individuals? What causes some people to settle their disputes with knives, guns, or fists? I wish I had the answers, but I don't.

I do know that America needs to come to grips with this growing phenomenon. Like scores of companies and organizations, the Postal Service has not been immune to the tragedies of workplace violence. As this nation's largest civilian employer, however, I believe we can be in the forefront of public and private efforts to create meaningful and realistic plans to help prevent violent incidents—before they happen.

We are taking very proactive steps to analyze, deal with, and—to the degree possible—resolve issues before threats or assaults occur.

One very important step we have taken is the establishment of a National Committee on Violence and Behavior, which has involved management and the leadership of our unions and management associations. I believe it is critical that both labor and management work together to eliminate violence in the workplace.

In looking for some common factors that might be prevalent in violent workplace incidents, communications seems to be an area where there may be some relationship. There is a need for everyone to listen to and talk to each other and keep open the lines of communications. But sometimes communications between top management and some level of supervision going down the line, and communications filtering up from employees, somehow gets lost. That's one area that corporations must be aware of because if there are stresses in the workplace, an early warning sign could be found in this communications line.

As one of the nation's leading experts on workplace violence, Dr. Mantell has certainly made a significant contribution in this book toward helping us to better understand this tragic phenomenon. But more importantly, his book addresses specifically the central issue of how we might prevent such tragedies from occurring in the first place.

Dr. Mantell has vast experience in dealing with violence-induced trauma. He expresses in the book his firm belief that correct personnel selection procedures are the most effective way to prevent potential problems in the workplace. I congratulate Dr. Mantell for a well-documented professional book that will go a long way in helping us to find realistic solutions to preventing workplace violence.

Marvin Runyon
Postmaster General and Chief Executive Officer
United States Postal Service
Washington, DC
December 1993

Preface

Violent crime has penetrated and gripped our society. The ticking clock of crime moves swiftly throughout the day, and a pervasive fear of violence in the workplace has become the most recent threat to the way decent people live.

This book provides a step-by-step preventive approach to the chilling reality that innocent men and women are being killed, maimed, and attacked at their worksites. Recent data suggests that the number of employees who kill their bosses has *doubled* in the last 10 years. Violence in the workplace is not an invention by the ever-hungry media but an all too real and spreading American phenomenon that has reached catastrophic proportions.

It has been called an *epidemic* by those who study disgruntled employees and angry spouses and the violence they perpetrate on innocent employees. According to a recent landmark report issued by the Chicago-based National Safe Workplace Institute, in 1992 alone, 750 men and women died at the hands of rage-filled co-workers. These cases, coupled with an estimated 111,000 workplace violence incidents that did not end in death, have cost American business approximately $4.2 billion (estimating, conservatively, that each significant episode runs upwards of $250,000 in lost work time, employee medical benefits, or legal expenses).

Reputation, credibility, efficiency, morale, productivity, absenteeism, and employee turnover are the not-so-hidden costs of violence in the workplace to the employer. The other victims, workers who themselves are not necessarily physically injured, pay dearly in terms of job satisfaction, a sense of well-being, and emotional scarring that often goes unseen for months and years, only erupting later in ways that are frequently misunderstood.

The most noteworthy sites of violence in the workplace in recent times have been at branches of the US Postal Service. With 750,000 employees, the Postal Service found itself victim to over 2,000 cases of workplace violence in 1992. When projected to America's entire work force of approximately 115 million men and women, this would mean more than 300,000 acts of violence in businesses throughout the country.

One study completed by the American Psychological Association found that among *first and second graders*, 45 percent said they had witnessed muggings, 31 percent had witnessed shootings, and 39 percent said they had seen dead bodies. More Americans have been murdered already during this decade than were killed in all the years of the Vietnam war. According to the FBI, there were more than 24,000 murders in 1991 and an estimated 23,000 homicides for 1992. Is our society a violent one? You don't need to be a criminologist to figure that one out.

Charles Silberman's aphorism that "crime is as American as Jesse James" certainly is correct. What's new, however, is that violent crime is no longer restricted to urban centers and ghettos. The offices, factories, school playgrounds, post offices, fast-food restaurants, hospitals, shopping malls, hotels, grocery stores, banks, convenience stores, and in fact, nearly everywhere people are employed and business is carried out have become the latest sites for disgruntled, unhappy, desperate, often psychiatrically impaired people to vent their rage.

Time magazine, in its August 23, 1993, cover story "America the Violent: Crime Is Spreading and Patience Is Running Out," summarized this by noting that "No place is sacred. All sanctuaries are suspect."

It is time for American business to recognize the critical role it must play in helping to prevent violence in the workplace and to protect the safety and security of its personnel at least as well as it does its products, recipes, documentation, and equipment.

This book provides a *practical, realistic, and cost-effective* blueprint for that effort. Our approach has been framed as the *benchmark for defusing violence in the workplace*. We offer a seven-step model (see accompanying illustration) that goes full-circle and encompasses all of the visible and invisible factors surrounding this problem, including:

1. Preemployment screening.
2. Informed, aware management trained to see the early-warning signs.

Seven-Step Workplace Violence Prevention Model

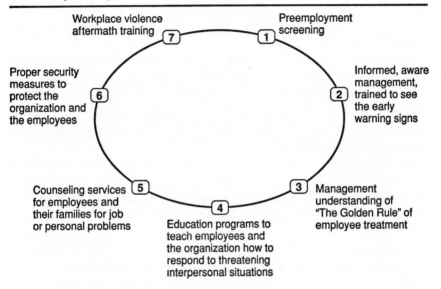

3. Management understanding of the Golden Rule of employee treatment.
4. Education programs to teach employees and the organization how to respond to threatening interpersonal situations.
5. Counseling services for employees and their families for job or personal problems.
6. Proper security measures to protect the organization and the employees.
7. Workplace violence aftermath training.

Our seven-step model, when applied, doesn't guarantee that workplace violence will never happen. No approach can provide such a promise. After all, even with Secret Service protection, the finest in the world, presidents of the United States are still attacked and even gunned down.

But this model and this book will arm you with the kind of *ready-to-use information* and understanding you'll need today; *safe* hiring, discipline, and termination practices; the *tools and tactics* you'll need to identify and reduce your vulnerability to enraged, explosive, or disgruntled employees; the *policies and procedures* you'll need to deal with the aftermath of violence should it, God forbid, occur; and the methods you'll need to effectively *secure your business operation.*

The single biggest deterrent to violence in the workplace is careful hiring. While not every business can employ an industrial or personnel psychologist, nevertheless, equipped with the material we provide in our chapter on the hiring process, you can cast a better net to prevent access by applicants who are "ticking bombs" waiting to explode in your company.

A second deterrent is a supervisory team, from one to several thousands, who are buoyed by the knowledge of the early-warning signs of emotional upset. Once skilled in identifying these indicators, they can take the proper intervention steps to deal with problems before they become invasive and malignant. Chapter 4, on picking out who may be a perpetrator of violence in the workplace, will provide the necessary information for any supervisor to feel more confident in this new era of disgruntled employees.

The Golden Rule of employee management—Treat your people as you would like to be treated—is discussed in Chapter 6 as a method for executives, managers, and supervisors to design improved ways of dealing with employees. While we take a strong position that management is often the victim—not the villain—in acts of violence, still, there are identifiable behaviors that you can take to improve employee treatment and reduce the risk of violence occurring "on your watch."

Steve Albrecht's extensive interview with convicted workplace murderer Robert Earl Mack is one of the centerpieces of the book. Mack's story is both chilling and thought provoking, as he discusses why and how he took the life of one man and critically wounded another at his worksite. There are many lessons to be learned from his actions.

We also describe the importance of educational programs aimed at teaching employees how to respond to conflict-based interpersonal situations. Recognizing that American culture accepts and glamorizes violent solutions to everyday problems, that young people are exposed to more and more violence in their daily lives and in the media, and that many people have had poor role models from whom to learn healthy ways of resolving conflict, US business is left holding the bag. It will need to become the educator of last resort.

We discuss in great detail methods for safely disciplining and terminating employees, the two most common and immediate sources of perceived provocation by disgruntled employees who commit violent acts. We provide you with clearly stated steps for reduced-risk discipline and safe termination procedures.

Finally, one of the particularly unique aspects of this book is Chapter 8 on protecting your physical and human assets, from a corporate security expert's perspective. Ira A. Lipman, chairman of the board and president of Guardsmark, Inc., which best-selling management author Tom Peters described as "the Tiffany of security firms," contributes a definitive piece of work on practical methods businesses can use to protect the security of their people and property. This chapter stands by itself as a "must read" for every businessperson in America concerned with issues of safety and security.

Violence in the workplace won't go away because you and your staff read this book. You may be able to rest easier, though, knowing that after you've gained the knowledge and used the tools we teach, you, your staff, your co-workers, and your organization will be better equipped to defuse the ticking bombs that might have otherwise exploded in your workplace.

Michael Mantell

Acknowledgments

Michael Mantell

This book is based on nearly two decades of work with corporations, management teams, unions, and grass-roots employees, all victims of perpetrators of violence in the workplace. I am sincerely indebted to these men and women for the privilege of working with them, and for allowing me, through this work, to gain the expertise I have in this field.

From McDonald's to General Dynamics Corporation, from Rohr Industries to US post offices around the country, from banks, schools, shopping malls, and hospitals to supermarkets, television stations, hotels, and manufacturing plants nationwide, the human resource managers, employees, and direct victims of violence have all, in their own way, contributed to this effort.

I would especially like to acknowledge Kenneth H. Vlietsra, Executive Director of the National Association of Postmasters of the United States, for his insights and guidance in dealing with the alarming rate of violence in the US Postal Service.

A very special gentleman, Ira A. Lipman, Chairman of the Board and President of Guardsmark, Inc., deserves my special appreciation for all his time and support, in addition to the very pivotal contribution he made to this work. His chapter on security measures, Chapter 8, has added a very significant dimension to the book, and one that I am certain will be personally invaluable to every reader.

I would also like to acknowledge Tom Graves, Cathy Dice, and Neil Solomon from Guardsmark, Inc., for their very special assistance with this project. Their expertise in corporate security has also been most beneficial and adds to the practical usefulness of the book.

Having served as chief psychologist for the San Diego Police Department and consultant to dozens of law enforcement agencies, civilian and military, for more than a decade, I want to acknowledge the men and women in these agencies throughout the country. They have contributed in many ways to my understanding of the spread of violence in this nation.

The many television, radio, newspaper, and magazine interviewers who have picked my brain over the years on this topic also deserve special mention. By interviewing me, they have helped me sharpen my thinking and dig deeper for facts and figures, and have prodded me to write this book. The staff of "Good Morning, America," and "Nightline," in particular, deserve my special appreciation.

I would like to express my appreciation to my coauthor Steve Albrecht for all of his patience with my schedule of patients. He has contributed very meaningfully to this project, not only in terms of his writing skills, but also with his sensitivity to the victims and their stories.

My secretary Stacy Cooper, the finest anyone could be blessed with, has been of tremendous value to me during this project. Let's hope this doesn't go to her head—though it would certainly be well-deserved if it did.

My family, naturally, requires special mention and appreciation for all of their support, encouragement, and patience. My wife Paula and my two sons Ben and Jonathan are most precious to me, and I thank them for all they have done in helping me grow personally and professionally.

My late mother and father, Edith and Sol, were the guiding force in my life. I miss each of them more than I could ever describe. I am certain they would have been proud of this work, and ultimately, I dedicate it to their memory. They taught me the value of human life and the importance of helping others.

I pray this book will prevent further violence from taking place, and in so doing, improve the overall quality of life in this country. With God's help, may it be so.

Acknowledgments

Steve Albrecht

A book of this magnitude requires a tremendous amount of synergistic effort. Thankfully, two authors can do about four times as much work if they have healthy quantities of help from the people you see listed below:

Thanks first to Major Garrett, Capitol Hill reporter for the *Washington Times*, for his 20-year friendship and help with the research phase of the workplace violence incidents across the country.

To Solange Brooks, from the Sacramento office of the California Department of Corrections (CDC), for her assistance with the Robert Earl Mack prison interview. And to Terri Knight, Director of Communications at the CDC San Luis Obispo Men's Colony, for her courtesy while I met with Mr. Mack.

I'm grateful to Dr. George Bryjak, Professor of Sociology, University of San Diego, for his insights into some of the causes of violence in the workplace.

Thanks to Jack Gordon, Editor of *Training* magazine, for his early support of the book project, and to *Training* reporter Robert Filipczak for his July 1993 story of our topic. Similar thanks to Patricia Galagan, Editor of the *American Society of Training & Development Journal*, for her encouragement.

David Klinghoffer, Literary Editor for *National Review* magazine, gets a gold star for the best title of a workplace violence article we've ever seen—"Fired! Ready! Aim!"

Secure thanks to experts Ron Davis, Director of Security, General Dynamics Space Systems Division, and Willard S. Cushman, Director of Security, Titan Corporation, for their knowledge and expertise.

Regards to labor attorney David Little, for his help with sticky employment issues as they relate to hiring and termination decisions.

I'm also quite grateful to *San Diego Union-Tribune* reporter Tom Blair for his thoughtfulness and inclusion of our book in his columns.

Sincere thanks to Tom Erickson, Vice President of Human Resources, Elgar Corporation, for allowing me to tread over old and surely painful ground regarding the shooting incident that claimed two lives at his plant.

A salute to Al Menear, jack-of-all-trades at *Police & Security News*, for his help with security industry contacts.

Thanks to Irwin Professional Publishing pros Cynthia Zigmund, Senior Editor, and Jeff Krames, Editor-in-Chief, for their publishing acumen and seerlike vision.

Love to my parents, best-selling business book author Karl Albrecht, for his support, direction, and quiet leadership, and Eileen Hodes, for her durability and stamina when it came time to transcribe the 1½-hour Robert Earl Mack prison interview.

Thanks finally to my wife Leslie, who had the good grace to give birth to our daughter Carly while I was trying to do the same thing with this book.

Contents

Chapter One

Workplace Violence: Can It Happen Here?

For those of us who have worked all of our teenage, young adult, and older adult lives—probably every reader of this book—the fact that the workplace is no longer a safe haven is hard to accept. To now have to factor workplace violence into our rock-solid beliefs about what work is and what our jobs do for us is almost unfathomable.

"Do you mean I have to worry about whether some employee I just fired will get a gun and come back and kill me?" wonders one plant supervisor from a furniture manufacturing company in North Carolina.

"Are you saying that if I suspend a worker for breaking work rules, he may come after me?" asks a personnel manager for a New England-based shipyard.

"Will I have to institute new security policies to protect my company and my people from other disgruntled employees?" wonders the owner of a small and growing accounting business in Seattle, Washington.

The simple answer to these highly disturbing questions is yes. What was unimaginable 20 years ago is now a cold, hard reality. But while the answer is simple, the solutions are not. This book will serve to guide you in a safe direction as we look to inform, educate, and force you to change the way you now do business.

We believe the information contained in these pages now falls into the "need to know" category. No matter how safe you think your company is or no matter how friendly and nice your employees appear to be, and no matter how good your labor–management relations are, this problem is growing and escalating at an alarming rate.

A survey conducted by the Pinkerton Security Service asked 100 security directors from Fortune 500 companies to rate their top 10 concerns. Two years ago, workplace violence wasn't even on the list. Today, it has moved to sixth place.

Our goal is to offer a conclusive model to prevent the continuing spread of this occupational workplace violence. And what you will read in this book is not found in any current management textbook. You won't see it in any of the old standard personnel handbooks. Nor will you find it taught in any MBA program. Few business school professors lecture on the topic for one good reason: *Workplace violence has never been a prominent business or social issue until now.*

Most senior managers and executives will admit they know of specific incidents of workplace violence; yet, they don't know how to deal with the instigators, the victims, and the related business, legal, and emotional problems their organizations face as a whole. They see these events taking place at other companies, on the TV news, in the newspapers, or even in their own firms, and they want answers.

In addition to a full-scale model for prevention, deterrence, and control, this book offers a clarion call for a hard look at a problem that has continued to grow at exponentially alarming rates over the last 10 years. We will offer a readily available solution for a frightening business problem that was virtually unheard of until the late 1970s and has now since tripled in incidents.

We realize the subject is timely, current, and filled with hidden hazards. Workplace violence has grown and evolved from an "underground" problem for business into a substantial hazard, not just for the 90s but well into the next century.

Some of what you will find here comes straight from the daily newspapers and right off the evening news. The workplace violence stories from across this nation read like a grisly who's who of injury and death on the job.

- A San Diego, California, General Dynamics plant worker, Robert Mack (whose exclusive interview with the authors appears in Chapter 5 of this book), shot and killed his supervisor and wounded an industrial relations representative when he was fired after 25 years on the job.
- A former Universal Studios driver, who thought his old firm had blackballed him, fired 36 shots into the Los

Angeles, California, MCA/Universal Studios headquarters. He injured seven people.

- A disgruntled supermarket employee shot and killed one person and wounded another at the store where he worked in Wilmington, North Carolina. Police killed him at the scene.
- A fired Dallas, Texas, car-rental employee came back to the agency and shot his ex-girlfriend and the office manager, wounding them both before taking his own life.
- A gunman in Kenosha, Wisconsin, who left a video tape saying the "world had done him wrong," opened fire at a McDonald's restaurant, killing two people and wounding another before turning the gun on himself.
- A woman in a Corona, California, hospital opened fire with a .38-calibre handgun, wounding a nurse and spraying the infant nursery with bullets. Before she was arrested, she told the horrified hospital workers, "Prepare to die."
- A fired Mount Pleasant, Michigan, sports editor used a pair of scissors to stab his boss in the head.
- A former IBM lab worker in San Jose, California, set fire to his former supervisor's house and office. Not surprisingly, the two fires came after years of threatening phone calls and letters.
- A Tampa, Florida, man returned to his former workplace and shot three of his supervisors as they sat eating their lunches. He wounded two others before killing himself.
- A San Diego, California, electronics worker for Ketema, Inc., suspended for a sexual harassment claim, left the plant with a gun and ended up wounding a female highway patrol officer before killing himself. (The human resources director for the company had been interviewed in the local newspaper about violence in the workplace only a year earlier.)
- An upset female worker at a Bennington, Vermont, battery plant shot and killed the plant manager and wounded two others after first trying to set the plant on fire.
- A terminated Woodlawn, Maryland, car mechanic came back to the garage and fired into a crowd of workers, killing two and wounding one.

- A Sunnyvale, California, worker at a defense contractor shot and killed seven people in the office after a female co-worker turned down his romantic advances.
- A Tustin, California, chemical worker stabbed two of his supervisors, one fatally, after they called him into their office to fire him.
- An 18-year employee of a print shop in Arkansas was put on disability leave for "mental instability." He returned to work with a gun and started shooting. In the end, he killed 8 people and wounded 12. Surviving victims said he "felt like everyone was against him and he wanted revenge against the owners and the supervisors."

Unfortunately, these stories only scratch the surface of the problem. There are countless other workplace violence incidents that take place every day and involve fists and feet, threats and intimidation, and fear and terror. Estimates from labor experts point to as many as 111,000 serious acts of violence on the job per year. These are not always the heralded "Fired employee goes on rampage with gun" that people usually associate with the subject of workplace violence, but disturbed workers who resort to other types of physical or emotional violence as well.

By the time a workplace violence incident makes the newspapers, it has usually escalated from a small problem to a fatal one. Just in the course of writing this book, we have heard of nearly one dozen homicide incidents across the country. The problem continues to eat at our social fabric like a never-ending cancer.

THE MYTH OF THE SAFE WORKPLACE

We're here to say there is no workplace that is entirely safe in the United States.

In fact, we're certain that the vast majority of working adults have either witnessed episodes of workplace violence in their own companies, heard about workplace violence problems from among their friends, peers, and colleagues who work at other firms, or seen or heard of dozens of workplace violence incidents on the TV news or in their newspapers. It's that prevalent.

The Southland Corporation, the parent company for the sprawling 7-Eleven convenience store chain, has told its employees—themselves frequent victims of violence in the workplace—"not to assume that the workplace is any safer than the rest of the world." In other words, "We'll do our best to protect you and the store from an armed robber or other violent intruder, but there are just no guaranties."

DEFINING OUR CONTENT

Before we can talk about what this book is, we need to spend a little time telling you what it is not.

While this book certainly deals with personnel issues—hiring, the culture of the company, discipline, termination, and so on—it is not a personnel manual. The subject of how to hire and fire has been covered quite extensively, and there are a number of good business books on the subject.

Our approach to the personnel side of workplace violence starts with what we know about problem employees. In many documented workplace violence incidents, the instigator has shown a number of warning signs prior to taking action. Many of those warnings appeared first during the interview process and continued to build in severity throughout the person's employment. We will offer a prescription for safe, legal, and effective screening, interviewing, and hiring to help you avoid the employee who exhibits the greatest potential for violence in the workplace.

Labor law is like quicksand mired inside a tar pit: It's slippery and sticky at the same time. With new legislation arriving to negate old hiring practices, affirmative action and equal employment laws changing with each new presidential administration, it's often hard to get a firm handle on how to hire someone.

Moreover, it's more than a bit nerve-wracking to know how *not* to hire someone who applies at your company. With many legal caveats in mind, we will address hiring issues from a more psychological perspective. What clues does the person who applies at your company give to you during the interview? What verbal or nonverbal messages can you pick up from the responses, either written or given in person? What can a careful background check or a review of the job application tell you?

While we don't seek to make you a labor law expert, we do want to offer new ways to look at an age-old problem: How do you hire good people and keep them? For more help, consult with your local experts who will know how to keep you from making legal or ethical mistakes.

And although the senior author is a nationally known psychologist and one of the leading experts on violence in the workplace in this country, this book is not a collection of "Tales from the Psychologist's Couch." You won't find any jargon-filled, deep forays into the inner workings of the human mind. Instead, we focus on practical applications based on years of research, interviews, counseling sessions, and evaluations of employees from all walks of life.

Thanks to news headlines, TV talk shows devoted to the problem, and business press articles focusing on homicidal employees, the many facets of workplace violence as a topic are constantly changing. Unlike many of the other new management issues—total quality service, teams, employee empowerment, reengineering, and change leadership—which all have a definitive beginning, middle, and end to them, the nature and scope of our topic changes every day. As more and more people experience episodes of violence in the workplace, however large or small, the problem—and more importantly, our responses as businesspeople—changes as well.

Although each of these new episodes of workplace violence are tragic, they do serve one positive purpose: We can learn from the pain of others. Each shooting or serious assault can give us new insights into what went wrong, how each organization reacted to the event afterwards, and how we may all prevent this kind of problem from ever happening again.

THE ROLE OF THE MEDIA

Thanks to speed-of-light news broadcasts, we now hear of the latest workplace violence incident within hours of its occurrence. The May 6, 1993, post office shootings in both Dearborn, Michigan, and Dana Point, California, were on our TV screens immediately. As happens in similar events, the media leapt into action and prepared lengthy profile pieces, in print and on TV, about this problem. The US Postal Service, long known as the "leader" in these types of workplace violence incidents, bears much of the brunt of these profiles.

With regards to the newest round of postal worker violence, the media dug into their collective archives and pointed to other episodes at other post offices. For two weeks after these shootings, stories appeared daily. Experts from psychological, legal, labor, and personnel fields readily offered their opinions and advice. With so much information about this subject bombarding readers and viewers, people were ready to connect violence in the workplace with everything from the New York World Trade Center bombing to the Navy *Tailhook* scandal.

But as we know from our observations of presidential campaigns, wars, and other significant news events involving tragedy, suffering, or personal discomfort, the media has a different agenda than just reporting the news. It doesn't just "report" the news; many times, it seems to create it.

As much as the newspapers in this country like to say they are in the news-gathering business, the more succinct reason for their existence is as profit-making entities. You make profits by selling plenty of newspapers. If you can't do it all with the classifieds, food store coupons, and space ads, you must do it with sensational news stories that stimulate your readers to buy copies.

And as much as the network and local TV news groups want you to believe they are on a mission to reveal the truth and inform and educate you as to the happenings of the world, their main goal is to run a profitable operation. Since we don't pay for the privilege of watching network TV, they must do it with commercial advertising sales. The way to get the average person to watch the commercials interspaced between the news is to make the news less dry and more entertaining. The TV set—whether it features your favorite "Cheers" rerun or Dan Rather and Connie Chung—is an entertainment device.

Disturbing stories about violence in the workplace help the newspapers and the networks to sell, sell, sell. "Here's yet another workplace violence incident to shock you, raise your apprehension level about your own workplace, and force you to tune in to hear the reasons how and why it happened."

More and more executives, managers, supervisors, and company owners are recognizing the problem and want solutions that can be put in effect immediately. "No one," says a wary executive, "wants to see their company parking lot surrounded in police crime scene tape and part of the lead story on the evening news."

And while this is not a "doom and gloom" book filled with one workplace horror story after another, we will discuss specific incidents not with the intent of pointing fingers and looking for likely companies, policies, or people to accept the blame but to give you illustrations that can be used as learning experiences. It's easy and provocative to talk about the decline of human values, how the good old American work force is not what it used to be, how big business treats employees like dirt and is only concerned with profits, and how society is really to blame for the murderous events taking place in our offices, on our factory floors, and on our parking lots. But finger-pointing doesn't solve problems; only actions will.

THE VILLAIN AS VICTIM

Here is exactly where our book parts company with other new workplace violence texts. We do *not* blame the victim—whether it's a company or an individual employee—for the murderous action of a disgruntled employee. Under no circumstances should you infer that we are blaming an organization for something a disturbed employee did against it.

With hope, this book will address some misconceptions you have about what workplace violence is and who is ultimately to blame. The disgruntled employee, who goes home and loads his gun, is ultimately responsible for his murderous act.

All too often, the media is quick to jump aboard the victim-bashing bandwagon. These stories often include the telling phrase, "If only XYZ Company had done this or offered that, maybe this whole tragedy could have been avoided."

We strongly disagree with this line of thinking. No company or supervisor, no matter how unjust, inflexible, or ineffective, went home and loaded the bullets into a homicidal worker's gun. *The victim is not the villain.* The choice these deranged people made was strictly and ultimately their own. It will be our contention throughout this book that although every organization should certainly look closely at its policies and the way it treats its employees, the person who commits these crimes, no matter how minor or catastrophic, holds the final responsibility.

Following the May 1993 post office shootings in Dearborn and Dana Point, Dr. Mantell once again found himself innundated with requests from the media for interviews. During one with NBC Radio, the reporter asked, "What's going on at the post office? What policies and procedures have to be changed to prevent this from happening again?" Dr. Mantell pointed out to the reporter that the question he just asked implied that he believed the US post office is at fault for the shootings. For CBS Radio, another reporter offered the same question, "Isn't the post office at fault?"

Clearly, the media's implication from the start is that there is obviously something "wrong" with the post office. We'll certainly agree that the post office—like any other organization—can and should do things differently to make the work less stressful and the facilities more psychologically beneficial places to work, but even if it *does not*, that doesn't make the post office responsible for the murder of one of its employees.

Referring, as one media report did, to the US post office as "America's newest shooting gallery" not only clouds the issue with hysteria but continues to point the finger of blame in the wrong direction.

Which leads to another misconception about workplace violence, relating to the victim. The "victim" is not just the person who was shot, assaulted, battered, or intimidated. The actual concentric circle of victimhood is much larger than most people might think. Especially after a workplace murder, the tendency is to focus solely on the dead person and his or her inner circle and forget everyone else nearby.

Other victims include the victim's family and friends; his or her co-workers; the eyewitnesses and nearby neighbors, who may not even work for the company; and the supervisors, managers, and executives of the firm where the incident took place. And it doesn't just stop there. If the incident involves murder, then the city where the incident took place is also a victim of the crime. The *victim* of workplace violence is a much broader category than most people realize.

When Marvin Runyon, postmaster general during the Dearborn, Michigan, and Dana Point, California, post office shootings, journeyed from his office in Washington, DC, to the California death site, he said he wanted to provide comfort and counsel to his people there. Admirable, yes, but what about the workers in the Omaha, Nebraska, post office or the Jacksonville, Florida, post office, or the Seattle, Washington, post office? What is being done for them, the "other victims" in the California and Michigan cases? Only by broadening our definition of both workplace violence and the workplace violence victim can we learn how to help everyone involved.

This book is *not* just another "nut with a gun at work" study. While sensational at-work crime sprees may sell newspapers and TV time, workplace homicides are only one part of our overall look at violence on the job. And while homicide is indeed a critical part of the problem, it is only one entry in an entirely larger series of issues—that is, how to recognize problem employees before you hire them, how to recognize their symptoms and danger signs once on the job, how to change negative behaviors, how to discipline or terminate those employees who act out with aggressive behavior, and how to safely and legally protect the many valuable assets—tangible and intangible—that make up the company. We will examine many types of workplace violence at all these levels.

THE PERCEPTION OF WORKPLACE VIOLENCE

Times are changing, and the workplace is just not as safe as we once thought. What used to be a rare occurrence has now become not only more commonplace but has even fallen into that rare category of significant life issues that people almost take for granted. While a new episode of post office violence makes front page headlines after it happens, where does the "Disgruntled employee kills boss" story now appear? In most large city newspapers, that story has become a filler on page 22.

We have already steeled ourselves to look at street crime murders with relative nonchalance and the feeling that, "If I don't know the victim or it didn't happen in my neighborhood, I'm not going to invest a lot of emotional energy in the problem."

In an article in *National Review,* literary editor David Klinghoffer says it correctly: "The phrase—'disgruntled employee'—strikes fear into the heart of law-abiding Americans. It has become almost commonplace for the worker with a grievance to take a gun (or guns), show up at the office, and shoot everybody. Indeed the single word 'disgruntled,' . . . is all you need to hear to know that something terrible has happened."[1]

Our hope is that this book will force businesspeople to address what is a growing, controversial problem and one that will continue to flourish unless certain steps are taken to protect potential victims, offer counseling to the survivors, isolate and if necessary punish instigators, and keep companies up and running.

Further, we will examine the changing culture in the workplace that often says, "It's okay to hit your boss" or the *entitled* employee who says "This company *owes* me something and if I don't get it, I'm going to act out my frustrations."

Like children who hit their teachers, employees who assault their supervisors or co-workers don't feel the same social stigma anymore. It has become "normal" to see workplace violence.

NATIONAL STATISTICS—STARTLING AND INCOMPLETE

If you've only given a little thought to the subject of violence in the workplace, it's time to update your perceptions. From a national perspective, the problem is very real. Just ask the families, friends, and co-workers of the estimated 1,400 people who are killed each year at work across the country.

According to an in-depth study conducted by the National Institute of Occupational Safety and Health from 1980 to 1988, homicides at work accounted for about 12 percent of job-related deaths.

In California, a state known for its population diversity and progressiveness, one in five on-the-job deaths was a homicide. According to records kept by the California Department of Health

Services, 154 employees, customers, and visitors were slain at the workplace in 1991. This figure represents 20 percent of all workplace deaths.

In New York City, US Bureau of Labor Statistics tell us that workplace homicides accounted for almost 70 percent of the 177 work-related deaths in 1991. This makes death by murder the number-one cause of death at work in New York City, as a follow-up *New York Times* piece was so quick to point out.

As Samuel Ehrehalt, the bureau's regional commissioner, so aptly puts it, "It suggests that if people here were not getting killed on the job in homicides, we would have quite a low rate of fatalities."[2]

The national media likes to roll out the workplace violence statistics like Easter eggs across the White House lawn. The headline "Murder on the Job Now the Third Leading Cause of Occupational Death" can only serve to strike fear in the hearts of anyone who works for a living. It's no longer possible to ignore this problem. Whether you own a business, work for a company, or just interact with people in other companies, no matter the size, you are a potential victim of workplace violence.

In studies of workplace violence in 32 states, 14 percent of all deaths on the job were caused by homicides. The statistical perspective is startling. Of every 100 people who died while at work, 14 of them were killed by some "one" rather than by some "thing."

Still, while vast quantities of statistics are bandied about by all sorts of sources, the validity can range from accurate to farfetched. Typically, some of the raw numbers for workplace violence incidents are skewed by several factors. As with many new problems, the federal government needs time to change its data collection and management techniques. And since individual states vary in the way they categorize these events, reporting procedures for these episodes can become quite murky.

A similar example comes from the FBI, which keeps track of seven major crimes in its Uniform Crime Reports (UCR). This group of felonies—murder, assault, rape, robbery, burglary, theft, and auto theft—is thrown together into a mishmash that the reader must then interpret and make sense from.

In his criminology textbook *Crime in American Society*, author Charles McCaghy says, "Are the Uniform Crime Reports worth anything? Yes, if you do not expect too much from them. They are published under the title 'Crime in the United States,' an exercise in wishful thinking. A more appropriate title would be: 'Crime Reported to and Observed by Police Which They Have Seen Fit to Officially Record,' but that would be too long and not very inspiring."[3]

His point is that about 87 percent of all crimes are reported to the police by victims or other observers, which means the police actually see about 13 percent of all crimes themselves. So for all its heft and importance, the FBI's UCR is merely a record of crimes they *know* about. And so it goes with workplace violence.

For all the at-work cases the police do find out about, there are certainly thousands they know nothing of. This is not to say that workplace homicides go unreported, since we know they do not, but rather, all of the other less severe (but equally important) workplace violence cases too often fall by the side.

And while underreporting is a major obstacle to accurate workplace crime data, miscategorizing the data is just as bad. Violence in the workplace as a crime faces the same reporting problem as another new and frightening event: carjacking.

Carjacking is on the rise primarily because today's criminals are more aggressive and car security systems are more sophisticated. The average car thief has already realized that he cannot easily defeat the alarms, steering wheel locks, or engine kill switches attached to many cars.

"Why waste time," he reasons, "on complex security devices when I can just wait for the owner to show up and let me steal the car at gunpoint?" Why indeed. Carjacking has become a crime of opportunity based on need. The difficulty with this crime, in addition to catching the crooks responsible for this evil mixture of violence and theft, also lies in the way it's reported.

Some criminal justice agencies—local police, prosecutors, state CJ divisions, federal justice groups, and so on—classify carjacking as a "robbery" and still others classify it as an "auto theft." You can see how this creates confusion and problems relating to underreporting and overreporting the number of incidents. Is carjacking a crime of robbery? Yes. Is carjacking a crime of auto theft? Yes again. But since there is no standard of classification for the crime, the statistics for carjacking are hard to fathom.

Does a rise in the local robbery rates indicate an increase in the crime of carjacking? Or does a rise in the auto theft rate mean carjacking is also on the increase? Who can accurately say? With these kinds of reporting problems, police agencies can find themselves having a hard time knowing how and where to allocate their personnel to best combat the problem.

The statistics surrounding violence in the workplace suffer from the same reporting problems. Much of the attention surrounding the problem focuses primarily on murder rates while on the job. While this certainly represents the epitome of the problem, it also underreports the entirety of the problem. National statistics are noticeably absent when it comes to assaults at the workplace, vandalism, sabotage, threats, or batteries involving severe injuries.

Most reports coming from the government—via the Department of Health and Human Services, the Department of Labor, the Center for Disease Control, the Department of Justice, or state and federal Occupational Safety and Health Administration (OSHA) offices—center on murder as the third leading cause of death on the job. Murder, as it relates to workplace violence, is now the hot topic.

But what about other less invasive workplace violence issues? Where is the statistical data for the hidden costs of workplace violence? There can be significant dollar costs stemming from the civil suits; the rising insurance rates for workers' compensation, health insurance, and physical plant protection; the lost productivity; the sick days taken by highly stressed employees; the fear that causes avoidance, apathy, or near immobility seen in frightened co-workers; or the significant financial damage one out-of-control employee can wreak on a company that cannot get a handle on his behavior.

Since violence in the workplace is such a new problem, the hard data gleaned from raw numbers just doesn't exist in highly organized forms. The reports generated at the federal and state level tend to focus on portions of the overall problem—that is, specific job categories, regions of the country, or demographic information. And the statistical information quoted by the media ranges from cautiously optimistic to wildly overreaching. Good, verifiable statistics for workplace violence are just hard to come by. And while this doesn't necessarily hinder our look at the problem, it does force us to make certain assumptions based on what we do know.

DRUG AND ALCOHOL ABUSE PARALLELS

In many respects, the topic of violence in the workplace follows the same sort of business time line as drug and alcohol abuse on the job did at the start of the 1980s. And, at least from a statistical standpoint, drug and alcohol abuse was also underreported or poorly classified in terms of its impact on the labor force. The government could offer reams of reports for drug abuse on the streets, but—like violence on the job—the numbers were not as easily applied to the workplace.

The reasons for this are the same, no matter which problem you want to analyze. Drug and alcohol abuse and workplace violence tend to be "secret" problems, ones that most businesses don't feel the need to make public. "No one," says one executive, "wants customers to think their company is full of drug abusers or overly aggressive or disgruntled nuts. It can make for a bad image."

This is hardly a surprising viewpoint. Certainly the image of the US Postal Service suffers each time it experiences a significant workplace violence incident. People read of these episodes and talk among themselves, "Another one! What's going on over there?"

With companies hesitant to declare drug or alcohol abuse problems among their employees, it's no wonder the statistical data is sketchy. Problems surrounding workplace violence can create the same closed-mouth tendencies.

Whereas in the old days, employee drug or alcohol problems were typically dealt with in an ostrich-like, "head in the sand" fashion, today, it's much more common and even accepted as one of many problems people may have in their lives.

Instead of quietly disposing of substance abusing employees—common practice in our less enlightened times—we now encourage them to seek medical treatment, attend counseling, or go to 12-step programs. In short, as business leaders, we actively try to intervene in these employees' lives. Using employee assistance programs (EAPs) and the promise—thanks in part to the new Americans with Disabilities Act (ADA)—of job security, we try to reshape these negative behaviors and make the employee a better person first and a better worker after that.

Before, we used to "scrapheap" (as one cynical executive puts it) these kinds of so-called problem employees. Now, their treatment and return to the workplace is increasingly more important. In the past, executives and personnel administrators felt quite uncomfortable having to deal with drug- or alcohol-dependent employees and all their related problems.

This new workplace violence problem, like drug and alcohol abuse on the job, has only recently been officially recognized or documented. Government and criminal justice agencies are only now starting to see workplace violence as a growing concern for business. In the past, their recordkeeping for these kinds of events had been at best, spotty, and at worst, nonexistent.

And like drug and alcohol problems, violence on the job can have a "swept under the carpet" ring to it, since many companies aren't thrilled with the negative publicity these events—large or small—can bring.

In some circles, like professional sports or in the entertainment industry, it's almost fashionable to admit to a drug or alcohol problem. The prevalence of treatment programs, where admitting your problem freely is part of the cure, has made this much more acceptable. When the problem came out into the open, it also became easier to solve. Thanks to a more intense focus from the mainstream media and the business press, drug and alcohol abuse at work is now perceived as a problem business can conquer.

Given the right resources, the proper exposure as a "must solve" problem, and a top to bottom commitment from the business owners, executives, managers, supervisors, and workers, workplace violence can become our next significant business problem to solve.

THE BUSINESS READERSHIP

The fact that you're reading this book indicates you have some interest in this problem. Looking at your own life and the places where you've worked, what kinds of things have happened to cause you to think more about violence in the workplace?

Have you been involved in a workplace violence episode of some magnitude? Have you only seen accounts of workplace violence on TV or in the news, and you're now trying to make some connections to your own company? Are you an executive familiar with this problem? A supervisor who has had threats made against your life? A manager of one or more potentially disturbed employees?

We start by defining violence in the workplace in its broadest terms, not in its narrowest. Ask the following question and answer first for yourself and then for your company: Have I or my company ever been the victim of violence in the workplace? You have if anyone you work with or for has ever:

- Punched a supervisor.
- Intimidated another employee with a threat of assault.
- Tampered with your computer system.
- Shot one of your employees.
- Vandalized your employee restrooms on a repeated basis.
- Returned to your company and stabbed an employee.
- Sent threatening letters or faxes to people in the company.
- Slashed the tires of cars in your parking lot.
- Killed themselves in or near your facility.
- Returned to your workplace as a disgruntled customer and killed someone.

For the most part, we believe people are too quick to say, "Well, we really haven't had any violence in the workplace. No one got shot or beat up or anything major like that."

"How about your office typewriters or your office equipment?" we would continue. "Has anyone ever deliberately damaged your keyboards, copy machines, fax machines, or postage meters?" We contend, under our broad definition, that those acts are covert violence in the workplace, too.

It ranges from the hostile union employee who assaults his management supervisor, to the factory worker who fights with a co-worker, to an executive who gets laid off or terminated and then refuses to turn in his ID badge and leave the building.

We see the potential business audience for this book as a large one, made up of:

- Business owners.
- CEOs, company presidents, and so on.
- Senior executives—vice presidents, assistant vice presidents, and so on.
- Personnel, training, and human resources development (HRD) managers.
- Managers of all types.
- First-line supervisors—management and union.
- Labor relations and labor union specialists.
- Attorneys—workers' compensation, labor, corporate.
- Law enforcement, related security professionals.
- Psychologists, counselors, social service providers.
- Worried spouses, friends, and colleagues of the above, and the most important:
- Surviving victims of workplace violence.

THE WORKPLACE VIOLENCE SPECTRUM

To better understand the definition of workplace violence participants, we've created a model to portray who these people are and what behaviors they exhibit.

The Workplace Violence Spectrum (Figure 1–1) is a time line that reads from left to right. If we start at the far left with the "normal" employee, who doesn't engage in any kinds of antisocial, dangerous, or destructive behavior at all, and we move to the far right end point, which signifies the homicidal killer at the workplace, we can fill in a lot of different kinds of behaviors in between.

The key to utilizing this simple model starts first with your ability to look at the employees around you and say, "Where does each person fall on this scale?"

If you were to examine most organizations, the majority of workers will never move beyond "left." They remain hardwork-

FIGURE 1–1
The Workplace Violence Spectrum

ing, reasonably loyal employees who don't create tension, threaten the safety of others, sabotage company assets, or otherwise exhibit any signs of the potential to commit acts of workplace violence.

However, as we move up the scale from left to right, the level of intensity increases. This leads us to define the participants in a building progression as it relates to covert and overt activities and indirect and direct confrontations.

The Normal Employee

The normal employee presents no threat of workplace violence. He or she can work with others, get along with supervisors and management, and solve workplace problems by positive, nonthreatening means.

The Covert Employee

The covert employee is the "closet" employee who engages in silent, hidden, or behind the scenes activities that serve to disrupt the workplace. This includes small-scale sabotage, vandalism, anonymous letter writing, threatening faxes, and questionable voice mail messages. He usually stays covert. Here, the level of destruction or damage is less intrusive against people and aimed more at objects. The threats tend to be indirect and nonverbal.

In some cases, he may increase the risk or "up the ante," but he probably won't go public with his behaviors. His actions are still fraught with problems, but not to the extent of actual confrontational violence against another employee.

The Fence-Sitter

The fence-sitter sits on the border between covert activities and actual violence. Here, the level of destruction, injury, or damage is more intrusive, aimed at inanimate objects or people. The threats tend to be more direct and verbal. He may lash out at someone in the company, or may target someone in the company for intimidation, nonphysical threats, or direct threats with no hands-on movements yet.

As we move more to the right, problem employees can become more overt, and we become more aware of the danger factor for these types of employees. The risk factors, for all parties, go up. This person may become more of a danger to himself, more of a danger to the people around him, and more of a danger to the company. The employee has moved into a highly suspect stage.

The Overt Employee

With the overt employee, the message is clear. The threat level is high and the potential for this person to attack other workers is a strong possibility. The activities range from assaults with great bodily injury, extreme cases of sabotage, vandalism, or intentional damage to company assets, machines, or materials, property or work items belonging to other employees, and any other symbol—tangible or not—that represents the company this person dislikes.

The Dangerous Employee

The dangerous employee is the homicidal employee. The threat level is off the scale. This person may be psychotic, armed to the teeth, and bent on cutting a wide path of destruction. The signs will usually be very apparent prior to most criminal activities. Threats, confrontations, and armed aggression move this employee to the most dangerous level.

THE COST OF WORKPLACE VIOLENCE: REAL AND HIDDEN

Violence on the job or even the mere threat of it can be perilously expensive. Statistics in an issue of "The Lipman Report," written by Guardsmark Security CEO Ira Lipman, point to some startling figures surrounding the costs of the traumatic and even long-term effects of occupational violence incidents:

> Stress-related claims cost, on average, $15,000 to $20,000 per claim, double the amount of physical injury claims. And, reports the National Council on Compensation Insurance, employees with stress-related injuries stay away from work longer than those with physical injuries.

A Kemper National Insurance Company study found that:

> [W]orkplace injuries—not necessarily from violence—reported within 10 days of their occurrence cost an average of $10,172, while ones reported after 30 days averaged $15,745. The study theorizes that early reporting leads to quicker treatment, while delays let problems fester and increases the chances of litigation.[4]

If these are the per injury figures for workplace injuries in general, what is the dollar value of the hidden, unreported, or untreated injuries related to workplace violence injuries?

And what about the hidden costs of violence in the workplace, those that don't appear with insurance premium rate increases or on the bottom line of a balance sheet?

The assembly-line worker who uses intimidation to coerce other people into doing his work for him, employs veiled threats of assault to keep his supervisor away, and causes an array of problems at work is not just harming the people around him. His behavior affects the entire organization.

By creating an environment of fear, that person can cause the people who must interact with him—his victims—to collectively look at the organization and say, "You have failed to provide a safe working environment for us. We're afraid to come in contact with this person, and so far you have done nothing to change this feeling."

If the company is lucky, someone or some group will finally tire of the hostile employee and his dictatorship of fear and intervene. If the company is not so lucky, a whiff of lawsuits will begin to fill the air. The workers who feel intimidated may file suit against the company if the disgruntled employee causes their own job performance to diminish. The supervisor who feels sick to his stomach and shaky may file a workers' compensation stress claim.

And the costs associated with this kind of pending workplace violence are often hidden or disguised, taking on other forms. The work group who fears this intimidating employee may take more sick days or other days off and watch their productivity and quality control fall to new low levels. We can't put a value on the rising cost of security services (i.e., devices, controls, and guards), or skyrocketing workers' compensation insurance premiums, claims costs, or even cancellation costs. All of this may result from the harmful activities of one bad employee.

In addition to the damage he can do to the physical assets of the company—keys, locks, computers, keyboards, machines, data, mailing lists, inventory, and so on—there is also the hidden cost of damage to the psychological assets. What about his victims, the associated bystanders, the managers and supervisors who must deal with people who are afraid to work? How about the people throughout the company who feel threatened not just by the instigator but also by what he represents—a hostile, displaced worker who may come back one day and harm them? What kind of negative impact does it have on their enthusiasm for their work or even the good of the company?

And what about the mass exodus of qualified personnel this person could initiate? What if the people around him all suddenly decided to quit, feeling—however truthfully—that their company either can't protect them or doesn't care to? Can you put a price on their skills and expertise, especially after qualified people leave the firm because they fear for their lives?

Finally, what does the assaultive worker do to affect the survival of the organization as a whole? Could one demented employee bring down the company? What does the threat of that occurrence do to the confidence of the entire work force there? The top executives and the management leadership? The shareholders for that company?

The rising tide of workplace violence incidents points us to two distinct but carefully linked factors: people and money. Controlling one without the other could lead to disastrous results.

A BUSINESS MESSAGE FOR THE TIMES

Our book teaches businesspeople at all levels how to put a sturdy "cap" on this hidden cost of fear. By recognizing potential problems at the earliest stages, businesspeople can avoid expensive litigation for work comp cases, stress-disability claims, psychological damages, and injury claims for everyone touched by workplace violence or even the threat of it. This is a definitive "how to" book that teaches prevention and protection, what to do, when to do it, and why to do it. We seek to educate our readers, change their understanding of the problem, and teach them strategies for protection and survival. The book tells interested (and worried) businesspeople how to select their employees with care, prevent potential workplace violence incidents from becoming full-scale problems, and protect the psychological, human, and physical assets of any company, regardless of size.

We offer business readers a bona fide model for creating a safe working environment in their own organizations. Unless you act accordingly before or after a significant workplace violence episode, your business will falter and may even fail. Your business can come to an emotional and physical halt unless you have the tools and the wherewithal to put it back on track and keep the doors open.

Regrettably, you can do everything right at your company and still experience some type of workplace violence incident. There are no easy answers to this vexing problem. So-called experts who try to provide quick-fix cures usually miss the crux of the problem—it starts with the people in the organization.

In its worst instances, workplace violence can ruin lives, ruin businesses, and tear at the fabric of our society.

But by taking a proactive, visible stance when dealing with this problem, companies and employees can avoid being victimized by the outbursts of the uncontrolled. We hope our book will cause the phrase "Safety at Work" to become the new order of the day.

ENDNOTES

[1] David Klinghoffer, *National Review*, "Fired! Ready! Aim!" April 16, 1993, p. 56.

[2] "Homicide Now Leading Cause of Death on Job," *New York Times*, February 24, 1993.

[3] Charles McCaghy, *Crime in American Society* (New York: Macmillan, 1980), p. 88.

[4] "Workplace Injuries," *The Wall Street Journal*, August 16, 1993, p. 1.

Chapter Two

Toxic World, Toxic Workplace

OUR TOXIC SOCIETY

It's not uncommon for people who are concerned about the problem of violence in the workplace to start asking questions about it. The first and most important question to leave someone's lips—whether a reporter working on a workplace violence story, a businessperson concerned for his or her own organization, or the survivors of a dead victim of workplace homicide—is *why*?

There are many reasons we can propose, but none of them stand alone as the single cause for this devastating problem. What becomes most clear when we examine these potential reasons is that they don't start and end with problems in the workplace; rather, they begin at home.

At this point in our understanding of children and child development, there should be no surprise to the statement "We reap what we sow." You don't have to be a child-rearing expert to see the validity of this idea. The old computer programming acronym GIGO—garbage in, garbage out—applies just as well to our children as it does to our machines.

What we do for our kids, or more importantly, what we do *to* our kids, typically guides the way they grow up into adults. Unhealthy childhood, unhealthy adulthood. Violent childhood, violent adulthood. No morals, scruples, or value for others as a child, none of these things as an adult. And so it goes.

Let's look at a profile of a typical workplace violence suspect. What follows is an evil mixture of problem incidents, failure histories, mistreatments, and day-after-day adversities that serve to draw a portrait of a problem employee. And this employee is not just "difficult" to deal with at work; he may want to kill you.

Let's look at all the ingredients for destruction that follow a person from early childhood to adulthood.

Our society faces ever increasing levels of child abuse. Studies tell us undeniably that violent acts against children lead those children who grow into adulthood to commit their own violent acts, typically against their own children. The social worker's case-books, the psychologist's file cabinets, and the judge's prison cells are filled with examples.

If little Johnnie's father and mother beat him, he learns to view this treatment as a part of the "right" way to raise children. Consequently, if he knows no other approach, his answer to the torment caused by his own children is to strike at them, too.

Writing in *Playboy* magazine, former prosecutor David Heilbroner offers a profile of the environment surrounding serial killers that comes startlingly close to the one of our own young Johnnie. Noting the tarnished upbringing of the serial murderer, Heilbroner says:

> The American killers' breeding ground is a lonely landscape of malls, single-family houses and apartment dwellers who maintain an almost paranoid insistence on privacy. American suburbia has evolved into a place through which people ride in the isolation of their cars and return to sit, docile, in front of television sets. Day to day, we encounter strangers more often than neighbors. The communal life of the European extended family, or a Latin American town, ensures that abusive parents or troubled children will be noticed. But in America, children can be subjected to the worst physical and psychological abuse from disturbed parents—who are themselves products of repression and frustration—and remain hidden until it is far too late. By the time one of these tortured individuals emerges into the world, he or she is an explosion waiting to be triggered.[1]

In addition to the child abuse he encounters, if his family is typical of nearly half the marriages in this country, Johnnie's dad will leave home following a divorce. So he sees marital breakup as the "right" thing to do in times of stress, arguments, and hostility.

And at the same time, we're seeing increasing levels of domestic violence at home, with the violence aimed primarily against women. Nationwide, only about 4 percent of men are the true victims in domestic violence assault cases. And typically, young

John sees his father beat his mother and again, he learns to view this kind of treatment of others as the "right" way to control someone in a marriage relationship. So for him to beat his own wife is not unusual. He's learned this behavior from his father, so it must be acceptable. By now, John has found that aggression and violence offer good ways to control the people around him and can help him release his anger by blaming someone else for his problems.

By the time he's reached adulthood, John has seen increasing amounts of violence on television, in movies, and in magazines. He sees people in the news or on the pages of the newspaper solving their problems with fists and guns.

And if that's not enough, as a child, he's probably been given a number of "visual training aids" that go with what he saw on television. His parents may have taken him to a toy store and let him pick out a plastic machine gun, a real-looking plastic Uzi, or an AK-47 assault rifle, complete with sound effects.

As he rose into adulthood, more and more of these factors pointed him toward a propensity for violence, or at least more of the ability to make the decision to be violent.

Couple this with a number of failure experiences in John's life, including perhaps a difficult stint in the military, one or more failed marriages, and a marked propensity to lash out at the supposed villains that surround him, and you have the early breeding ground for a workplace violence instigator.

When John stumbles through a number of low-paying, low-skill jobs that offer him no real satisfaction, he starts to look around for people to blame. When the economy goes bad and cutbacks are imminent at his company, this person does not see his own layoff as a sign of the times but as a personal affront to himself.

By now, John's self-esteem is in tatters. The most important things in his life, starting with his job, to which his sense of self-worth is glued, are in shambles, and his other significant relationships with his spouse, family, and fair-weather friends have also been ruined. And John now sees the world differently than most people. He feels he is certainly not to blame for his problems, other people are.

If he starts to feel disconnected from our growing, mobile, and discordant society, the inward pressure really begins to mount.

With no healthy friendships or outlets for effective communication with anyone on a deep level, he may feel like he is removed from the mainstream, thereby adding to his delusional thoughts, which start with, "Nobody likes me," and build to "Nobody knows who I am," and end with "I'm gonna get a gun and change all that."

If he does happen to hold a job, he may work at a place where people above him or around him don't care about him as a person, only his output. "Tighten more fender bolts!" his shop supervisor may scream at him. "File more papers," his office supervisor may yell. If he works at a place where management is more concerned with marginal utility—that is, the production of work units—and people don't seem to care about each other, he feels even less connected to the real world. His enemies list, whether it exists only in his mind or actually on paper, has already taken shape.

Give John poor if any access to psychological services, support, or counseling, and he now feels like he has no alternative, no apparent options for change, and no real solutions save for one—make someone pay for his pain.

Finally, give John access to as many alcoholic beverages or illegal drugs as he can take and more guns than we used in all of World War II and you have just concocted the recipe for someone who may one day explode.

Critics of this scenario are quick to leap up with the retort, "Yes, but hasn't society always been that way? Didn't kids always play 'GI Joe' or 'cops and robbers'? Haven't parents always gotten divorced?"

This argument misses the point of our description of the workplace violence suspect. There's no difference in the way kids play then and the way they play today (save for the price of their toys). The difference lies in the *way* kids then and now perceive *how* they play. In the above description of the characteristics, the most important ingredient—and the one kids of yesteryear had and today's children don't—lies in the role of the family.

In bygone days, after the kids came home from playing "Bang! You're dead!" games with their friends, they went to the dinner table where the values taught were that real violence was bad and that respect for other people was very important. Most parents were careful to model nonviolent behavior in the home. It was okay to play cops and robbers, but the line between what was real and what was pretend was carefully etched by most mothers and fathers who knew the difference.

And when the kids sat down in front of the television, their access to extremely violent shows was limited not only by the low number of shows but by parents who controlled what they watched. As the child watched TV, his or her parents served to interpret what was seen against the backdrop of family and human values. The context of that environment is much different now. The glowing screen serves as an electronic babysitter for parents who just aren't there, either because of job commitments, divorce, or any other reason.

TV critic Ken Tucker, writing in *Entertainment Weekly*, points to the way people of all ages cling to old TV reruns for some proof that the "nuclear" family actually exists:

> Look no further than the enduring, still-growing cult for "The Brady Bunch": People of all ages snicker at the corniness of this family of straight-arrow suburbanites, but one reason its episodes are watched over and over is that viewers also wish, on some level, that the security and closeness of the Brady clan were still common in American life.[2]

According to the American Psychological Association, the average American child, watching just three hours of television per day, has by age 12 seen 8,000 murders on TV and witnessed over 100,000 acts of violence.

Writing in *The New Yorker* magazine, TV critic Ken Auletta puts it this way:

> America, the country most strongly addicted to the moving image, is perhaps the most violent of Western societies. On average, a violent crime is committed here every 17 seconds. The entertainment industry alone cannot be blamed for this, anymore than guns alone can be blamed for gun-related deaths. But the connections are inescapable. If there were fewer guns, fewer people would be shot to death; if there were fewer violent images, fewer people might be moved to seek violent solutions.[3]

Violence starts in the cradle and explodes in the workplace. Parents and schools have all those years in between to prevent that from happening, and we're all failing miserably.

THE SELF–ESTEEM GAP: A BROKEN BRIDGE

Through our research and experience, we place much of the cause of violence in the workplace on the diminishing self-esteem of the American worker. And this lack of individual self-esteem finds its roots in many of our other societal ailments, like those listed for our fictitious worker John.

In the majority of workplace homicide cases we have studied, the root cause of these incidents starts and ends with the perpetrators and their total lack of self-esteem.

When the unhealthy worker says, either aloud or to himself, "The owner of this company doesn't know who I am or care about me. He doesn't give a damn about what I do," he's preparing himself to make that leap from relative anonymity to the front pages of his local newspaper.

The healthy worker says, "So what if the president of this company doesn't know me by name? I've got my job to do and I do it and then I go home. I have my friends here at work and away from work and it doesn't really concern me. It might be nice to know the guy, but his affairs are his business and mine are mine."

The disgruntled employee thinks differently. His thinking starts with, "I'll show him who I am and he'll never be able to treat me this way again." And then it ends with a gun.

But how does someone really say, "I've gone past the point of just simple anger. I'm not just going to punch my boss. I'm going to go to my house, get a gun, drive back to my job, and shoot him"?

By looking at our model, The Broken Bridge of Self-Esteem (Figure 2–1), it becomes easier to see how this dramatic leap into homicide can occur.

On the left side of the Self-Esteem Bridge, we see the abstract concept that is the person's Values. It's a self-described set of beliefs he or she has about what is right and what is wrong. On the right side, we see the abstract concept Respect for Human Life. These two concepts are connected by the person's self-esteem level.

But look at the connection for the disturbed employee bent on homicide. It's broken in the middle; there is no longer a connection

FIGURE 2–1
The Broken Bridge of Self-Esteem

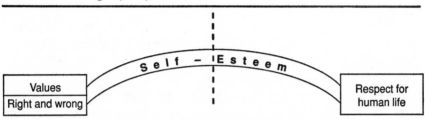

between human values and respect for human life. Once this rupture occurs at whatever point in the disturbed employee's own breakdown, it becomes easier for him to make the decision to harm other people to avenge his own pain.

The underpinning of most emotional disturbance is a lack of self-esteem. Most therapists will say that increasing their patients' self-esteem is the number-one priority of their sessions.

THE WORKPLACE AS PROVIDER

The workplace, above all else, gives people the security of a living. It's a job first, so that people can meet their basic needs of home, food, clothing, and so on. At the other end, it gives people a sense of identity, self-worth, and self-esteem.

Over the years, it seems the role of the workplace has changed from the place where we go to earn money, to the center of our universe. Now, more than ever, people are judged not so much by who they are but by what they do. And in no case is this more evident than with men.

Eavesdrop on any dinner party, backyard barbecue, or similar social function where some of the people know each other but not everyone knows everyone. The conversations between men typically center first on the pleasantries of life, the weather, the food, the standing of the local sports team. But rare is the conversation that does not somehow shift directly to work.

People in social situations spend the early parts of their conversations "feeling each other out." Social dynamics involving tone of voice, body language, body proximity, gestures, and facial expressions tend to monopolize the beginning stages as people try to become comfortable with each other.

After these boundaries and ground rules about space and sound have been established, the bulk of the postpleasantries conversation shifts to what it is that we "do."

Whereas women, whether or not they work outside the home, tend to spend much of the time talking to strangers about their husbands, families, or children, men usually cut right to the chase. It takes very little prodding from the other party to learn that the man near them is a plumber, a lawyer, a doctor, a repair technician, a realtor, or a salesperson.

Rare is the man in a social setting who will not make at least a passing reference to his work. The phrase, "Boy, I'm really tired. I put in a long shift down at the plant today," will usually be enough to start an entire new discussion about what it is that he does for a living.

Bestselling self-help writer Robert Fulghum (*It Was on Fire When I Lay Down on It*) has his own unique way of countering this job-identification paradox that says, "I *am* somebody, because I do X for a job."

Instead of carrying around a stack of business cards with his job title embossed in ink, Fulghum prefers an even more descriptive symbol. His business cards simply say, "Fulghum." When puzzled recipients ask what it means, he says, "I'm Fulghum. It's what I do and it's who I am."

Alfred Korzybski, the founder of the science of general semantics, said that the English language doesn't function as well as it could for the job of describing our experiences. He felt the language we learn as children causes us to perceive reality in certain biased ways.

Psychologist David Bourland and Albert Ellis, PhD, working independently with theories developed by Korzybski, described an unusual approach called E-Prime. Bourland saw that forming sentences without using any form of the verb "to be" (be, am, are, is, was, were, been, being) forces us to focus on action and concrete description.

For example, E-Prime would outlaw the phrase "I am an engineer." Instead, the phrase "I work as an engineer" would describe the person best, since it correctly identifies only one part of his or her existence. He or she also may "be" a friend, a voter, a citizen of a certain country, a spouse, or a parent. Categorizing the person as "an engineer" limits our perception and understanding of him or her. Robert Fulghum's simple but specific business card is a good example of E-Prime.

THE FACTORY AS FAMILY

Unfortunately, today we've seen the employer take over as the role model—a job that was once filled by the family. As a result, we watch in amazement as people make requests of their employer that they probably wouldn't make of their own mothers, including asking for food, education, recreation, medical care, psychological care, and plenty of tangible and intangible "warm fuzzies" that help people pull themselves out of bed and head out to work.

It's not enough anymore just to be a good place to work. Today, the company must also offer a host of other "perks and benes" to make the job attractive for even the most mundane position.

Does the plant have a nice cafeteria? I want to be able to eat a good meal at work. What about the health plan? Will they pay for everything or do I have to come up with some of my own money? Do they offer a dental plan? I want to get my teeth fixed. How about a vision plan? My kids need glasses.

How about the vacation policy? How many extra paid days off will I get? How much sick time? How many breaks do I get each day?

What kind of educational benefits can I get? Will they pay for me to go back to school? Help me get my high school diploma, college degree, master's?

Will they teach me English as a second language? Improve the way I speak or write? Pay for me to study at home or on the job?

What kind of recreational activities do they offer? A company softball team? A bowling league? A company health spa? Outside office picnics every other Friday? Casual dress days?

What about wellness programs? Will they help me quit smoking? Fix my alcohol or drug problem? Help me lose weight?

These things are what many people look for when they go to work for a company. The implied questions they ask are largely self-directed: "How will this job improve the quality of my life? What will I get—besides the ability to work and collect a paycheck—to work here? What do I get, as opposed to what do I have to give?"

We're here to say this "what's in it for me" approach is wrong. People, in our opinion, should not look to the workplace as their provider; they should look inward, back to themselves, and more importantly, to their families for the support they need.

The nurturing environment that was the family is now provided by the job. "The family," says one wry observer, "is now General Motors."

In the 1970s, when TA, or Transactional Analysis, was in its heyday, the concept of positive "strokes" was all the rage. In the era of "I'm OK–You're OK" books and programs, strokes were something you gave or received. Logically, positive strokes—"I like you, you look nice today, that was a nice casserole"—were much better to receive than negative strokes—"I don't like you, you look like a slob, you shouldn't eat that fattening casserole."

Whereas we used to look to our family and close friends for our positive, emotionally pleasing strokes, for many, those people either don't exist now or don't give us the attention we so desperately seek. With the widely discussed "nuclear family" on the increasing decline, people started to look elsewhere for their strokes. In addition to time spent at home, where else do we spend the majority of our adult lives? At work.

But if you have a good family, you don't need to look only to your job as the sole source of your positive strokes. Strokes from our bosses, colleagues, or employees are certainly nice to get, but if you don't get them, you can go home to a good family and know you are thought of as valuable, worthy, and capable.

It is our position that the profile of a homicidal workplace violence suspect will reveal gaping holes in the family structure. Here's the parallel that illustrates this best: What happens to the worker who grows up in a pain-filled, traumatic, dysfunctional family where he is abused, neglected, or otherwise raised poorly by people who don't care for his needs?

What happens when that person, who may be marginally or completely antisocial by now, goes to work, ostensibly in search of the missing strokes?

And what happens to that same person who doesn't get any positive feedback, praise, or support from the people at the workplace?

And what if that person must live and work every day in the same type of dysfunctional environment at work that he suffered through at home? The answers to these questions are chilling.

When he has had enough, he may see violence against others as his only resource.

THE LOYALTY MYTH

The employee who places all hope on the workplace to make him or her feel supported and positive about life is treading on icy ground. With our business economy in constant transition, worklife is not just about treatment at work anymore, it's about longevity and personal survival in the company.

The days of starting your career with one company fresh out of high school or college and staying there through your retirement seem long gone. Even civil service positions or military service—historically known as "cradle to grave" employment situations—are falling victim to the "downsizing" axe.

The face of long-time employment has changed. Employees either change jobs on their own volition, or the job ends and they are then forced to seek other work. Because working for some company—as opposed to being self-employed—involves this constant risk of layoffs or other terminations, it's difficult for employees to feel very loyal to a firm that may give them a pink slip within the next week or month.

Business owners and executives who criticize the average American worker as disloyal should place themselves in their shoes. How can you ask for loyalty to a company that does not reciprocate it?

Company loyalty, while it may exist in certain industries or with certain firms, is no longer a two-way street. The presence of aggressive labor unions who feud constantly with management have succeeded in creating an adversarial relationship where both sides now say "I'll be glad to give you yours as long as I get mine first."

Employees see long-time co-workers terminated after 19.5 years just so the company won't have to pay retirement benefits, and they get rightfully outraged. They see ham-handed top management dissolve their pension funds to fight ill-advised takeover or buyout strategies, and they get discouraged about the future. They hear constant rumblings from management about "making do with less," cutbacks, plant closings, the more frequent use of temp workers, or widespread layoffs, and they get understandably fearful for their own economic survival.

The one-job-for-life experience is just not a reality anymore. Most people will admit, "Yes, it would be nice to work here forever, but that's probably not in the cards."

This belief is based on their own experiences, what they have seen in their own companies, and what they have seen across the nation.

Few jobs are guaranteed anymore, and people know it. "Why should I give my all to the company, when I could be laid off tomorrow," is a common lament of the employee who has been hired and fired many times already.

Jack Gordon, the well-respected editor of *Training* magazine, points to the number of changes in the quality and quantity of the labor force. "Many hourly wage earners feel like they have no future with their company. With so many layoffs and so much downsizing, it's hard for them to feel very secure. The violent employee, stuck in a low-wage job and feeling he may be headed for a layoff, may think, 'There's no worth to my job. Why not punch the boss? I can always go and get another (low-wage) job just like this one.'"

INTERVENTION STRATEGIES

A southern California manufacturer of sporting goods began to suffer some extensive inventory losses. The firm's internal security office conducted an investigation and discovered that the equipment was being stolen by some employees in the shipping department. These people would send the goods to nonexistent customers, mail them to their own homes, or give them to outside associates posing as truck drivers.

After the investigation revealed the depth of the problem, several people were immediately fired. The shrinkage flow slowed and business went on as usual.

The company was well known in the sporting goods industry, and it offered a variety of T-shirts depicting various sports activities. One of the employees fired in the theft ring decided to use a company T-shirt to send his former managers a message.

He took a shirt out to the desert, tied it to a fence post, and proceeded to shoot it full of holes with a handgun. He returned to his old job late one afternoon and waited in the parking lot astride his motorcycle.

As one of his supervisors started to leave the lot, the man drove up to his driver's side window and tossed the T-shirt at him. "This is for you," he said. "Just consider it a message."

The implication was quite clear. The shaken manager returned to his office as the ex-employee raced out of the parking lot on his motorcycle.

We believe that although the firm should hold no responsibility whatsoever if this obviously disgruntled employee goes back and kills somebody, they do have a duty to react to this clear sign of a pending workplace violence problem. Anybody who would go out of his way to create such a clear-cut symbol of rage, aggression, and hostility, needs help.

Should this company intervene in this employee's life? Absolutely. Here's how the intervention could work:

Manager:
Don't leave just yet. Let's talk for a minute. Will you do that with me?

Employee:
Yeah? There's nothing to talk about.

M:
I think there is. Obviously you're upset and angry. Let's talk about it.

E:

Yeah, I'm upset. I'm not happy with the way I was treated here and that shirt is just a way for me to show how mad I am.

M:

Okay, that's a good place to start. I want to talk with you about this and get to where we can find some solutions.

E:

Like what?

M:

Maybe you and I can sit down with the plant manager and talk about your grievances together.

E:

All right. I'd be willing to do that.

Is this "perfect world" thinking only? Not anymore. Most companies, when faced with this situation, would just be glad they were rid of him. Then, when he returned a few months later with something in his hands other than a T-shirt and assaulted an employee, someone in the company will cry out, "Gee, we're sorry that happened. We should have looked harder at the warning signs. We should have recognized his problems."

But for every guy who comes back to the job site and kills, there is a tremendous number of people who will use something like the T-shirt as their symbol of extreme frustration, and you'll never hear from them again.

Going over the line and committing an act of workplace violence is a tremendous bridge to cross for the person who does it. The difference between shooting a "symbolic" T-shirt and shooting another human being is a huge one. It requires an extraordinary amount of energy to come to that point.

To go back to the workplace violence spectrum shown in Figure 1–1, this particular disgruntled worker crossed the line in terms of his highly overt activity. He could have delivered the T-shirt anonymously or left it under the manager's car windshield wipers, but instead, he chose a very intrusive, destructive act with a high degree of threat attached to it.

The T-shirt example illustrates an important point: Not all workplace violence is based on physical contact. As we will reiterate, there is more to the subject than just fist and guns. The *threat* of fists and guns can be equally destructive, if not more so. The employee who threatens his boss in some concrete yet nonviolent way—"If you don't give me a day off next week, you're gonna be sorry you ever met me"—is just as destructive as the employee who punches his boss.

Why? The stench of intimidation fills the air and harms the boss just the same as a punch.

THE FINANCIAL IMPACT OF NONLETHAL WORKPLACE VIOLENCE

A story that illustrates the "value" of intimidation as a workplace violence weapon of choice starts at a US nuclear power plant.

Building one of these energy behemoths takes years of work and hundreds of millions of dollars. As is typical in many large construction projects, the general contractor in charge of construction employs hundreds of tradespeople ranging from carpenters and welders to pipefitters and electricians. And as is common with this kind of project, the job site is typically a union shop, with different trade unions representing various groups of workers.

It's almost a rule of membership that construction unions and their members despise the worksite management and the people ultimately in charge of the building before and after its completion. While union–management hatred is hardly unique anywhere in the world, the construction trades seem to consider antimanagement fervor as a near rite of passage.

Many of the arguments that stem from these union groups have a ringing familiarity: "Management doesn't understand us, appreciate us, or listen to our complaints. They have no respect for our people or our needs. They offer unfair (fill in the blank—wage packages, pension plans, work hours, etc.) and we can't support them because they don't support us."

In this particular nuclear power plant construction job, this animosity seemed to stay at normal levels. Workers offered their usual gripes about management, but there were no news headlines surrounding any of the work. The building continued and business went on as usual.

Only after the plant was completed did troubles start to rise to the surface like fish after food. During the plant's testing periods, many of the critical water flow and radiation containment pipes were found to have cracks in them. Further inspections revealed shoddy welds, poor pipefitting, and potentially dangerous construction techniques.

An immediate review of the inspection sheets for these pipes showed nothing unusual. The inspector (surely perceived as a "management type" by the blue-collar workers) had supposedly inspected the welds and had, in fact, "signed off" on them. But the pipe weld inspection reports and the state of the pipes now were clearly out of sync.

After an investigation, it became dangerously clear that the inspector should never have let these welds pass. Something must have happened. Why else would he approve critical work areas like nuclear water containment pipes if the welds were not right?

When the real story came to the surface, the specter of workplace violence had struck again.

Some of the workers, in their haste to move on to other jobs, told the inspector if he didn't sign off on their welds, he could expect problems. Using threats of violence, physical and psychological intimidation techniques, and supposed safety in numbers, the work crews successfully frightened the inspector into approving their shoddy work.

Ultimately, federal government inspectors forced the construction company to redo the welds before they would certify the reactor facility. The cost overruns required to refit these dangerous welds ran into the millions.

Had they been built right in the first place or corrected after the first inspection, this extra cost would never have seen the light of day. But thanks to the workers' threats and the inspector's fear for his health and safety, millions of dollars were added to the project.

This case of physical intimidation and, in effect, workplace extortion shows the now-not-so-hidden cost of this problem. The money spent for reinspections, fines, cost overrun penalties, new welds, and the labor involved to correct dangerous work goes right to the bottom line.

This workplace violence incident—and it clearly is one even if no punches were thrown—forced the cost of those sections of pipe and indeed, the entire project, to go up dramatically.

Your understanding of violence in the workplace should start with the fact that not all episodes are caused by punches or bullets. The woman who works at a construction site filled with men may find her lunch pail gets "accidentally" crushed by a pile driver, or she may dodge a brick that "accidentally" fell from a nearby ledge. She may have her tools stolen, her work sabotaged, or threatening notes painted like graffiti on the walls where she works.

Perhaps a group of employees wishes to take control of their work area. Using pushing and shoving or even punches to keep other frightened employees in line, this band of thugs on the job can dominate an entire work section of a firm.

Maybe a group of line workers assaults an employee who has worked "too fast or too hard" and made them look bad in front of their supervisors. "Let's get this guy!" says this mob of workplace violence instigators, "He's the one who (ratted on us to the boss, made us redo a job, speeded up the assembly line—take your pick). In these instances, the tacit ringleaders called the shots.

And even if the line workers don't resort to physical violence, they may use subtle or even blatant sins of sabotage against their new "enemy's" work. Tales like these abound on automobile assembly lines. Disgruntled workers have not only vandalized their own work as a way to "get back" at the company but have purposely damaged the work of others to send them a message or vent their frustrations in an even more destructive way.

For more horror stories about life on the auto line, read Ben Hamper's chilling but true tale of his years as a riveter for GM. His 1991 book *Rivethead* (Warner Books) gives us many insights into the mentality of the workers, the supervisors, the managers, and the executives who toil for one of America's "Big Three."

THE TOXIC COMPANY AND TOXIC BOSSES

And just as there are bad employees, no discussion of workplace violence would be balanced unless we focused some attention on what could be called psychologically unfriendly companies, where employees are controlled through a culture of suppression and fear.

A grid model describes this best. Figure 2–2 looks at four types of employees in the Toxic versus Nourishing Organization model.

The left, vertical side of the model measures the climate and the culture in the organization. Is it emotionally healthy? What is the degree of "toxicity"—bad feelings, mistreatment by supervisors and co-workers, or the potential for workplace violence—or "nourishment"—the good feelings, the unity of purpose at all levels of the organization, or the positive, pleasant, and even nurturing working conditions.

The right, horizontal side of the model measures the individual maturity of the employees. Are they low or high? Do the employees care for one another or just themselves? Is there turmoil, mistrust, and ill-ease among the good workers, who may feel controlled, threatened, or manipulated by the bad ones? What is the relative level of maturity of the people who do the work and interact?

As the figure indicates, the best of both worlds occurs in a highly nourishing work environment coupled with a mature, positive, productive employee with a healthy sense of worth and self-esteem.

But the highly nourishing, healthy work culture mixed with an employee with weak or poor self-esteem and maturity makes for a marginal worker.

And the emotionally mature employee working in a highly toxic environmental culture may feel stifled, threatened, or apathetic. The company is in jeopardy of losing this person due to his or her sense of hopelessness about the future there.

The worst of all worlds appears in the lower left corner of the model. The employee who works in a highly toxic organization with a predominantly negative culture, and is himself very immature, emotionally underdeveloped, or loaded with weak or poor self-esteem, could be a potential ticking bomb. With little or no positive support from either co-workers or supervisors, and with dangerously low maturity, morale, or self-esteem, the borderline employee can be a bad mix for the organization.

In terms of the potential for violence in the workplace, this person may be the worst employee the toxic organization could have inside it.

FIGURE 2-2
The Toxic versus Nourishing Organization

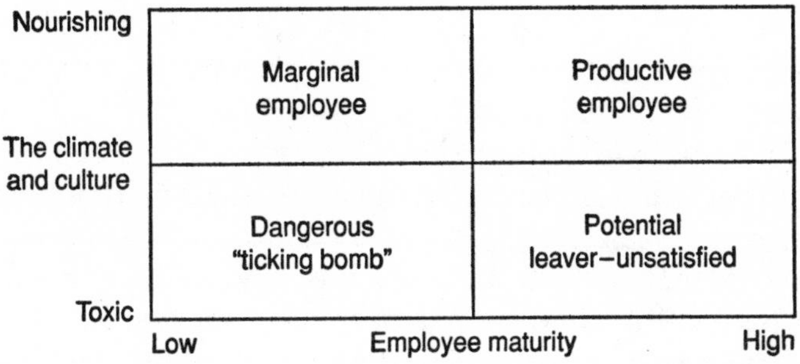

How employees react to certain situations depends largely on the culture, mission statement, and beliefs that are grounded by the organization. So-called toxic company cultures are fraught with stress, tension, low morale, and anxiety. This can foster feelings of rage and helplessness in many employees and the desire to commit violence in the borderline or marginal ones.

There are noticeable differences between toxic organizations and nourishing ones, including the systems, policies, and environment related to how the company treats its employees, promotes its supervisors and executives, and controls or does not control the people who work there.

"There's no such thing as a perfect company," says Tom Erickson, a vice president of human resources at Elgar Corporation, a San Diego, California, company where two people were slain by a former employee named Larry Hansel. "I think all companies have some sense of toxicity in them. The better companies are always striving to improve the quality of worklife and make changes in the culture that make the organization a better place to work."

And supervisors are not without their own personality problems. (We will look at this particular problem in more detail in Chapter 6 on discipline.) A colleague who has a number of people working under him made a joke in passing when he heard about the topic for our book. "Employee violence?" he said with a wry smile. "How about a book about managerial violence? You know, for frustrated managers who assault their own employees?"

He then proceeded to rattle off a whole litany of employee crimes: "You people are lazy and worthless. You rob me blind, you break my machines, you steal my inventory, you drink and take drugs on the job, you argue with me when I ask you to work hard, and you cheat me out of a full day's work by your tardiness, two-hour coffee breaks, and leaving early."

He said this with a twinkle in his eye, but we can't help but wonder if his sarcasm isn't actually more accurate than he wanted to portray.

There are managers and supervisors who are to blame for creating or instigating their own workplace violence incidents. San Diego, California, labor and fair employment attorney David A. Miller frequently represents workers who have been mistreated by their supervisors and their organizations. He has strong feelings about the relative toxicity of some organizations he goes against in court.

"I meet with a number of clients who tell me they have been treated very unfairly by supervisors. I hear stories of abuse and other indignities and I'm surprised there are not more cases of workplace violence."

He feels that since organizations must hire all types of people, they must first "look what's going on in their own house."

"People," he states, "want to be treated with honesty, respect, and dignity. You can take even the most mild-mannered employee and psychologically torture him at the workplace for long periods of time and even he will be capable of overreacting."

Miller points to the differences between our work culture and that of the Japanese. "In Japan," he says, "worker loyalty, camaraderie, and team spirit are the most important assets to the company. In America, the customer is considered the most important, not the employee."

To assert his belief that organizations may bring on their own misery when it comes to employee problems, Miller cites a letter written by a business reader for the editorial section of the *San Diego Union-Tribune*. Commenting on a story about downsizing at the local General Dynamics plant, the writer said:

When is American business going to realize that employees are a company's most valuable resource? A little show of appreciation from the employer in the form of a "thank you for a job well done" can go a long way toward increasing production and that all-mighty bottom line. Wake up, Corporate America, employees are living, breathing human beings with feelings.[4]

And these employees have strong feelings about the impact of occupational violence on their lives and careers. When the US Postal Service set up a telephone hot line last year to receive reports of threatening incidents, the employee response was overwhelming. In fewer than six months, the service received 1,128 calls. Violence in the workplace is not just a management–employee problem; it's a people problem closely tied to our culture.

How we perceive each other, as employers, as employees, and as the collective members of society, may well dictate how we treat one another in the future.

ENDNOTES

[1] David Heilbroner, "Serial Murder and Sexual Repression," *Playboy*, August 1993, p. 150.

[2] Ken Tucker, "Vintage Watches: Why We Still Love'Em," *Entertainment Weekly*, July 30, 1993, p. 22.

[3] Ken Auletta, "What Won't They Do?" *The New Yorker*, May 17, 1993, p. 45–46.

[4] Brooke Willis, "Employers Must Learn that Employees Are Valuable Assets," *San Diego Union-Tribune*, March 31, 1993, p. 13–14.

Chapter Three

Why Hire Trouble? Safe Hiring Practices

With the notion of disgruntled employees and the havoc they raise continuing to grow everywhere we look, two obvious questions come to mind: "Why hire a problem employee when you don't have to?" and "Why start out with someone who already violates your sense of trustworthiness or integrity?"

The answers to these questions should relieve you, at least a bit. The fact is, you're not under any legal obligation to hire anyone just because they apply. The concept of "forced employment" is long gone. This means people don't *have* to work for you anymore than you *have* to hire them. No matter how the labor law attorneys scream and shout, you still have a choice about whom you hire and where they work for you. This is not to say the sky is the limit, however. Most businesspeople know, from a hiring standpoint, that they may not discriminate against people based on a number of factors, including their sex, age, race, creed, birthplace, religious beliefs, disabilities (visible or not), marital status, criminal record, military service, clubs or memberships, sexual preference, or medical history.

But no matter what the law says, you and your co-workers will have to work with anyone you choose, so the people you pick must be compatible with your company at all levels—from the mission and direction, the policies and procedures, the work goals, and the people who seek to fulfill them.

With workplace violence on the rise, the not-so-simple solution to the problem of weeding out potentially bad employees is this: Hire the good ones and turn the bad ones away. Stop the problem of violence in the workplace, at least at your own company, before it ever begins, by being very selective about the people you choose.

Two short parables illustrate this point.

One fine spring day, a group of picnickers sat beside a flowing river, enjoying their lunches and their own company. As they ate and talked, a cool breeze covered them. All was good.

One of the people happened to look over at the river and noticed something floating in the water. As he watched the object get closer, he was horrified to see that it was a baby floating on a raft. Dropping his sandwich and kicking over his soda can, the man raced to the river's edge and dove in. He swam quickly over to the baby's raft and pulled the child into his arms. All the other picnickers came over to the river's edge to help him and together, they rescued the baby.

As the man dried himself off, the other guests looked at the baby and all asked, "Where did this child come from?"

Looking upstream at the river, a woman in the group saw two more babies coming down the swift river, each clinging to a raft. She yelled to the others and this time several people leapt into the water and rescued the two new babies.

As the group pulled babies and wet swimmers to shore, three more babies came floating by on rafts. Before anyone on the shore could move, six more babies approached, and behind them a dozen more babies, and behind them, three dozen more babies followed.

By now the entire group of adults was in the river, trying desperately to save these children. As fast as they could rescue the babies, more would come down the river toward them.

Finally, someone in the group said, "We can't possibly rescue all these babies. Why don't we go to the top of the river, at the source, and see how they are getting into the river in the first place?"

And so they did. Reaching the source of the river, they were able to prevent the babies from leaving the shore and going into the water.

The moral and the point to the story is simple: If you've got problems, go to the source. If you're plagued with bad employees who may threaten your safety or the existence of your business, then go to the source and prevent them from coming down your own corporate river.

Another example: A small village in Switzerland was known around the world for its great ski runs. People came from across the globe to ski there. The conditions, the location, the weather, the hotels, and everything else fit together to make it the finest skiing experience possible.

And people being people and human nature being what it is, everyone who came to this ski village already thought he or she was an expert at skiing. Because they had a noticeable tendency to ignore the warning signs posted along the trails or to disregard the "Beginning," "Intermediate," or "Expert," signs posted at the top of each ski run, some people fell and broke their legs. Not only did this ruin their ski vacation, but it caused some bad publicity for the little ski village.

One part of the mountain was particularly treacherous. Interviews at the local hospital told the town elders the majority of injuries came from one area on this mountain.

With the reputation of the ski village at stake, the town elders got together to try to fix this reputation-threatening problem. The mayor of the ski village said, "We only have $20,000 in our budget to fix this problem. What are we going to do?"

The town elders discussed and debated the problem for several days. They voted and came up with what they thought was an ideal solution. They called General Motors and asked them to build a special ambulance just for ski accidents. They decided to place this snow-equipped ambulance at the bottom of the most dangerous mountain to wait for any bad falls.

So GM built their ambulance and sent it overseas. The town elders parked the ambulance at the bottom of the mountain. Whenever someone fell, the ambulance would race to the scene, pick the injured person up, and get him or her to the hospital in record time.

As the hospital admitted yet another injured skier, someone in the admitting office called the mayor and said, "You know, for about $1,000, you could put up a fence at the top of the dangerous mountain. That would keep the people away from this area and consequently, out of the hospital."

This chapter is about setting up fences and going to the source of the river. Instead of looking back with regret after a bad employee has caused problems, we will tell you how to stop the problem employee from ever gaining access to your company in the first place.

NETWORKING: PREQUALIFYING YOUR APPLICANTS

The old adage "It's not what you do, but who you know" certainly applies in job hunting. Referrals from friends who already work at companies that interest you can mean the difference between sandwiching your résumé in a pile with 300 others or getting an interview with the personnel manager.

So if networking works for you as an individual, why not try it in reverse? When a new position opens, ask your employees to help you fill it.

"We've found that the best way to get good people, who agree with our mission statement, core values, and are compatible with the way we work, is to network," says Tom Erickson, vice president of human resources at San Diego–based Elgar Corporation.

He says that whenever the firm has an open position, it asks its employees to spread the word among friends, colleagues, and peers. "We recruit by networking first," says Erickson, "especially at the executive and managerial levels."

Through networking, it's easier to find qualified people than with just ads in the newspaper. Further, the Elgar employees who recruit new people can often vouch for them along many different levels, including education, background, work experience, and just how well they get along with others.

PREEMPLOYMENT SCREENING, TESTING, AND EVALUATION

Labor law experts suggest that you don't just go around collecting résumés and applications when you post a new position in your company. If you have to hire someone, advertise for the position in various ways, carefully screen the candidates who apply, and fill the spot. Gathering piles of résumés and applications just for the sake of doing something creates an unnecessary paper trail that could have legal ramifications later on.

Some companies utilize pen-and-paper psychological tests for all applicants for certain positions. In some organizations, jobs involving security clearances, major financial transactions, or the use of proprietary data all fall under a special category requiring these kinds of tests.

For a relatively inexpensive investment, these tests can help weed out the obvious problem candidates. Typically, companies will contract with a qualified outside psychologist (or an in-house professional if the company is large enough) to give the exam to large groups of applicants, screen the results, and prepare a detailed report on each person. Since this is often done on a volume basis, the results far outweigh the minimal cost.

With these reports in hand, the personnel manager can make a more informed decision about borderline candidates.

But the use of psychological screening written tests is not without its perils. In Oakland, California, the Target Stores chain was forced to award $1.3 million to 2,500 prospective security guards who were asked to take the well-known Rodgers Condensed CPI-MMPI written psychscreen. An attorney for the plaintiffs suggested that a number of the test questions for the long-used exam "are extremely invasive on matters of sexuality, religion, bodily functions, and the like." Under terms of a class-action suit settlement, the Minneapolis-based 500-store chain agreed to ban the test in its 113 California retail outlets.

The caveat here is clear: Check with qualified labor law experts in your state. Some screening instruments may have a court history behind them.

APPLICATION REVIEW

If your company does not use prescreening tests and relies primarily on the interview process in order to hire, you may be able to gather information just by reviewing the candidate's job application. Here are some points to consider as you read over the hard copy:

- What is your first impression when you look at the form? Is it legible, clear, and "within the lines?"

A slap-dash effort on the application should give you an immediate feeling that the candidate may not be serious about the position, may be trying to hide certain damaging information, or may not have the job skills you require for the particular position.

- Do you get any immediate sense of hostility or evasion when you look at the document as a whole?

Angry, intense people don't always express themselves in angry, intense ways. But their emotions may be evident if you look at the small signs. You don't have to be a handwriting expert or a psychologist to see hostility on a printed page. Noticeably hard pen pressure, excessive smearing, or overuse of underlines and exclamation points may indicate repressed anger.

Conversely, the person who writes extremely small letters—far smaller than would be considered unique penmanship—may also have some underlying psychological problems relating to self-esteem.

- Is the application full of missing information, date gaps, or questionable addresses?

People who want to hide past problems may leave large holes in their applications. Ask careful questions if you see date gaps of longer than 30 days. Focus in on sketchy job histories, scant mention of military service, and out-of-town job references, personal references, or residences with gaps of 30 days or more.

Be especially wary of applicants who say, "Oh, my last job closed down and the other two went out of business, so there's no one to call about me."

People who lead itinerant, transient lifestyles often use the "no contacts available" ploy to hide damaging information about their pasts. We recall one gas station owner who hired an attendant even though each of his three former employers went "out of business." No wonder the others went belly-up; after three days on the job—spent carefully storing away the cash receipts from Friday, Saturday, and Sunday in a place other than the station floor safe—this person locked up one night and headed out of town for good.

There are perfectly legitimate people who have come to you from out of state, but those that can't give you real phone numbers and addresses may be hiding something.

- Be wary if you see "None of your business" or "Why do you need to know?" responses on an application.

Legitimate people should have no valid reason to omit information, refuse to answer valid, legal questions, or hide the truth. If they do, you don't want them. No sense getting into a debate with someone over why you need to know the names of at least two verifiable references.

BACKGROUND CHECK CRITERIA—THE CRITICAL FIVE

In our view, if you hire anyone today without doing at least a rudimentary background check, you're taking a big risk. At the least, your final steps before bringing someone aboard should include a check of their work history, military history, criminal history, credit history, and driving record.

First check with the labor law experts in your state to see what your limits and constraints are for this kind of data. Privacy laws differ across the nation, and you may need to get the applicant's permission to get some of the information.

Viewed separately, one negative history report—like credit or criminal—may not mean that much, but taken as a whole, the information could serve as an alarm bell for your applicant.

Work History

Verify gaps in the candidate's employment, ask why the applicant left the previous company, and get an idea of relationships with past supervisors and co-workers.

Military History

Dates and cities are not nearly as important as evidence of discipline problems. If the candidate says, "I received a two-day suspension for missing my ship when it left port," you need to find out the story behind the suspension. Was there a legitimate reason the applicant missed the ship? Or was it because of a drinking problem, an arrest, or an accident?

Criminal History

In most states, criminal convictions are a matter of public record. Asking about arrests is illegal under the labor code; asking about *convictions* is acceptable. In fact, many organizations ask job applicants on the application, "Have you ever been convicted of a crime? If so, state the date and nature of the offense." Coupled with a statement on the application that says, "Making false statements with regard to this employment application is cause for dismissal," you can put the responsibility back on the shoulders of the applicants to explain their past histories.

You'll want to know if the candidate has an extensive criminal record—a critical factor if the person is going to be put in a position of financial trust. Would you hire someone who told you, "I was convicted of mail fraud, embezzlement, and check counterfeiting. But that was three years ago"?

Any convictions for crimes of violence, spousal abuse, child abuse, workplace assaults, theft, burglary, arson, animal abuse, auto theft, robbery, and so on should force you to think hard about this person. There is a difference between an otherwise normal person who may have had a brush with the law—a drunk-driving arrest, for example—and someone who seems to have made a career out of traveling to and from jail cells.

Credit History

Like the criminal history check, a credit check can point out certain indications. Would you hire an accounting clerk who had filed personal bankruptcy three times? Would you hire a minimum-wage cashier who was in credit card debt to the tune of $60,000 and teetering on a home foreclosure? What about a person with five liens attached to his property? The choice is yours, but you have to weigh the information in front along with the needs of your company. If you can't honestly tell yourself you can trust the person to handle your firm's money or proprietary data, why take the chance?

Driving Record

While this may seem harmless enough, it's often overlooked. If you have to hire someone to drive a bus, a company van, a delivery truck, or even a forklift, why not ask them to bring in a copy of their current Department of Motor Vehicles record? Failing to verify a good driving record could lead to many financial and legal headaches for you if your new employee wrecks a car in your fleet and the insurance companies discover he or she was driving with a suspended or revoked license.

Do you want to hire a parcel delivery driver with three hit-and-run convictions on his record? Twelve speeding tickets in two years? A long history of unpaid parking tickets or traffic arrest warrants?

As with all of these history checks, the same rule applies: Review the information carefully, discuss any discrepancies with the applicant, verify errors in the reports, and use the data as another benchmark for your decision.

The old story about the man and the snake applies here: As a man was walking down a road, he saw a snake lying in an open canvas bag along the side of the road.

"Help me!" said the snake. "I'm badly hurt!"

"What do you want me to do?" said the man as he looked at the wounded snake in the bag.

"Carry me home in this bag and nurse me back to health. I need food and water right away," said the snake.

"No, I think not," said the man. "If I do that, you'll only bite me later and I'll be sorry."

"No! Trust me," said the snake. "I'll be good."

So the man wrapped up the snake in the canvas bag and took him home. For days, he tended to the snake until one day, he was ready to set him free. As he reached into the canvas sack to lift the snake out, it bit him hard on the arm.

Wincing in agony, the man cried out, "What did you do that for? After all I've done for you, nursing you back to health. This is the thanks I get?"

"You knew I was a snake," came the reply, "when you took me out of the bag."

ALPHABET SOUP: LABOR
DEPARTMENT LESSONS

Hiring has never been more fraught with legal peril. Many companies who find themselves in legal hot water may have the best intentions, only to discover they have flagrantly broken the law. The best advice: Get good legal help from qualified counsel before you make any significant changes to your hiring policies.

Labor law attorneys are now warning companies to be careful of state and federal labor code "blacklisting" statutes that protect applicants from unjust or unfair screening practices.

And with regard to the July 1992 Americans with Disabilities Act (ADA), the rule of thumb is clearly mandated: "Don't pry into an applicant's personal life."

If you're already up to speed on the legal requirements for safe interviews, the following can serve as a quick review for you. In any case, experienced veteran or new personnel manager, get sound advice from established legal and human resource professionals.

The labor board for your state, your in-house corporate counsel, outside attorneys on retainer, or professional personnel organizations like the Personnel Management Association (PMA), the Society for Human Resource Management (SHRM), or the American Society of Training and Development (ASTD) can all offer help with safe interviewing techniques. As of this writing:

- You can't ask about an applicant's spouse or even if he or she is married.
- You can't ask when or if a person attended high school or college, only where.
- You can't ask if the person has children, only if there is anything that would keep him or her from working normal business hours or traveling, if it's required for the job.
- You can't ask about health issues, but you can ask the applicant to take a physical exam or a drug screen if it's required for all candidates.
- You can't ask how a person became disabled.

- You can't ask any specific questions about diseases (e.g., AIDS, cancer, alcoholism, mental illness).
- You can't ask specific questions about drug or alcohol use.
- Make sure your job descriptions fit the jobs you're hiring for. If it's no longer necessary to lift 50 pounds for a warehouse job, change the written description to match the job as it is now.
- Watch what you write during an interview. Any notes you take may have to appear in a courtroom later.[1]

Asking previous employers for references is another shark-infested area. Thanks to the proliferation of lawsuits over this issue, most employers will not give any pertinent information about a former employee. If you're looking for something other than name, date of hire, and date of departure, you probably won't get it.

But some employers will go so far as to answer yea or nay should you ask them if they would rehire the applicant. One way to phrase this question might be, "If you were given the opportunity today, would you rehire this applicant at your firm?"

If they choose to answer this question, you can add it to your own decision-making process.

ASKING THE RIGHT QUESTIONS: THINKING LIKE A PSYCHOLOGIST

Unless you have a psychologist do your interviewing for you, don't pretend to be one. But you can get a great deal of information by asking the right interview questions and carefully listening to the answers.

More often than not, the people in your personnel department (if you have one) are well-trained interviewers, with years of experience. Arm them with the kind of information they should be searching for, not just to identify competence to do the job in question but for the signs of potential violence in an applicant. The next chapter discusses these in much detail.

While it's not necessary to *be* a psychologist to safely hire someone, it never hurts to *think* like one. The following questions are certainly not foolproof, but they will lead you toward the areas that point to the credibility and more importantly, the volatility, of a potential employee. (Before you begin, check first with in-house or outside counsel for the validity of these questions in your state.)

Are you satisfied with what you've accomplished in your life?

In what areas do you feel qualified to give advice?

In what ways are you aggressive?

In what ways do you intimidate people?

Who are people that you would never intimidate?

When do you fail to confront people when you really should?

What specifically arouses your aggressiveness?

What do you do to control your anger?

What do you do to avoid arguments?

What are five acts of courage you admire in others?

When do you feel intimidated by difficult people?

In what ways can you be tricky?

When is it hard for you to admit you made a mistake?

Which people do you dominate in your life and how?

When are you able to show compassion for other people?

How do you react when things don't turn out as you expected?

When have you taken insults well?

In what hidden ways do you try to exercise power?

Which minority group do you have the most trouble getting along with?

In what ways does your gruffness express itself?

On what occasions do you lie?

In what ways are you difficult?

In what ways do you try to dominate your spouse?

What foolish things have you done out of misguided courage?

In what ways are you deceptive because of pressure from other people?

Do you feel more pleasure in avoiding arguments or in arguing?

Can you differentiate between a worthwhile argument and one that's not worthwhile?

With which people do you tend to argue most?

With which people do you tend not to argue?

How many friends can you count on in your life?

If you ask no other questions during the interview—besides name, address, phone, and "When can you start?"—make sure you cover these next "must" seven questions. Skip these only at your peril, especially if you're interviewing an applicant who fits several categories for workplace violence potential:

1. When have you felt that you have been treated unfairly in your life?
2. What did you do about it?
3. What would you have liked to have done about it?
4. Why do you feel you had been treated unjustly?
5. What complaints have you had about your supervisors in the past?
6. What could a supervisor do to make you angry?
7. What has a supervisor done in the past to make you really angry?

Any comments you hear from the applicant about unjust or unfair treatment in past employment should raise an immediate red flag in front of your eyes. In nearly every case involving disgruntled employees who resorted to some type of violence on the job, their perception of unjust or unfair treatment has been one key to their motivations.

In interviews with you, the problem employee may not even seek to hide his anger or aggression toward past employers. "I've been treated unfairly. My last boss was such a jerk that I had to leave. He wouldn't give me a day off when I really needed one and I got so upset that I just quit."

If you hear the applicant give you an unsolicited comment about some past problem on the job, don't skip over it in the vain hope it's somehow not important or it will go away. Chances are, if you get this kind of information voluntarily, there's a good reason for it.

Negative comments about the applicant's home life also should serve as a warning sign. Violence at home should warn you about violence at work. Studies, interviews, and police and social worker caseloads point to a clear link between domestic violence and workplace violence.

If during an interview the subject of spouses comes up and the person says jokingly "Boy, sometimes my wife makes me so mad I want to strangle her!" you should not smile pleasantly and move on to the next question. Ask why now or face the consequences later.

Finally, consider asking the job applicant to answer the following hypothetical scenario:

"Let's suppose a supervisor of yours really started to treat you unfairly. This person talks down to you, dumps more work on you, passes you over for a promotion, that type of thing. You are really starting to get upset about the way this supervisor is treating you. What would you do?"

If the applicant says, "Well, I'd go to my supervisor's boss and talk to him or her about the problem."

Your reply: "Suppose your supervisor's boss wasn't interested in talking to you?"

If the applicant says, "Maybe I'd go to the personnel manager, or the union rep, or the president of the company."

Your reply: "Let's say those people were out of the office or on vacation and you couldn't talk to them. You're getting madder by the minute at your supervisor. What now?"

In most cases, using this scenario, the applicant will give you a normal response—that is, "I'd try to find someone else in my work group to talk to about it," or "I've never had that kind of problem with a supervisor before, but I'd either chalk it up to experience and try to ride out the storm or I'd seriously think about getting another job."

On the other hand, you should be able to spot an abnormal response to this scenario right away. If the person says, "I'd wait for my supervisor out in the parking lot after work and confront him," or "I'd find a way to get back at him," or "I'd be just as nasty to him as he is to me," then you know you've struck a nerve. The signs are on the wall; don't forget to read them.

DISCOVERING PERSONALITY DISORDERS: CAREFUL QUESTIONS MAY REVEAL SOME FATAL FLAWS

We recommend that whoever is doing the early preemployment screening, whether it's the personnel manager, human resources executive, or job supervisor, look for certain specific personality difficulties. It's not necessary to do deep analysis on people; just gather the data and let their answers speak for themselves. The responses you hear should give you enough information to make an accurate decision for the all-important question: Do I feel comfortable hiring this person or not?

WHAT TO LOOK FOR IN APPLICANTS WITH POTENTIAL PERSONALITY DISORDERS

These types of people may exhibit the following characteristics during your interview process. You should make note of any responses that clearly indicate these factors:

1. *Tenuous stability under stress.* These people exhibit behaviors and thought patterns that are usually rigid, and they are not as able to adapt to new difficulties or disruptions like most of us do. Anxiety, depression, or psychosomatic symptoms may be present in their lives.

2. *Lower than average self-esteem.* This can interfere with their ability to work and/or affect the relationship with a supervisor, since poor self-esteem can lead to an overreaction to criticism.

3. *Poor interpersonal coping skills.* These people may lack the social skills necessary to function well in the workplace. This is especially true if their work involves an interpersonal component that makes them have to interact constantly with co-workers and supervisors.

4. *Episodic periods of anxiety or depression.* Even small or otherwise minor stressors can trigger these feelings. And in some cases, internal thoughts rather than external occurrences bring them on.

5. *Blames and punishes others or self.* People with passive–aggressive, paranoid, or histrionic disorders tend to blame and punish others for their own problems.

6. *Repeats vicious cycles.* These people engage in self-defeating patterns that can escalate and intensify with time.

The following series of questions may reveal the presence of these noticeable personality problems. They may seem a bit intimidating to ask at first, but the areas they cover are critical. (Check with your legal department or outside attorneys for permission to ask these questions in your state).

SCREENING FOR HIGHLY PARANOID PERSONS

1. Do you often worry that people might be planning to harm or take advantage of you?

2. Are you concerned that certain friends or co-workers are not really trustworthy?

3. Do you usually take what people tell you at face value, or do you frequently try to figure out what they mean?

4. If someone insults you, how long does it take until your relationship gets back to normal? Are there some people you've never forgiven?

5. Do you think it's best not to let people get to know you too well?

SCREENING FOR ANTISOCIAL PERSONS

Before the age of 15:

1. Have you ever run away from home?

2. Have you ever used a weapon in a fight?

3. Have you ever been intentionally cruel to animals?

4. Have you ever lit fires to cause damage?
5. Have you stolen without confronting the victim? Or by confronting the victim?

After the age of 15:

1. Have you ever been unemployed for long periods while not attending school?
2. Have you ever been involved in illegal activities that could have gotten you arrested?
3. How often do you get into physical fights?
4. Have you ever been so angry that you started hitting or throwing things at your spouse or partner?
5. When you want something, would you mislead someone about what they can expect from you?

SCREENING FOR BORDERLINE PERSONALITY PEOPLE

1. Does it seem like people who were your best friends at one time turn out to be your worst enemies at other times?
2. Do you switch from loving, respecting, and admiring them at one time to despising them at another time?
3. Do you spend money impulsively?
4. Has anyone ever told you that you were irritable or that your mood seems to change a great deal?
5. Have you ever noticed rapid mood changes where you can go from depressed to normal to angry to anxious all in the same day?[2]

RATIONALIZATION ROAD HAZARDS

The average human resources person wants to justify certain kinds of borderline responses by looking at the context and saying, "Well, that's okay, I guess. I might have done the same thing if I were in that position."

You must be careful to weigh the person's responses based on the needs of your organization, not against *your* moral compass. If your personal feeling is "Hey, what's the big deal?" then maybe you need to look at your own ethics and values as they pertain to what is good for the company.

Police departments across the country have fallen into this moral trap. Courts have found several police agencies liable when they hired recruits with a known penchant for unnecessarily aggressive behavior, domestic violence against a spouse, or documented child abuse problems.

By saying, "Well, that's OK if the guy shoved his wife once two years ago. It's not that important to us now," these departments overlooked key red flag areas in the applicant's history. Their own biases about police officer aggressiveness, the macho code that dooms many officers to failure, and their inability to see domestic violence at home as the window to violence at work have forced some police agencies to pay out large settlement sums to the victims of these unchecked officers.

Too many times we want to overlook an applicant's red flag responses and purposely ignore the serious consequences they bring up. Look at each person's response with the context in mind, but keep your perspective, too.

One of the biggest problems we face when we hire may come from within ourselves. As paradoxical as it sounds, we *want* to believe the people we interview and ultimately hire. The hiring process is a give-and-take encounter, where both sides offer something of themselves to the other.

We don't use robots to interview prospective employees, we use people. And since most people strive to be at least cordial to one another, the interview process is often full of conversations, asides, and remarks that have little to do with the actual job at hand, but rather, serve to build rapport between the interviewer and the interviewee.

This rapport building serves two functions: it helps to put the job candidate at ease and, to a larger extent, it helps to put the employer at ease as well. Even people with years of experience in personnel and hiring may secretly admit that they find the entire interview process to be a stressful experience.

In most instances, interviewing is hard work. In some cases, where large blocks of employees need to be hired to fulfill certain

work demands—defense contracts, government contracts, short-
or long-term production schedules, and so on—the personnel
and human resources people may have to hire hundreds or even
thousands of people in a short period of time. The clock ticks and
the production supervisors point to their watches, hold the work
orders in their hands, and scream, "Get us qualified people and
get them yesterday!"

Forced to cope with people stacked like cordwood in the waiting
room and reams of résumés or job applications, it's no surprise
that some interviews can deteriorate in quality. "We need people,"
thinks the harried personnel supervisor. "I've got to make a choice
and get someone on the job now."

This can really take its toll the longer the interview process
takes. It's no surprise that after weeks and weeks of application
reading, interviews, follow-up letters and calls, and sorting
through the mounds of paperwork that seems to accompany every
applicant, even the most enthusiastic personnel worker can get
jaded. This is even more true if you've been doing the same
job—hiring and/or firing—for many years.

People new to the hiring experience tend to be much more
careful, largely because they're probably afraid of making major
legal mistakes, or they don't want to be responsible for hiring the
wrong person, or because they have less time in grade to feel
burned out. The long-time personnel specialist may be able to
spot good employees right away, but he or she can quickly lose
enthusiasm during a major hiring period. During these hectic
times, it's hard to keep track of the sea of faces that have passed
by your desk in search of a job. Burn out, in such instances, is a
distinct possibility. It's easy to get careless, make snap judgments,
and create future problems with bad choices.

The human mind looks for ways to justify things. As employers
wishing to hire the proper applicant, we look for ways to rationalize the past and current behaviors of other people. Too often, in
our own mind, we want to give someone the benefit of the doubt
for something he or she has done that may not be particularly
heinous but still gives us pause.

The employer who asks for trouble starts by saying, "I have
questions about this applicant's work history, and even after several tries I've still not received a satisfactory answer. He'll probably
be all right. Let's hire him anyway."

What makes interviewing so difficult is that on the one hand, the candidates want to put their collective best foot forward, so they spend their time trying to tell the interviewer what he or she wants to hear.

On the other, the interviewer wants to make the correct determination about the prospective employee because the decision to hire or turn away the person is fraught with legal, fiscal, and emotional issues. This is especially true in our rocky economic times.

In states located in the Rust Belt—particularly in steel and auto manufacturing firms—where hiring and firing is done on large scales, many people in the labor pool are in desperate need of work and will say or do almost anything to get a job.

And in the Silicon Valley and the Aerospace Belts, middle to upper-level managers, engineers, and executives may all vie for similar positions with the high-tech, computer, and defense companies who still have contracts and work. This can put tremendous pressure on the interviewer to separate truth from fiction and choose wisely.

Failing to ascertain real and valuable information about past work performance, work history, job skills, education, military history, credit history, criminal record, past performance evaluations, and reasons for leaving the last employer can cause a chain reaction of future problems that begin when the newly hired employee walks through the door.

THE LUXURY OF THE MULTIPLE INTERVIEW

If this were a perfect world, businesspeople could take plenty of time and care to screen each job applicant with a battery of tests, skills assessments, and in-person interviews conducted in several locations and under different circumstances.

But most companies have to make do with the standard advertise-interview-select process that is commonplace to hiring. Often, the sheer numbers alone make any deviation from this process expensive and unnecessary. Consider that in only one year, a large employer may interview 25,000 people to fill 2,000 positions nationwide. These numbers certainly call for a streamlined interview process.

If you're charged with hiring assembly-line workers, then a careful review of the application, a brief background check, and a thorough interview that covers all the factors you deem appropriate could be good enough. As the level of sophistication for the position rises, so should your interviewing efforts.

Some human resources and personnel managers swear by the multiple interview as an ideal evaluation tool. They say it allows them to see the applicant in a variety of situations. Often, the employer will meet with the job candidate for one interview and then schedule a "roving" interview that introduces him or her to other employees, supervisors, or the work area itself.

For more sophisticated positions, the second interview may take place in a social setting, such as over lunch, or during an after-work drink. Typically, for these "away from the office" encounters, two or more representatives from the company will go along to help with the evaluation and to add their own input into the interview process.

The president of a large computer systems company puts it this way: "My second interview for new salespeople always takes place at lunch. When we get to the restaurant, I suggest to the applicant that he or she order for both of us while I take care of some paperwork at the table. You'd be surprised how much you can learn about people from the way they treat waiters and waitresses. It's funny, but I know immediately if the candidate treats these people like 'peons,' he or she will be wrong for our company. If they can't get along with all kinds of folks in a social setting, I worry about how they will get along with my customers."

With time and money constraints at issue, this amount of interview work is rarely feasible. And in most cases, it might not even be necessary. Historically, the majority of workplace violence incidents involving serious assault cases or murders have involved blue-collar, entry-level, or middle-management employees.

We don't recall any memorable cases involving a member of a company's board of directors going on a shooting rampage. This is not to say it won't happen, just that the documented cases point toward employees on the lower end of the skills/salary spectrum.

Unless your company is choosing a new CEO or a president, the luxury of a multiple interview is usually just that—a luxury.

So it all depends on the time, money, and effort you want to put into the candidate's interview. While we're not trying to suggest pie-in-the-sky solutions to hiring, the multiple interview offers you the opportunity for a good second look at someone.

YOUR HIRING HANDBOOK: WHEN IN DOUBT, DON'T

Whenever you schedule hiring sessions and before you make any decisions, keep these rules in mind:

1. *There are always going to be more applicants available than jobs you can give them.* Therefore, you have the luxury of being choosy about whom you hire.
2. *Consider every contact you have with the applicant as another opportunity to obtain information.* Whether the person meets you in your office, speaks to you on the phone, writes you a letter, fills out a job application, submits a résumé, or sits for an interview, use that contact to find out more about the person. See even seemingly short encounters as an opportunity to collect more data.
3. *Where there's smoke, there's fire.* If you see warning signs, either during the interview, based on the information you read on the application, or as a result of a background check, entrance exam, or prescreening test, go with your true feelings. Either dig deeper and ask the applicants to fill in gaps or answer questions to your complete satisfaction, or don't hire them. Hoping someone with a documented, significant workplace or personal problem will "get better" is a risky proposition.
4. *Better to be safe for your company now than sorry later.* If you have real doubts about an applicant's veracity, moral turpitude, or ethics, don't hire!

Jet pilots for our major air carriers must go through a strenuous certification process in order to get and keep their licenses. Experienced pilot trainers take new pilots on "shakedown" flights to evaluate their skills at taking off, landing, instrument flying, and so forth.

To grade the new pilot properly, each evaluator asks a simple question: "If this pilot was flying a plane and my family was aboard, would I feel comfortable?"

If the answer is yes, the new pilot passes the training phase and goes to work. If the answer is no or even a qualified maybe, it's back to flight school.

If you can't give your new hires the same vote of confidence, why bring them aboard? If you wouldn't leave your children with a babysitter who had a questionable job history, a shaky job application, and poor references, why would you hire someone you didn't feel you could trust with the assets of your company?

This is not to say we have to love everyone we hire. You may not have the time nor the inclination to develop a lasting friendship with everyone you hire. The key to good hiring is to establish strict and legal policies and procedures and follow them. No one can fault you for doing your best, just as long as you don't deviate from the laws.

TRUSTING YOUR GUT INSTINCTS

If you feel the hair on the back of your neck rise every time you deal with a certain employee at your company, those are probably valid warning signs. If you get an odd sensation in the pit of your stomach when this person is around you, this is a genuine feeling.

People are usually highly intuitive in their feelings toward one another. First impressions are often right on the mark. While it's true that people can change their opinions of others and often do, how you perceive someone in your initial meetings usually remains the same.

Think about this in your own life. Review the first meetings with your truly close friends. Did you hate each other at first sight and then grow closer over time? Not likely. Most of us feel some kind of affinity to another person, and if it grows in strength, then we can point to a solid friendship.

Conversely, if we don't feel any positive alliance with someone we first meet, chances are those feelings will not change with time. All of this certainly applies to the hiring and interviewing processes that take place every day in business.

What happens if the applicant has a sterling résumé, solid experience, and all the on-paper qualifications, yet goes out of his or her way to rub you the wrong way during the interview? Will this person get the job?

And what if the applicant makes you feel physically uncomfortable? Would you hire the person who made you feel threatened, intimidated, or apprehensive? What about the person who applies for a position and makes you feel like you owe him or her a job? That your job applications, testing processes, and screening procedures were biased, unfair, or not politically correct? Could you say yes to this person's request for a job and safely bring him or her into your firm?

If you don't feel you can trust certain applicants, or you wouldn't feel comfortable with them, why hire trouble? In the worst case, maybe a potentially good employee gets away from you and goes to another company who hires that person on the spot. Maybe your first impressions were totally wrong and you let a winner go. But then again, consider that most of us can count the number of times on one hand when our gut instincts let us down. It's far better to err on the side of what's right rather than make assumptions, create rationalizations, and hire someone who may turn out to be a problem employee later.

Destructive employees are like bad apartment tenants: It's always easier to turn them down in the beginning than to turn them out in the end.

THE MYTH OF THE PERFECT EMPLOYEE

"Computers," said artist Pablo Picasso, "are useless. They can only give you answers." One benefit of working with computers is that they are inanimate objects that do not require food, shelter, praise, or a paycheck. For that, we have employees. If a computer malfunctions, you can either have it repaired or you can go to the computer store and buy another one. People aren't so interchangeable, so when something goes wrong with one of them, you can't just go to the factory and get another.

And just as there are no perfect computers, there are no perfect employees. Try as we might, the occasional bad apple still slips through. Sometimes what makes this even worse is that the employee who turns bad started out as a potential shining star. A case in point:

A southern California police agency hired an applicant who passed all its tests with high marks. His entrance exam score was in the first category, his physical abilities test score was top notch, and his background looked impeccable. He had been a minor league baseball player of some note, had attended college, married his high school sweetheart, and begun to raise a family. This candidate scored well on his oral interviews, polygraph test, and medical exam. He was sent to the next police academy for enrollment.

Through the police academy, the new cadet scored well on his written and hands-on tests, he provided leadership and motivation to his classmates, and he impressed the academy instructors with his discipline, enthusiasm, and police skills.

By the end of the academy class, the cadet had scored well enough on classroom and physical training exams to be named the Honor Graduate, the best student in his academy.

The new officer went into the field and completed his field training hours with little difficulty. All who saw him thought he was a good cop, a good partner, and a friendly guy. During nearly five years on the job, the officer was a model employee.

During the time the officer worked an area near the beach and coastline of his city, a frightening series of sexual assaults were taking place. The police put extra patrols in the beach area, but the number of assaults grew to seven, and many women who lived in the beach community were scared to go out at night.

One night, a man came to a hospital emergency room with a gunshot wound in his hand. He told the ER doctors he had been robbed and shot as he worked on his stalled car on the freeway. As with all gunshot wounds, the hospital called the police, who came to investigate for themselves. As they talked to the man, they noticed he was covered with beach sand. He also happened to be an employee of the police department. He also happened to be the model police officer in this story, the honor grad, the hardworking, enthusiastic officer everyone liked and believed in.

When the officer's supervisor came to the hospital, he found many holes in the story of this alleged attack. When two men and a woman reported an attempted rape at the beach, things started to fall apart for the officer. When detectives found his flashlight—with his name and ID number engraved on it—at the scene of the beach attack, they arrested the model officer on suspicion of robbery and attempted rape.

When the officer was brought to trial, many questions came from the public, the media, and other police officers. "How could he have done this?" and "How could he have even become a cop in the first place?"

A careful review of his initial application, background check, psychological exams, and interviews revealed no warning signs. For all purposes, the officer was a model candidate for the job—and yet, he was later responsible for seven sexual assaults. The puzzled background investigation detectives and preemployment psychologists all agreed: Had this candidate applied for a police position anywhere else in the country, he would have got the job in a flash. His credentials were without question; he simply went bad.

As frightening as this sounds, the real truth is that hiring a new employee is more of an art than a science. You can only do the best you can do. You can interview and interview and interview a candidate until you're both weary of looking at each other, you can screen and screen and screen some more, and you can test and test and test. But in the final moment, hiring an employee for your company is still a judgment call. We try to choose wisely, but we must recognize there are limits to what we can do.

Follow your instincts, be conservative, stay within proper state and federal legal guidelines, allow other qualified people to help you make good decisions, and keep the real needs of your company in mind.

ENDNOTES

[1] Marc Hequet, "The Intricacies of Interviewing," *Training* magazine, April 1993, p. 31.

[2] Mark Zimmerman, *The Interview Guide for Evaluating DSMIII-R Psychiatric Disorders and the Mental Health Status Examination* (Philadelphia: Psych Press, 1992), pp. 100–110.

Chapter Four

Caution! Disgruntled Employee Ahead!

Assuming today is like many other days for American business, somewhere a "disgruntled employee" feels cheated, betrayed, endangered, dissatisfied, harassed, bored, or just plain upset. But what makes his or her situation different are the two words *disgruntled employee.*

David Klinghoffer, writing in *National Review*, noted that historians will quite likely recall this time in history as one of "great disgruntlement." In Klinghoffer's words, "More and more, we Americans are an irritable, uncivil, bitchy, self-pitying, dissatisfied, disgruntled group of people."[1] Indeed, the art critic Robert Hughes refers to our environment as the "Culture of Complaint."

But there is a difference between being "uncivil, bitchy, self-pitying . . ." and being referred to as a "disgruntled employee" these days. Uncivil people usually don't kill their bosses. "Disgruntled employees" most certainly do. And they are doing it in record numbers. Just the words can send shivers up and down your spine, especially if you are a typical human resources professional charged with disciplining or terminating an individual who you think of as disgruntled. "Will he come back and kill me?" may now be a legitimate question.

When you hear the words *disgruntled employee,* you probably recall newspaper headlines describing the aftermath of violence in a local factory, or you might see images in your mind of your local television news showing bodies being carried out of a local business establishment or even recall actual live scenes of violence in your own workplace.

CASES AND INCIDENTS

George Cook, 56, regional vice president of Merrill Lynch's Boston office, was described in the *Boston Globe* as "very, very understanding, the kindest guy you could ever come across" by his friend Charles Mohr, then president of Colonial Management Associates. Another Merrill Lynch vice president, Paul Knouse, told the *Globe* staff reporter, "Cook's strength's were his administrative skills and his ability to get on well with people."

Still, Lonnie Lee Gilchrist, Jr., dismissed by Cook the previous day for poor performance, was charged in 1988 with pistol-whipping him and fatally shooting him four times. Cook tried to flee from Gilchrist inside the firm's 36th-floor office at One Financial Plaza but was unsuccessful and died of his wounds.[2] Is that the headline you recall when you hear the words *disgruntled employee?*

Or perhaps on the West Coast you flash back to the Hewlett-Packard electronics plant in Roseville, California, in April 1992, when Eric Houston was terminated from the assembly line. You may recall headlines that screamed that young Eric used a shotgun and a .22-calibre rifle to kill four innocent people.

This young man was described by the *New York Times* as a "disgruntled former student." Student? Yes, you see, Eric didn't return to Hewlett-Packard to commit his violence. Instead, he paid a visit to his former alma mater, Lindhurst High School in Olivehurst, and took out his rage on those he held responsible for preparing him for such a lousy job. Does Eric come to mind when you hear the words *disgruntled employee?*

Perhaps you recall another disgruntled employee, Pat Calden, who shot and killed three of his former managers and wounded two other innocent employees at the Fireman's Insurance Company in Tampa, Florida, in January 1993. He turned his gun on himself and took his own life.

"Disgruntled employee." The phrase may jar you to recall Paul Hannah, a technician of the Illinois Bell Company. This disgruntled employee faced the possibility of being suspended from his job for refusing to take a drug test. He allegedly murdered a union steward.

Or does your memory take you back to Killeen, Texas, in October 1991? Remember the national headlines? George Hennard gave new meaning to the notion of "drive-up service." He drove his truck right through the large, plate-glass window of Luby's Cafeteria and executed 22 people in random fashion. He also turned the gun on himself. He never worked for Luby's, but did lose his job as a merchant seaman two years earlier. Luby's was the workplace where he decided to spill his rage.

And then there are the many acts of violence you may recall at US Postal Service branches. Perhaps while the phrase wasn't yet fashionable, still, back in the summer of 1985, Patrick Henry Sherril coolly walked into his former place of employment, the Edmond, Oklahoma, post office, and murdered 14 of his fellow co-workers. He didn't like the way he had been disciplined the day earlier. He also turned the gun on himself.

Perhaps you recall Thomas McIlvane's headlines when the two famous words *disgruntled employee* were uttered. Thomas was dismissed from his employment as a mail carrier in Royal Oak, Michigan, in November 1991. He "looked possessed" and was called a "ticking bomb" by a co-worker because he exhibited many "warning signs" and had made many threats to his supervisors in the past. What was his response to being dismissed? He returned to his place of employment and murdered 3 supervisors, wounded 14 others, then of course, committed suicide.

Ridgewood, New Jersey, newspapers carried the story of Joseph M. Harris, another disgruntled employee—a mail sorter at the local post office. He used a samurai sword to stab his former supervisor to death. Then, he returned to the post office and murdered two other co-workers with a gun.

"Workplace Violence Becomes Epidemic" shouted the headlines in the May 24, 1993, issue of the *Federal Times*. Yes, as you are preparing for another day of hiring, disciplining, terminating, or just working with others in your law firm, bank, factory, retail store, restaurant, school, supermarket, travel or insurance agency, hospital, government installation, local car wash, or post office, workplace violence is rising dramatically around you.

As you prepare for another workday, in the midst of shaving, putting on your makeup, fixing breakfast, or doing whatever your morning rituals are, you hear those two words, *disgruntled em-*

ployee, coming from the radio or TV news. Again, images begin to pop into your mind. This time you may summon up media pictures of May 6, 1993, in Dearborn Michigan, and in Dana Point, California.

In Dearborn, the pictures appear in the aftermath of the violence committed by Larry Jasion. Jasion was a postal employee who wanted a job that required less standing due to his "bad legs." He requested an administrative clerk's position in the vehicle maintenance facility at Dearborn. Instead, someone else got the job.

Then there was the problem he had with the music that his co-workers were playing at work. He didn't like it. He filed a union grievance about the playing of loud rap and heavy metal music. He lost the employees' vote, 10 to 2.

He decided to take matters into his own hands and pulled a .38-calibre handgun from a doughnut box, murdered one co-worker, critically injured another, and wounded his supervisor. He then shot himself to death.

When investigators searched, they found two other small-calibre handguns and extra ammunition inside the doughnut box. Since 1969, Jasion had registered at least 13 guns.

Back to the West Coast, you may recall the results of Mark Richard Hilbun's own disgruntlement. He was suspended in September 1992 and terminated as a mail carrier in December 1992. Able to bypass the beefed-up security measures established by those already concerned about the possibility of violence, he allegedly shot and killed Charles Barbagallo, a letter carrier, and shot and wounded Peter Gates, a mail clerk.

Hilbun, it was later learned, allegedly murdered his mother before coming to the post office to continue his rampage of violence.

Fortune magazine recently noted, "Maybe it's time to start handing out bulletproof vests along with IDs. Homicides committed by disgruntled employees and former employees at the workplace are on the rise. That kind of killing was virtually nonexistent before 1980. But since 1988, the number of office slayings has increased disturbingly, to an average of 18 a year."[3]

So you've heard the phrase *disgruntled employee* until you're sick of it? You think to yourself while you're driving to your workplace listening to yet another case, "What's wrong with people these days? Are they all crazy? Are people losing their minds? Doesn't American business deserve a 'normal' work force?"

Perhaps you are also trying to answer other questions: "Who are all of these 'disgruntled employees,' anyway?"

"How can I tell if someone is so disgruntled that he or she may actually come back and act violently towards me or someone else in my workplace?"

There are probably few remaining business professionals today who haven't considered these and similar questions.

From the transportation industry to food processing, from computers to construction, from the world of retail to the many shipping and delivery services nationally, and from the medical profession to manufacturing corporations, no industry is considered immune any longer from violence in the workplace.

Master control operators at broadcast stations, apartment managers, industrial maintenance machinists, room service waiters, librarians, utility company file clerks, cemetery groundskeepers, probation officers and cops, the pizza maker, and the bank teller all share in the potential to commit acts of violence or sabotage in the workplace. No job brings with it a guaranty of freedom from violence.

According to much-noted US Bureau of Labor Statistics reports, homicide is now the third most frequent cause of death in the workplace in America. In some locations nationally, it ranks first. It is the leading cause of death for women at work, and workers who are 65 years old and up had the highest fatality rate among all age groups.

More specifically, the National Traumatic Occupational Fatalities project reported that from 1980 to 1985, 42 percent of all women who died in work-related incidents were victims of violent crime. For men, the same study found that 12 percent of on-the-job deaths were the result of violent crime.

Of course, this doesn't necessarily mean the violence came from a disgruntled employee. As we stated earlier, the statistics that are available now do not allow for a clean breakdown between those acts of homicide that were committed by a disgruntled employee and those perpetrated by an outside individual in the course of a criminal action.

Shouldn't you be able to identify the worker most likely to commit one of these heinous acts in your worksite? Wouldn't you feel more equipped to deal with business's most important security problem if you had understood the profile factors surrounding one of these people? Wouldn't you and your family feel more secure if you knew what warning signs to look for in your employees or co-workers?

The answers to these questions are the same we have heard from businesspeople we've spoken with from all around the country—an apprehensive yes.

So what are the common characteristics of those employees who commit violence in the workplace? Drawing a profile of a potentially violent employee is not an easy, or necessarily safe, thing to do. For one, if you're wrong, you may get fatally surprised. In an interview with *Training* magazine in July 1993, Dr. Mantell was quoted as having "the strongest voice against overdependence on 'profiles' to ferret out dangerous employees."

His concern is that there are, of course, exceptions to every rule. With an issue that has life and death, real bottom-line implications, overdependence on anything may be too cavalier.

While you are busy keeping your security department focused on one employee recently terminated in Orlando who fit the profile, you may be shocked to learn that someone disciplined months earlier, who did not seem to fit the profile at all, just randomly shot at co-workers in the parking lot of your St. Louis office. *Profiling* is an inexact science at best.

We do know that there are certain high-risk types of employment that have greater than the average number of acts of occupational violence (e.g., criminal or disgruntled employees). These have common characteristics:

1. They are involved in the delivery of services or goods to the public.
2. They are typically involved in an activity that carries with it the exchange of money.
3. The environment is best described as unsecured.

READING THE SIGNS

Let's see if you feel safer having a checklist to use in another potential life and death situation. The FBI's William Carter provides this profile for executives to use in another form of workplace violence. First, we'll tell you what the danger signs are, and then, we'll ask you to figure out what the signs are trying to predict:

Excessive weight for the size.

Too much postage.

No return address.

Mailed from a foreign country, or via airmail or special delivery.

A rigid or lopsided envelope.

Common words are misspelled.

Restrictive markings, such as Confidential or Personal.

Incorrect title for the addressee, or a title without a person's name.

Handwritten or poorly typed address.

Protruding wires or tinfoil.

Oily stains or discoloration on the outside of the package.

It's obvious, isn't it? Package and letter bombs frequently give clues to alert you to beware, to get some professional help right away, and to proceed with extreme caution. Would you open a package that had 1 of these indicators? 2? 3? 6? 10? Or would you need to have all 11 before you decided not to risk your life or the lives of those around you by opening the letter or package?

Similarly, with human ticking bombs, there are indicators in the workplace that should alert the hiring authorities, personnel managers, co-workers, and others to be cautious, to proceed with extreme care, and to get professional help in dealing with the potentially life-threatening actions that the human ticking bomb can display.

Aren't the ticking letter bomb and the ticking human bomb similar? If you would use caution before opening a letter that meets some or all of the indicators described above, then you would want to use caution before engaging with someone who meets the criteria described for a human ticking bomb.

What should your safety zone be? In other words, how many of the following items do you need to see before you become concerned? There is no perfect answer. Just as with the letter bomb, how many do you need to feel safe? In our experience, we don't need many more than a few before we would take conservative, perhaps even life-saving, measures.

As an employer, the value of the profile is in what it does and doesn't tell you. Some of these characteristics may even be discovered in hindsight, after the employee is long gone. But as these common threads pile up, coupled with the threat of job loss, aggressive behavior during discipline sessions, or other antisocial activities at work, it becomes clear that you can't just sit back and hope that if you ignore 19 of 20 warning signs, then nothing bad will happen. It doesn't mean it will, but you had better be prepared to react and intervene just the same.

It is now possible to draw on nearly 15 years of experience in this field and create a general profile of perpetrators of violence in the workplace. What follows is just that, a compilation of the most commonly seen characteristics among those who commit violent acts in the workplace:

COMMON CHARACTERISTICS OF PERPETRATORS OF VIOLENCE IN THE WORKPLACE

1. *Disgruntled regarding perceived injustice at work.* Many cases of individuals who have committed violence in their own or another workplace indicated they were angry, mad, annoyed, or disgruntled about some perceived injustice they felt at work.

Perhaps in your own workplace, you have dealt with people who complain about work conditions, pay, the way they are treated by management, or some policy or procedure in the company. These should not be brushed off too lightly for many reasons, the least being that the way your employees feel they are treated by management will likely result in the way they treat your customers. It could also be the beginning of a seed of destruction, the kind that leads to an eruption of violence.

Some of these perpetrators believe that others either threaten or persecute them. Some may be paranoid. As a manager, your job isn't to diagnose psychiatric impairment, but you should know some of the signs of potential trouble.

There are three types of paranoid disorders of which the average employer should be aware. The first is *paranoid personality disorder*. Here, your employee will have a long-standing set of maladaptive behaviors grounded in misinterpreting the words and actions of others as threatening or demeaning. Some may feel that supervisors don't take them seriously and they may feel mocked, exploited, or easily slighted.

Paranoid schizophrenics are severely ill and have a range of psychotic symptoms during the active phase of their illness. They may typically display the need for assistance in self-care, social relations, or in work. These workers are unlikely to be able to tolerate the demands of most work environments when they are in the active phase of untreated schizophrenia, caught up in delusions or in hallucinations of a systematized nature.

One noteworthy statistic, according to the National Institute of Mental Health Epidemiologic Catchment Area Study, is that only 43 percent of people with schizophrenia are working, compared to approximately 56 percent of the general population. Those with paranoid schizophrenia are most likely to be working, especially when their illness is in remission.

Delusional paranoid disorders are seen in employees who do not have bizarre hallucinations or delusions. They may be excellent workers, rarely miss work, and have few if any performance or conduct problems, as long as work does not involve their systematized nonbizarre delusional beliefs.

These employees are difficult to identify. However, they can be highly suspicious, angry, hostile, and violent. This disorder usually begins in midlife.

Are your disgruntled employees who perceive injustice paranoid in one form or another? Who knows? In all likelihood, unless you have excellent, detailed, and honest health records that you can access, you probably won't know, either. Don't guess. If in doubt, get some consultation from your company's psychologist, employee assistance program (EAP), or other mental health consultant.

2. *Socially isolated, may be a loner.* Some people have little else in their lives but work. They have little or nothing to do in their lives to keep it interesting, enriched, or fulfilled. Even in work, these people are alone.

These are the men and women who avoid socializing during lunch times and coffee breaks, and who don't join in company social activities. They are clearly the loners in their work group. When you try to seek them out, to invite them, they seem more than just shy. Perhaps they act like they lack the social skills necessary to interact effectively.

Others in the company may avoid these people as well. Co-workers may shun them because they appear to be out of step with everyone else. When invited, they appear angry, dull, or fearful.

3. *Poor self-esteem.* Self-esteem is crucial for success. This is accepted as a given by most thinking people today in any corporate atmosphere. Yet so many employees suffer from a lack of self-esteem, it may be industry's biggest personnel problem. Why?

A young child may be raised today in a typically dysfunctional atmosphere. Perhaps parents are separated, divorced, or one parent has simply never been available. In this atmosphere of emotional neglect, perhaps abuse may also have been evident—if not physical, then certainly emotional.

Where is this child going to develop any self-esteem? In school? Unlikely. Who is there to help him or her with homework, to share in the day-to-day successes and failures, and to be there to cheer him or her on in the face of frustration? Who is there to teach these children that "they can do it?"

Television, movies, magazines, music videos, and billboards will be there, selling the message of what good self-esteem may be based on to an unhealthy extent: sex, drugs, and violence. Unfortunately, these are the makings of self-esteem for many in our culture.

With no healthy outlet for anger, and few if any opportunities to develop a positive self-image, many young men and women grow up with little inside save for the great sense of gnawing anger and frustration that builds with age. Work becomes the only outlet, and one that also carries with it the opportunity to "prove" you are "somebody." Unfortunately, work typically gives these people another experience in which they are "proven" wrong.

With low self-esteem, the average worker has difficulty tolerating frustration, criticism, or any negative message. This is the platform from which much of workplace violence springs.

4. *Cries for help of some kind.* Employees who commit violent acts toward others in the workplace may have asked for some kind of attention before they lashed out. Requests for help come in many varieties.

Some will ask for attention from the EAP department. Others ask for attention by taking excessive time off. Still others may display conduct or performance problems as a way of drawing attention to themselves not for negative purposes but for positive ones, for help of some kind. They just don't know how else to get it.

It's not uncommon to have heard from some who have committed violence that they would have liked to have taken advantage of an EAP, but none was offered to them, in spite of the company having an excellent EAP available. They just wanted it offered. They didn't want to have to access it themselves. As we will see in Chapter 5, this is exactly what happened in the case of Robert Earl Mack.

5. *Fascination with the military.* To begin, we strongly urge human resources (HR) managers to avoid, at all costs, the generalization that Vietnam veterans are all prone to commit violence in the workplace. Of course, they are not.

And yet a bad reaction to combat experience may appear during an interview or background check. A national survey of more than 1,300 Vietnam veterans showed combat-experienced soldiers had a 23 percent arrest rate and a 12 percent conviction rate, both figures much higher than noncombat soldiers. Psychologists and other experts studying this phenomenon point to Post-Traumatic Stress Disorder (PTSD) as an important factor. They believe some Vietnam-based soldiers have never gotten over their war experiences, and their aberrant behavior is a result of this failing.

We do see so many examples of those who commit acts of violence in the workplace who either dress in military camouflage, act like they are about to engage in military-style combat, or give other evidence of a clear obsession about the military.

We are not analyzing why, necessarily, but our theory is that the military gives these men the self-esteem they are looking for. To be a real "GI Joe" or "Wyatt Earp" is what many of these men want. Life hasn't allowed them to become their ego-ideal, so they affect the dress, style, and role of the "macho man."

6. *Gun or other weapon collector.* In an article written by Bob Filipczak for the July 1993 issue of *Training,* Bruce Blythe, president and CEO of Crisis Management International of Atlanta, Georgia, noted that in his consulting he advises his clients that they should be wary of members of the National Rifle Association (NRA) or veterans of combat. He contends that those with access to guns and those who have killed before may find it easier to use that gun and kill again.

In our experience, it is certainly farfetched to be wary of NRA members and veterans. Many of these people are as outspoken against violence in our country as anyone. They are among the most responsible members of our society, frequently touting gun-safety measures, the need for training, and responsible gun ownership. To be wary of these people is simply irresponsible and may be likened to going on a witch-hunt, creating hysteria where there is no need to do so. (After Blythe's comments were published in the *Training* article, outraged NRA members flooded the magazine with angry letters and calls.)

That being said, however, those who commit violence in the workplace do seem to have an inordinate availability of weapons, frequently guns, and more often than not, not just handguns. Semiautomatic and full-automatic assault weapons are being used with greater regularity in occupational violence than ever before.

If one of your problem employees appears to have a fascination with the military to an unhealthy degree, talks about owning assault weapons, is under a great deal of stress, and fits many other areas of this profile, then there is cause to be concerned.

7. *Temper-control difficulties may have been observed.* Once an employee demonstrates temper control difficulties at work and begins to make threats [see item (8)], it is clear to us that more than smoke is blowing in the wind. A serious problem is in the making, and the HR manager, plant manager, shop steward, store owner, department manager, or whoever is directly in line for

supervision better make a serious note of this and take preventive intervention-based action.

8. *Threats may have been made.* Here, the disturbed employee has revealed himself as a candidate for violence. The threats may be directed at the company as a whole—a symbol for this person's perceived injustices or his private persecutor—or at the leadership of the company—the "suits" who continue to hold this person back from his career improvement—or at specific managers, supervisors, or co-workers.

9. *Few, if any, healthy outlets for rage.* Individuals prone to explode do so typically with no apparent warning. This is, in part, because they have no outlet for that rage and anger. They have no healthy way of expressing frustration.

Remember in Chapter 2 we described a common scenario of a family that offered no accepted, appropriate method for learning anger control. Hitting, throwing things, breaking what's not yours, stealing what's not yours, immediate gratification, drugs and alcohol—these methods are all too common in the background of the most explosive in our work force.

10. *Excessive interest in media reports of violence, especially in the workplace.* Is there such a thing as copycat workplace violence? We are not aware of any studies that have investigated the question, but our educated guess is that there is such a thing. Based on acts of suicide reported in the media and the aftereffects it has on the suicide rate, copycat crime rates, and other similar data, there is no reason to believe that copycat occupational violence is not a factor.

It is also our belief that some of the homicides taking place at Postal Service branches may also be touched by this copycat phenomenon.

In fact, it is not surprising to learn that a perpetrator of violence in the workplace is also quite familiar with other acts of such violence. Indeed, if you hear one of your employees, a problem employee especially, ruminating about an act of violence that recently occurred, and that person fits other characteristics of this profile, then, again, the responsible thing to do is to take preventive measures. Talk over the concerns you have with the employee if at all possible and suggest counseling.

11. *Unstable family life.* So much has been written about this area that not much more needs to be said. The fact is that those

who are given to creating havoc in their workplace via violence are frequently found to have had chaotic family lives. It's impossible to ignore this connection.

Talk of unhappiness at home, or never mentioning home life, may also be a tipoff. We are amazed at how little co-workers really bother to get to know each other. Aside from gossiping about others, really getting to know something about the person who works alongside you, for you, or has coffee with you every day, is something that can sometimes help in preventing the buildup of such loneliness and emptiness that taking a life finally becomes easy.

12. *Other employees are concerned.* If HR managers would only pay attention to the concerns of their employees, they might hear the seeds of concern being sown. That is, employees frequently, in retrospect, recall feeling "concerned" about Joe, who just killed three of his fellow employees, including his HR manager.

Employees talk about this concern in many ways. The environment must be arranged so that someone in the workplace can listen when employees share their concerns. The HR manager, or someone in a similar position, needs to feel reassured that the climate he or she has established allows for the open expression of these types of concerns.

Tattling is for children. Sharing concerns that are genuine, that involve corporate and human life and death, is for responsible employees. The difference may be a thin line, but so is the difference between life and death when violence breaks out in an office, factory, restaurant, or post office.

The informed HR manager can feel assured that he or she is on top of behavior before it turns violent only when the climate is open and employee communication can be exchanged without threat of negative consequences.

13. *Chronic labor–management disputes.* Any employee who carries with him other indicators of this profile, has a long history of ongoing labor–management disputes, or has numerous unresolved physical or emotional injury claims may have become so frustrated that with all of the other elements, an explosion of some kind may occur.

While many of these points are to be taken as red flags, and none by themselves stand out as the central indicator, an employee with many gripes, complaints, and/or feelings of having unresolved actions against the employer should always be taken as a person with serious potential to commit some kind of act of lethal or nonlethal violence in the workplace.

As we mentioned in the opening chapters, nonlethal, covert forms of violence may take many forms: plugging up the executive washroom's toilets with tissue, forcing the executives to use the employee's bathrooms; and popping off one cog on the end of a plastic crank to do much damage to a car on an assembly line. "Brooming" a carpet instead of really vacuuming it, stealing from hotel guests, and placing their carts in locations where they are not working so that the hotel workers may relax in another room are all favorite ways that hotel housekeepers have of using nonlethal forms of violence against the hotel bottom line.

One worker in a museum told us she once took home cassettes used to play music in the museum lobby and randomly just taped the loudest, most raucous noise for a minute or two, throughout the tapes, brought them back, stacked them neatly, and waited with baited breath for the museum to open the next day. Not all workplace violence is lethal.

When many disputes continue with the employee feeling little in the way of support, too frequently being found to be wrong, and having low self-esteem, there is only so much air that this human "balloon" can hold before it bursts.

14. *Numerous unresolved physical or emotional injury claims.* This person may come to the supervisor with a grocery list of ailments, ranging from the real to the surreal. But what may be given short shrift by the boss could be intensely personal to the disturbed employee. These psychological or physical injuries could indeed be psychosomatic or they could be the stress-laden indicators of real health problems, mental or physical.

Some of the surviving suspects in workplace homicides have made statements about apparent seizures, strokes, blinding headaches, blackouts, or other mind-altering central nervous system attacks.

15. *Problems with working conditions.* Employees who constantly complain about working conditions may be quite free of violent tendencies. Simply complaining about working conditions by itself is probably not much to worry about. However, an individual who is highly overreactive to a new corporate procedure or policy may be someone that should get some individual attention.

Too expensive to have to meet with every average laborer who shouts about a new policy? Think again. Which danger signal on the letter bomb list did you choose to ignore?

16. *Complaints of heightened stress at work.* The chronic complainer who always feels overburdened by the pace, the workload, or the physical or psychological demands of the job may be trying to tell you something. Those who cope by griping to the nth degree are usually trying to vent their growing feelings of rage, anxiety, or impending perceived lack of control of their work environment or personal space.

17. *Male between the ages of 30 and 40 years old.* We have seen few acts of lethal acts of violence in the workplace committed by women. On the other hand the nonlethal acts of sabotage or vandalism reported above are often caused by men and women of all ages.

In our experience, and what the actual cases tell us, the more serious, homicidal acts of violence in the workplace are committed by males, frequently between the ages of 30 and 40.

18. *Migratory job history.* This often reveals itself in the initial hiring and prescreening process, but it may become known if the employee speaks to other co-workers about bouncing from place to place over a relatively short period of time. This means that the employee may have lied about his employment history during the hiring process and/or that he may not be able to hold a job due to outbursts, confrontations, or other antisocial behavior at work. This information can create two problems.

19. *Drug and alcohol use and/or abuse.* Whether this takes place at home or at work, the signs of impairment are usually evident to even the untrained eye. Examples of the "maintenance" alcoholic or drug user who can appear perfectly normal at work are rare. Most people who abuse alcohol or drugs show the signs of physical and psychological deterioration.

For alcohol abusers, these signs in combination may include the odor of alcoholic beverages on their breath or clothing; glassy, bloodshot, drooping, or watery eyes; sweating; flushed facial coloring; an unusually disheveled appearance; noticeably slurred speech; and problems walking, focusing on small objects, or using motor and cognitive skills that involve details or high concentration levels.

Just as street criminals use drugs or liquor to gird themselves
for a robbery or burglary, some assailants in workplace homicide
incidents have prepared for this traumatic event by "numbing"
themselves with these chemicals.

And even if the substance abuse occurs at home, as we have
seen from other social problems that occur there—domestic violence, child abuse, emotional abuse, psychological distress, and
so on—the aftereffects can follow the disturbed employee straight
to the worksite.

20. *Psychiatrically impaired.* This phrase fits the seriously disturbed employee who at first may or may not display the impairment. As time goes on, this person may show a gradual psychological erosion, or this condition may deteriorate so rapidly that a
monumental psychotic episode follows a seemingly unrelated
event.

Cases exist where a so-called "normal" employee has left one
job and taken another, only to return with a gun to the first
employer and begin shooting. The evolution from the silent employee who "seems to have a lot on his mind" to the deranged
killer has come full circle.

The psychiatrically impaired employee needs immediate counseling from a qualified mental health professional. This is not the
job for a manager to do; now is the time for some form of EAP
to spring into action.

So the operant question raises its ugly head: "OK, so I've got
an employee who has exhibited a dozen or more of these characteristics," says the worried personnel manager at a manufacturing
firm. "Now what?"

The first step toward heading off the potential for violence in
the workplace is to admit that it may be possible. If you have a
disturbed employee who leads you to believe a violent episode
may be in the offing, a sturdy discipline session is *not* the answer.

It's time to offer counseling services for this person, and not
under the threat of termination, either. To put it bluntly, this is
a guy you'd better treat differently. In the next chapter, we will
look at an actual workplace violence case study and see what went
wrong.

What about the harried or cynical executive who says, "That's
not how I do business. Better to just fire the SOB and get it over

with"? Our response is, "Be ready to accept the consequences for your inability or unwillingness to treat this person in a manner that may be totally foreign, but completely necessary, for the situation."

By failing to heed the warning signs or abide by the Golden Rule of employee treatment, you may in fact set off a chain of events in the disturbed employee's psychological life. What we know about history tells us plenty about what might happen in the future.

We believe that all supervisors and hiring personnel should be trained in identifying and dealing with these indicators of potential human explosion. Seminars lasting anywhere from 15 minutes on video, to an hour for a classroom presentation in a cursory manner are minimum. Half-day and full-day seminars are valuable for more in-depth coverage of the topics, especially in training managers and supervisors how to deal with these issues when they are spotted.

Supervisors also need to be trained in other early-warning signs of emotional upset, not just indicators of explosiveness. These early-warning signs may be considered yet another way to sensitize the ears of supervisors to listen for the ticking inside the now-famous "disgruntled employee."

EARLY WARNING SIGNS OF EMOTIONAL DYSFUNCTION

Consider these additional factors when studying the previously discussed characteristics related to potentially dangerous employees:

1. Changes from usual behavior.
2. Noted anxiety and irritability.
3. Mention of sleep disturbances.
4. Depression, withdrawal, and comments about suicide.
5. Excessive drinking or drug use.
6. Noted sexual problems including harassing behavior.
7. Excessive altercations with others.

8. Being more accident-prone—either physical or traffic.
9. Being argumentative—feeling persecuted
10. Talk of physical complaints.
11. Talk of home problems.
12. Loss of interest and confidence in life or work.

As you can see, there is some level of overlap between these early warning signs and the aforementioned list of common characteristics of perpetrators of violence in the workplace. Once these indicators, or any of those from the list of danger signs described earlier, are identified in an employee, then the material should be kept highly confidential and classified, and discussed only with those who need to know.

Who needs to know? Perhaps a potential victim. Security personnel, certainly. First-line supervisors should be the first to know, and if they are not notified, ask yourself how is it they were not aware of this material if indeed they were doing the job of supervising in a correct manner? What kind of counseling, discipline, or other sanctions do you bring against a supervisor who doesn't know this material first? There can be no good reason why he or she shouldn't have been the first to spot small problems brewing.

The responsibility of the supervisor, in our model, includes having a working knowledge of both of these lists of danger signs and the ability to intervene and deal with them in a sensitive, professional, respectful manner. Above all else, the supervisor should know when, how, and where to get additional help in handling someone with any number of these indicators.

This is an essential ingredient to help a company cope with the growing problem of violence in the workplace. Having supervisors who are not knowledgeable in this component is destructive. If you are able to pick up on the small warning signs before they grow big, you are protecting yourself, your company, and its employees better than you can ever imagine.

If you can skillfully paint the picture of a person with a serious problem and have intervened early enough for most individuals, future violence is no longer a threat.

Of course, we are not suggesting that violence can always be predicted by just being aware of what to look for. Despite your best efforts to not act like a victim, despite all the best alarms and locks, you can still be mugged, robbed, burglarized, raped, or shot by a criminal.

So, too, with workplace violence. You can take all of the finest security measures in the world and they won't always protect you from the completely "out of the blue" form of random violence that plagues our society. James Jordan, the father of basketball great Michael Jordan, was simply resting on the side of the road in a fine luxury car on a nice summer evening in 1993 in the United States of America—yet random violence still took his life.

Of course, it can happen even in spite of the best corporate efforts. We are all too familiar with that fact. Some analogies apply here: We don't disregard traffic signals because some people run through red lights anyway; or we don't ignore the FBI's danger signals about letter bombs; or we don't tell our children to leave the doors and windows open when they are home alone because criminals will break in anyway.

We still must take the most responsible steps available to us to protect ourselves and our businesses from being victimized. Knowledge can be helpful when traveling in a foreign country if you want to avoid becoming a crime victim. Being aware of what streets to avoid, what areas are unsafe, what to look for among the population that might indicate signs of criminal activity about to take place can make most of us feel more secure in traveling with our families.

So, too, with our corporate lives. Ensuring that supervisors are knowledgeable, are on the lookout for potential signs of madness erupting into violence, and are skilled in knowing what to do to initiate the corporate safety plan is essential.

Remember, our model to help corporations cope with ticking human bombs begins with establishing safe preemployment screening factors, continues with training for supervisors in these indicators, includes skill-building in dealing with people who display some or all of them, reiterates the need for positive employee treatment, moves on to healthy approaches to discipline, and includes accessible, free, or very low cost confidential counseling or psychotherapy services for the employee and his family for all personal matters, whether or not they are directly related to work issues.

This counseling or psychotherapy should not be time-limited. Ideally, though, a minimum of 20 visits per year is reasonable. The model moves on to safe termination practices, security, and measures, and ends with critical incident group and individual debriefing services in the aftermath of violence.

To omit any of these very important ingredients is like ignoring just one traffic light in your city. Sure, you may be safe, but would you feel comfortable with your spouse or children driving freely through the area you chose as the one with the unheeded traffic light?

We think not, and similarly believe that all of the components of our workplace violence model are critically important and should reflect every corporation's commitment to safety for all its employees. We are confident that with the publication of this book, this model will rapidly emerge as the standard for all companies to adopt.

ENDNOTES

[1] David Klinghoffer, "Fired! Ready! Aim!" *National Review*, April 26, 1993, p. 56.

[2] "Merrill Lynch Executive Slain," *Boston Globe*, April 8, 1988, p. 1.

[3] "News" section, *Fortune*, August 9, 1993, p. 12.

Chapter Five

Problem Employees, Problem Behaviors: A Case Study in Workplace Homicide

THE ROBERT MACK INTERVIEW

What we know for certain is this: On January 24, 1992, in San Diego, California, Robert Earl Mack, a 25-year assembly-line employee for the General Dynamics Company, shot and wounded his supervisor—James English—and shot and killed an industrial relations representative—Michael Konz—following his dismissal at a termination hearing.

Mack was born and raised in San Diego. He has four brothers and five sisters who all live in the city. He was married once and divorced, with three children from the marriage and two stepchildren with his live-in girlfriend.

What makes 44-year-old Robert Mack so interesting is not so much that he killed one person and wounded another at his worksite—thereby becoming one of the many statistics that make up the subject of violence in the workplace—but that he is still alive to tell his side of the story.

As the majority of workplace violence incidents show, the suspects in these cases often kill themselves immediately after they commit their homicides. In comparison with most nonwork-related homicides, where the incidence of postepisode suicide is rare, workplace homicides seem to be littered with not only the bodies of the victims but of the perpetrators as well.

In this respect, Robert Mack is an anomaly; a rarity if you will, who is one of the few surviving murderers from the worksite.

And not only is Robert Mack still alive, he is also remarkably lucid, rational, and in short, not noticeably insane, like some of his workplace homicide counterparts.

When brought to a pretrial hearing in Orange County, alleged Dana Point, California, post office murderer Mark Hilbun looked gaunt and disheveled. Press accounts tell us that Hilbun had gone on a hunger strike of sorts while in jail and refused to eat his meals. This, coupled with his bizarre behavior during his flight to avoid arrest points many fingers toward his clearly disturbed mental capacity.

Larry Hansel, locked in the same San Luis Obispo prison facility as Robert Mack, showed many signs of mental instability during the court proceedings following his arrest for killing two Elgar Corporation executives in San Diego, California.

No, for all he is—a convicted workplace murderer who also severely wounded another man—Robert Mack is far from crazy. While he admits to having several near "blackouts"—after he unceremoniously received his termination letter from his employer of 25 years, and after he shot and killed an industrial relations manager and wounded his first-line supervisor—Mack is a rational, communicative, soft-spoken man.

To put his case into perspective, Mack was not fired because he did "crazy things" at work. He was not involved in workplace violence acts prior to this one, and he did not draw attention to himself as "someone we'd better watch out for." For most of his 25-year career as an assembly worker in the General Dynamics plant, he did his job and he went home. Only in the latter stages of his work there did his performance start to deteriorate.

Following a long period of absenteeism, tardiness, and unexcused movements inside and outside the plant, Mack's supervisors, particularly James English, his direct boss, began to lose patience with him. Because of his seniority, security clearance, and job designation as a "floater," or one who could work in a number of different plant areas or around different missile projects, Mack could move about the inside of the plant at will.

He already had a reputation for frequently going in and out of the plant, ostensibly to "run errands" for co-workers, or to buy snack items for himself and others when the local "roach coach" lunch wagon would arrive at the plant.

In the months before the shooting, he complained of car trouble, and since he took the bus from his home to the plant early each morning, he would often arrive late to punch in. Sometimes he would be late a few minutes, other times a few hours, and still other times he would not show up at all saying he missed his bus or had car trouble.

For the most part, he was a good, loyal GD employee. But his attendance problems began to grate on his supervisor. The supervisor's attempts to discipline and later terminate Mack for his inability to follow attendance policies and work rules led to Mack's final downfall as both a normal employee and a rational human being.

Mack's very existence, the fact that he lives, should tell everyone who looks to problem-employee profiles to weed out potential killers to be wary. Mack doesn't fit all of the elements in the profile of a workplace killer. Some of the factors in the profile clearly apply to him and others are not even close. And yet, it happened. One person was killed, another injured.

While the profile can serve as an important data source, it's far from foolproof. Even if you think you know what to look for, you'll always find exceptions.

As we've just pointed out in Chapter 4, profiles can only offer you *general* considerations, not written-in-stone absolutes. The danger is when someone in the personnel department says, "Well, this applicant or employee only meets one or three or five of these criteria, so he can't be so bad," or "We don't have anybody that sounds like this profile candidate at our company. So therefore, we have nothing to worry about."

In a sense, if you have an employee who is making threatening statements, acting out highly aggressive behavior, and making you feel nervous and even fearful, consider yourself somewhat fortunate. As paradoxical and even strange as this sounds, it's true. With the disturbed, vocal employee, you and the people around you are getting a warning of the violent behavior that may follow. It may be possible to successfully intervene in that person's life—with psychological counseling, discipline procedures, extra security precautions, or even acute mental health care—to save his life and the people around him. The Robert Macks of the world don't give us much warning. And as a result, tragedy can strike around us and we never had a clue.

The "silent killers," who sit at home or at work and brood about their treatment and inwardly curse their fate, are the ones who can send chills down the collective spine of the company. Robert Mack is an extreme example of what you can find in the real world; a person filled with such internal turmoil that he strikes when you don't expect it.

What follows is an exclusive interview with Robert Mack, which took place with Steve Albrecht on May 20, 1993, inside the California Department of Corrections San Luis Obispo Men's Colony, where he is serving two 17-to-life terms for the General Dynamics shootings. (The interview took place over a $1\frac{1}{2}$-hour period and has been edited and excerpted for clarity, quality, and length.)

Along the way, we will make comments, rebuttals, and observations about Mack and his story. His account of what happened is his opinion, his singular view of the events that went on around him, and his reaction to the injustices—real or otherwise—he perceived around him.

What, we ask ourselves, do Robert Mack and the profile characteristics for workplace violence perpetrators have in common? What is correct about Mack as it pertains to the profile? Incorrect? Not conclusive either way? What can we learn from his actions, prior to the shootings, during them, and after the incident? What did General Dynamics do right or what did it do wrong in its handling of the Mack termination proceedings? What assumptions did either side make about the other? What perceptions or misconceptions did each side bring to the room where Mack was fired after 25 years at the only company where he had ever worked?

We'll examine one real-life termination event that had tragic consequences. We'll also look at why this particular termination failed the employee Golden Rule humanity test.

What this interview reveals, either directly or tacitly, shows us what goes on in the mind of an employee who felt he had reached the point in his life and career where he saw no other alternative but to bring a handgun to the plant and start firing.

Steve Albrecht: SA.
Robert Mack: RM.

SA:

What kind of jobs did you hold prior to coming to General Dynamics?

RM:

None. That was my only job.

SA:

So you're 44 right now, then you'd have been 19 years old when you started working for them? Straight out of high school? You've been working for them a long time.

RM:

Yeah, straight out of high school.

SA:

What was your first job for them?

RM:

Plastic fabrication.

SA:

So you moved up the line?

RM:

Yeah. I moved up the line.

Since Mack spent his entire adulthood working for one company, there is certainly no evidence to indicate any connection to profile point 18—migratory job history.

SA:

What I'm interested in is what was going on prior to this incident happening and what was going on with you. What thoughts were going on in your head that led up to this shooting? What were you thinking a year before, a month before, a day before? I'm interested in what you were thinking about prior to this and what led you to this step.

RM:

Well, the thoughts in my head were somewhat naive. I didn't understand that this situation was coming to what it was.

SA:

You mean your discipline hearing?

RM:

The discipline hearing. I understood my supervisor [James English] had some kind of a problem with me.

SA:

Was he your direct supervisor?

RM:

Yes he was.

SA:

He didn't work on the floor though, right?

RM:

No, he worked on the floor. He was my first-line supervisor.

SA:

Was he a union member as well?

RM:

No.

SA:

Oh, he was management?

RM:

Yes, and these disciplinary things that he was putting upon me, it was like he was checking me out. There was a meeting that I overheard where the general foreman was talking about absenteeism. I heard him saying that the company would fire you and make you lose your house, your home, your cars, and your discipline for yourself at home. And this could cause your wife to leave you, so you might lose your wife and kids.

Clearly, Mack's self-esteem is distinctly tied to his life as a working adult with a real job. To lose a job would cause you to lose face, to lose your possessions, to lose it all.

The stage is already being set for a bitter labor–management showdown between Mack and English (profile point 13—chronic labor–management disputes).

Mack discusses the root of his problem with his supervisor—his increasing number of absenteeism and tardiness incidents:

RM:

Okay, to hurt my situation there, they denied my hours change. So that Saturday I was late. That Monday, I was four minutes late and then on Tuesday, I think I came in somewhere around an hour or so late. These were all events that happened in one session. And before I had a chance to realize how close I was [to being fired].

Mack continues to talk about problems with his supervisor, his work schedule, and his inability to get to work on time:

RM:

And so they kept messing around with my second shift [work schedule]. This is all at Christmas time, everybody's Merry Christmas and Jingle Bells and stuff like that. There was another incident I didn't understand. I didn't realize that English took a vacation day, one of my Christmas paydays away from me. He took the whole day away from me.

SA:

Because of absenteeism and being late?

RM:

Yeah, because of absenteeism. There was a flaw in the absenteeism part. I told them I got there at 5:30 AM, and the gate showed me punching in at 5:31 AM, and so they denied me my pay for that entire week. And I struggled and tried hard to get to work on time. That was the thing that started the whole ball rolling for a stretch, because I kept going back to payroll with my time slips. That was the pay for 5:30. Then they found out two days later, it was 5:31, so they canceled my paycheck.

SA:

So they held it up?

RM:

For that day, right.

SA:

That was James English who did that?

RM:

He did that.

SA:

Did you feel like he was building something against you?

RM:

It seems like it, but I was trying too hard just to get the money that I had worked for.

SA:

Was it like he had it in for you?

RM:

At that time I wasn't really thinking that he had it in for me but I was a little too naive.

SA:

But you feel that way today, that he had it in for you?

RM:

Yeah. So he docked me for an hour. That was another thing they weren't supposed to do. They weren't supposed to dock me for an hour.

By now, Mack is facing profile point 1 squarely on—disgruntled regarding perceived injustice at work. He feels his supervisor, English, holds a grudge against him and wants to go out of his way to dock Mack for his tardiness.

At this point, Mack's late arrivals have caused his relationship with his supervisor, English, to rapidly deteriorate. Mack is in jeopardy of getting suspended and even fired. His foray into profile point 16—complaints of heightened stress at work—is building rapidly.

SA:

The next day they were going to suspend you?

RM:

The next day. But that day, they took me down to the meeting to suspend me.

SA:

Right.

RM:

So, when I found the general foreman after our talk there, I told him and he said, "Oh no, Mack, no." I said, "Yeah, we just left from down there." He said, "I don't have any idea why English wanted to suspend you, you know your work and everything is OK. You're fine as far as I'm concerned." I said, "Well, you need to tell this to Mr. English, because he just took me down there to get me suspended."

SA:

Right.

RM:

So, he said, "Well, I'll tell you what, we'll talk about it tomorrow morning in my office and not down in Industrial Relations." And the next morning, I came in there, and Mr. English took me to IR to go before the general foreman.

SA:

So the shop steward didn't make the meeting?

RM:

He didn't make the meeting at all.

SA:

Did you think you were in a bad way right then or . . . ?

RM:

I was in a bad way because now I had no [union] protection over me. So, I went on down to IR and the general foreman says, "Don't worry about it Mack, I'll take care of everything." Okay, supposedly, he's gonna take care of everything. Then we got into the room, and they asked about me going in and out of the gate. OK, well that was fine, because I do it all the time. But they wanted to investigate it further. So, what they did was put me on suspension pending an investigation.

SA:

No pay?

RM:

No pay. All right, this is after Christmas, this is after New Year's, the day after and the next day. See how everything happens so closely together?

SA:

So did you go home right after that meeting?

RM:

Well, yeah, after the meeting there I did. They held me up and told me that I'd be on suspension until further investigation. They took my badge and everything and they sent me home. So I was at home for three more days. Now let's back it up. I went through Christmas trying to get my money that I did not get from the previous time.

At this point, Mack is feeling the financial pressure from the first procedural hold on his holiday paycheck. Now suspended, he faces an uncertain future with no pay.

RM:

Okay, this is starting all the stress rolling because I did not have a good Christmas at all. And I was waiting and waiting and waiting to go back to work. I had come back to work after two weeks, so now I had to go two long weeks without any pay. So what little Christmas money I had left over, I had to use that.

SA:

So you were hurting by then?

RM:

I'm hurting by then. This is a Merry Christmas and Happy New Year's and all that other stuff. So now I'm hurting for cash, OK? But I have three days off on suspension. Well, those three days turned into three weeks.

SA:

How did you know that you weren't going to come back after the three days?

RM:

Well, they called me and told me that my interview was scheduled for a date.

SA:

To come back, you mean?

RM:

Yes, but by then, it was not to come back to work; it was for a termination.

SA:

Like a hearing?

RM:

A hearing for a termination.

SA:

Let me see if I understand this. They suspend you for three days and then they told you not to come back for three more weeks until this hearing date?

RM:

Right.

SA:

So you sat home all that time?

RM:

All that time without pay. No welfare, no unemployment. No nothing, no organization, no nothing.

SA:

No help from the union?

RM:

Nothing from the union either.

Mack is just about to receive a formal termination notice in the mail, after sitting home on unpaid suspension for three weeks.

RM:

So when I got this letter in the mail . . .

SA:

Telling you what the date was?

RM:

Telling me what date to come back there. When the letter came in the mail to me, I said to myself, "I finally got a letter to go back to work." I had sat out all this time here without any money and then I finally got a letter to go back to work.

Thinking it's a letter inviting him back to work, Mack does not open it right away. Little does he know that the letter really will tell him he is fired from the only job he ever held as an adult.

RM:

All right. So I didn't open it as soon as I got it, because I wanted to read it by myself and see when I'm supposed to come back to work. But this letter had termination in it, instead of coming back to work.

SA:

So how soon after you got the letter was the day of the shooting?

RM:

About a week.

From the day he got the letter until he fired the fatal shots that wounded English and killed Konz, Mack sat home and grieved about his fate. For the first time in his adult life, he was now unemployed. His self-esteem level is about to hit rock bottom.

SA:

What I'm interested in is the point when you got the letter. What were your thoughts and feelings?

RM:

Like my whole career is gone. I got a letter, right? And the letter said "termination."

The following description of Mack's state of mind and his intense reaction to the unceremonious termination letter he received after 25 years of service sounds much like a psychotic episode (profile point 20—psychiatric impairment). He truly believed he was having a breakdown and describes it with emotion:

RM:

And I was stunned by termination. I tried to ball this letter up and it wouldn't ball up. It was still in my hands. So I tried stomping it with my feet and the letter was still in my hands. Then the letter burst into flames, and I sat there and shook it and tried to get it to go out until it finally went out.

SA:

That's what you were thinking, or that's what was happening?

RM:

That's what was happening. And it kept saying "termination, termination, termination." But I plugged my ears up so I couldn't hear the word termination. So, after that incident there, then it finally cooled down. I went and got some cold water and put the letter on top of the TV. When I came back into the room, "termination, termination" was what went through my head, termination. I've lost everything, everything I've worked for is gone. I'm not going back to work. What will the people think? How will I tell the people?

This last statement gives us a further clue as to Mack's poor self-esteem and his belief that his very existence as a human being had suddenly ended because his job had ended. He continues to address a theme that says, "People won't like or respect me if I don't have my job."

Mack describes more examples of his psychotic episode in full force now. The termination letter has turned into his constant tormentor and the object of his physical and mental suffering:

RM:

Everything was racing through my head, you know. And I went and sat down on the side of the bed and the TV burst into flames. Termination, termination. So I turned the TV off and I got into bed. I was laying in the bed and my pillow burst into flames—termination. Every time I would stop to sleep this letter would appear. It would appear and sometimes, it would chase me around the house and say "termination, termination." And no, I couldn't turn this off because it was consistently chasing me, consistently appearing for maybe five days in a row. Every time I napped. I couldn't sleep at night. I had to leave my leg hanging over the side of the bed, swinging it. So in case the letter came, I'd be able to wake up.

Mack locked himself in his home and agonized over what had befallen him. He had always been a closely guarded man; in his neighborhood he seemed to keep to himself and his family (profile point 2—socially isolated, may be a loner).

SA:

So you stayed at home and stewed for five days?

RM:

Yeah.

SA:

So by the time the five days went by, you were pretty wound up, pretty tight?

RM:

I was wound up pretty tight.

His feelings of rage and his emotional and physical instability are at a peak now. He has thought of nothing else but his pending termination hearing.

Mack plans his own death to coincide with his termination hearing appearance.

SA:

So, let's move up to the day of the hearing.

RM:

The night before, I figured it was time to terminate myself. I couldn't stand it anymore.

SA:

Why?

RM:

It was too much pressure on me.

SA:

You wanted to kill yourself?

RM:

Right. So that morning, I got up and I went out and got a gun.

SA:

From the house or from somewhere else?

RM:

Yeah, I bought one.

SA:

You bought it from somebody?

RM:

I bought it from somebody.

SA:

So you decided that you wanted to kill yourself at work?

RM:

Yes. If I would have killed myself at home it would have been a domestic problem. So, I had to go back to work where the problem all started from.

SA:

At that time did you think English was the cause of the problem?

RM:

I was still naive. All I knew then was that my life was over with. Everything was torn up. Everything had bottomed out.

SA:

OK.

RM:

There was nothing else left for me.

SA:

How did you get to work? Did you take the bus?

RM:

No, my girlfriend drove me.

Mack tries to "make his peace with the world" during the trip to the 1:00 PM termination hearing with his girlfriend in the car.

RM:

And I wanted to tell her some things, like, "Just take care of things around the house. Try to make the good life for yourself out there."

SA:

You're trying to sort of wrap things up?

RM:

Right. So then, I told her a few little small things, you know, good-bye and I loved you. I did everything I could do to take care of you all.

SA:

So when you got down to the [General Dynamics] plant, she dropped you off at the gate and said, "I'll pick you up in an hour or . . ."?

RM:

No, I told her to go ahead on. Well, I knew I wasn't coming back. I was going on because this was my own doing. It had nothing to do with her.

Mack is now armed with a .38-calibre revolver and is ready to confront his accusers—namely his supervisor, James English, and the industrial relations manager assigned to his termination hearing, Michael Konz.

SA:

So you went into the plant?

RM:

I went into the plant with the gun on me.

SA:

Did you know what you were going to do then?

RM:

I knew what I was going to do then. Mr. Konz came and got me. So I came on inside the gate, and then we went to a [interview] room in there. Now, I was originally charged for going in and out of the plant gate, so I should have been suspended for three days, but it was really for three weeks.

Now, I was also charged for absenteeism, and I told them no, I should have been back to work here after those three days. I should have been back to work by then. I was at the point where I was arguing with them.

SA:

So you didn't have any union representation there?

RM:

The union was there.

SA:

Were they going to bat for you?

RM:

Yeah, they were going to bat for me. But the whole scenario had changed because they were going to fire me for something different now.

SA:

Did that change your way of thinking or were you still on the same path?

RM:

I was still on the same path. My life was over regardless of what it was for.

Mack's security clearance for the company was like a badge of honor for him. He was always careful not to speak of his work to his friends and neighbors. The fact that he had a security clearance and worked on defense-related projects was a tremendous source of pride for him.

He makes the connection between his tardiness and absentee-ism and the impact it has on General Dynamics. He makes the analogy that if his attendance problems caused the company to lose money (red ink), he was going to pay them back with his own life (red blood).

RM:

So, then I kept wanting to talk so I could tell my side, and they wouldn't let me talk. What I had planned to tell them was that I held my top secret clearance to the utmost. I didn't reveal any secrets or anything and I hadn't revealed any secrets to the enemy sources. I came to work and gave my best that I could do at my job, while I was at work. If it meant so much to them for that one minute I was late, or if it meant so much to the company and it put them so far in the red for the late days I came in, and the work I did put them so far in the red, then I was willing to give my blood back to them. I was willing to give myself back to them in blood, for their red ink.

The stage has been set for Mack's murderous actions. He speaks of the way the termination hearing has gone poorly for him and another psychotic attack is imminent:

RM:

They kept telling me to shut up and so I did. And I kept trying to talk about my absenteeism. I sat there in anger, trying to get my words out, and then my mouth started getting dry, and I couldn't get any saliva in my mouth. My head started tingling, my hands started tingling, and then I knew I had to get up and get some water. These are the same symptoms that came when the big flash came.

SA:

The day at the house, when you first received the termination letter?

RM:

Right.

SA:

It's like an anxiety attack you're having?

RM:

Right. I had to get some cold water, so they took a break, a recess break.

SA:

Did you get some water or anything?

RM:

I wanted to get some water. And when I went to get some water, this big blur came over me. And that's when the shooting started.

SA:

You had a blackout?

RM:

Yeah, something like a blackout. I call it a stroke, because I lost a lot of my memory and stuff like that.

SA:

When you "came to," were the cops there already?

RM:

No. After the shooting took place, I went outside [the hearing room] or I was already outside when the shooting took place. I had already shot one man in the back of the head.

SA:

English or Konz?

RM:

And English had already been shot and now Konz has been shot now.

SA:

Right.

RM:

After shooting Konz, there was this Mexican man who was in the room. He worked in that room there. He was jumping up and down saying, "Don't do it, don't do it" and that caught my eye. And when that caught my eye, it made me look back around to where I could see there were two men laying down on the ground.

SA:

You had figured out what you had done after you "came back around"?

RM:

After I came back around. And so I asked the dude in there to go call my mother because something was wrong, OK? And he ran and hid. So that's when I went in and called my mother.

SA:

The cops came soon after?

RM:

The cops came soon after.

SA:

How did you feel afterwards? I mean did you feel relieved or sad or . . . ?

RM:

No, I was still in a daze, like I was still in a haze. It was still hazy, even when there was a security guard there. He had a gun and he walked right past me with the gun pointing in the wrong direction.

SA:

He didn't know what you were doing?

RM:

He didn't know who I was. So I told him, "Hey, hey I'm over here, I'm over here," just like that. And I had the gun to my head. And he said, "No, don't do it, don't do it." And then I put the gun down and I went in and called my mother.

SA:

Did you think that he talked you out of shooting yourself or you just decided that you didn't want to do that?

RM:

Well, maybe so.

SA:

You talked to your Mom?

RM:

So I talked to my mom. My mom said, "Don't do it" [commit suicide].

SA:

Did you tell her what you had done?

RM:

Yeah, there are two people who were down, two people who had been shot. And she said, "Oh, son what did you do that for?" I told her, "I don't know. I don't know what happened." But the two people were down.

After speaking to his mother, Mack sat and waited for the police to arrive and then quietly gave himself up. The badly injured English and the mortally wounded Konz were rushed to the hospital as a sea of law enforcement and emergency personnel descended on the area near the termination hearing room.

SA:

When you think about it now, when you look back when you have some quiet times, can you recreate the shooting or is it still a blur?

RM:

Well the shooting is still a blur, I'm not able to recreate the shooting yet.

SA:

The day you decided to go to the plant with the gun, did you sort of preprogram something in your head like, "Here's what's going to happen. I'm going to do this, then I'm going to do this, and then I'm going to do this?"

RM:

Yes, right.

At this point in the interview, Mack makes a quick shift from speaking of wanting to kill himself to wanting to kill the others in the hearing room with him. He makes an odd connection with a number of outside agencies who he thinks will be interested in what he has done and the treatment he received from General Dynamics prior to the shooting.

And Mack, as a black man, insinuates that his suspension and termination were also part of a race issue because his supervisor, English, was white.

SA:

So you set up kind of a plan, a scenario in your mind?

RM:

Right, yeah.

SA:

And did that involve shooting somebody?

RM:

No, it didn't involve shooting anybody but myself.

SA:

Killing yourself?

RM:

Right, but I had to make sure that I killed them . . .

SA:

Why?

RM:

I would have both the company there and the union and there'd be a big investigation over it. It would involve the Department of Defense, there would be a civil rights investigation, because my civil rights were being violated, the NAACP would look into it to find out what happened, seeing how they treated me.

SA:

Was it racial?

RM:

It was a racial thing. One or two other things like that would have to be named in that investigation.

From here, Steve tries to search for some kind of "prevention prescription" that will help other organizations avoid this problem for themselves.

SA:

If you think about it in terms of the [shooting] scenario you thought out in your head, is there anything anyone could have said or [done], or anyone who could have intervened to have changed your scenario?

RM:

Well, yeah, if I would have told my girlfriend, my fiancée, if I would have told her, I'm sure she would have stopped the whole thing.

SA:

I guess what I'm looking for is what kind of signs did you give off prior to this that they could have recognized?

RM:

Oh, I was tremendously upset.

SA:

On the job? All the time?

RM:

Oh yeah, I was tremendously upset there at the meeting. I kept trying to talk and they wouldn't let me.

SA:

Right. But prior to that, prior to being suspended, were you upset at work where your work had suffered? And did people notice a change in you, like they said, "What's the matter?"

RM:

Well, there was no time for them to notice a change in me because I was never there.

SA:

Most of this change took place at home?

RM:

Most of all of this took place at home.

SA:

Did you get the feeling that you had nothing to lose when you went to the termination hearing?

RM:

I already lost everything.

According to Mack, he showed no outwardly visible signs of his distress at work to others. The events that followed his suspension for attendance problems and his termination occurred so rapidly, that he didn't have much opportunity to interact with his co-workers. One day he was on the job, the next he was suspended.

SA:

Did you think of anybody who you feel is responsible for this? Do you blame the company or people inside the company or is it just you, or a combination of everything?

RM:

I think it was a combination of everything. I think that the company made it all come together.

SA:

The combination of your feelings, and the way the company made you feel, and the way people inside the company made you feel?

RM:

Right.

SA:

So if they had treated you differently, do you think it would have worked out another way?

RM:

Yeah, if they had treated me differently.

SA:

If you hadn't thought you were going to get fired, would you have crossed that line?

RM:

I'd have never have crossed that line, or if I knew I was being fired for a just reason, I wouldn't have had a problem.

Here, Mack fails to see his attendance problem as a bona fide suspension or termination issue. He was even late to the termination hearing itself. He is clearly attempting to rationalize his murderous behavior as something that was "not my fault."

He attempts to link his actions with the apparent suicide of another GD assembly plant worker in the parking lot of the facility. (Mack told me a GD worker had sent the news clipping to him in prison.)

SA:

So you felt like you were actually being fired for the wrong reason?

RM:

Right.

SA:

Why do you think other people at General Dynamics haven't done this kind of thing yet? Why do you think there have not been more workplace violence incidents at General Dynamics?

RM:

Let me tell you why. There was one here last month [April 1993] for an employee who went out in the parking lot, got a gun, put it in his mouth, and shot his head off.

SA:

At General Dynamics?

RM:

At the Convair Division [where Mack worked as well].

SA:

It didn't make the newspapers?

RM:

No, because it was a domestic problem.

SA:

Was he an assembly worker, too?

RM:

He was an assembly worker.

SA:

Do you think he had the same kind of problems you did, with the way the company treated him?

RM:

I think there was something in the way that the supervisors put the pressure on him that particular day, whether he would be terminated, or whether [the supervisor] was going to put some kind of destruction into his life. That's the same way I feel.

SA:

Do you think that General Dynamics has policies that lead to this kind of [workplace violence] behavior?

RM:

They have a policy there that makes you lose your wife, your house, your kids, cars . . .

SA:

Do you feel that their policies put people in fear for their financial well-being?

RM:

They put them in fear. Yes, that's true.

SA:

How do you think you're different than the guy who's also treated like you but doesn't go back and do what you did? What's the difference between a guy who works for a boss who's a jerk and doesn't do anything, and the guy that works for a boss who's a jerk and does take some kind of violent action against him?

RM:

Some people are afraid. Some things [the company does] put a lot of fear inside of them.

SA:

So they're afraid to react or afraid to do something?

RM:

They're afraid to react plus [the company] is trying to create that atmosphere where it equals fear.

SA:

The company's trying to make people fearful?

RM:

Well, the company makes you fearful because they give out directives and tell you what to do. If you don't do them, you'll be terminated.

SA:

So this is all about control?

RM:

Control.

SA:

So you are under their control?

RM:

Yes.

It's hard to make much sense of this last exchange. Is Mack saying the work rules at General Dynamics make people afraid?

SA:

Did anyone at General Dynamics talk to you or ask you what you were feeling? Did anyone take you aside and say, "Gee, Robert, you know, let's help you do this or I can see you're having problems, or I want to help you through this . . . ?"

RM:

They should have done that.

SA:

Who should have recognized that? The union people? Management people?

RM:

The union people and the management people, but they kept telling me to shut up, to shut up and be quiet.

SA:

During the hearing?

RM:

During the hearing. That was my most frustrating point. I was banging on the table . . .

SA:

The signs they could have seen in you, when you were excited, you were banging on the table, you're trying to tell them . . . ?

RM:

They could have avoided all that by stopping that [hearing].

SA:

Do you think that if they had communicated with you in person rather than by the mail that it might have been a better way?

RM:

Oh, yeah.

SA:

This letter, it's like you had to read it away from the plant and you had . . .

RM:

I had no idea. I had no idea what was gonna happen.

SA:

So do you think if somebody had at least called or maybe come out to your house or . . . ?

RM:

Right. Come or call, or said, "Hey Mack, we got something different going on now. We are going to talk about your absenteeism," then I would've had a chance to speak on my own behalf. I never had a fair trial.

Again, Mack tries to draw a distinction away from his own attendance problem, which, regardless of whether it was for tardiness, going in and out of the plant during work, or absenteeism, is still a violation of company policy for probably every business in the nation. It's as if he's trying to make his situation different than another employee with a similar attendance problem.

SA:

If you had a chance to talk out your problems either with the manager or the labor union people, or the shop steward, or anybody like that, do you think this all could have been prevented?

RM:

Yes, I do. I would have been able to explain the situation to them.

SA:

During the three weeks' [suspension] time, do you feel like they sort of abandoned you? I mean, everybody just sort of cut you off and . . . ?

RM:

Well, everybody just left me cut off until it was time for them to pick me back up.

SA:

Does the company offer counseling, in terms of mental health counseling, for people who are really upset and have problems that they really need to talk about? Do they offer that?

RM:

The company did not offer me that type of thing.

SA:

Do they offer it in general?

RM:

Now, the day after the shooting, they implied the counseling and things like that. But now it's in effect.

SA:

Would you have taken the opportunity to go to counseling if they had offered it to you?

RM:

Yes.

SA:

In terms of your feelings, for mental health counseling, you would have gone if you had had a free chance?

RM:

Yes.

People who don't wish to see something, simply don't. If you don't want to know something is available, you won't. Dr. Mantell remembers San Diego police officers telling him they had no idea his police psychological services program was in effect, even six or seven years after the program was already in place.

These statements by Mack are completely untrue, says Ron Davis, director of security for General Dynamics. He takes great offense at Mack's claim that he was not offered the chance to speak to a counselor about his many problems.

We have an aggressive EAP program here, in terms of psychological counseling. We have constant access to psychologists and we do lots of referral work. Our firm retains psychologists in a well-entrenched program that's been going on for 15 years. Everyone in the firm— management and labor both—has been trained to know about what we offer and everyone is well aware of it. We have posters everywhere and telephone hotlines for counseling, so nobody could ever say we haven't thought of our employees in terms of their EAP needs.

For the potentially dangerous employee who refuses to accept the fact that psychological counseling programs exist, and may in fact be a necessity for him, a forced intervention by the employer may be the only hope.

Could Robert Mack have changed his erratic attendance behavior if his supervisors had asked him to speak to a mental health counselor during his suspension? Could General Dynamics and a therapist have saved his career, and ultimately, those of James English and Michael Konz? We will never know.

SA:

How do you feel about what happened now? What thoughts go on now? Do you feel relieved, or regretful, or do you wish it hadn't happened, or wish you could turn back time?

RM:

Everyday, the same incidents come to me in my mind. There's not a day that goes that it doesn't come to mind.

SA:

Like flashbacks?

RM:

Sometimes little flashbacks or trouble sleeping. I still have trouble sleeping. I'm on medication now that makes me sleep.

SA:

This is kind of a hard question to answer. If you had to do it over again, everything being the same, would you have chosen the same route or . . . ?

RM:

No. But then again, I was at the point where there was nothing left in my life.

SA:

Right. So, your mindset was, I guess, you thought about killing yourself first and then everything just sort of happened after that, right?

RM:

It happened after that.

Steve attempts to seek solutions to these kinds of communication problems between employees and management:

SA:

If you were the people at General Dynamics, what would you recommend that they do to avoid these kinds of problems in the future? I mean, if you could say, "I'm going to tell everybody what they need to know." What would that be?

RM:

They'd have to change their ways. Change their ways toward terminations, change their ways toward talking and being with the people, change the old ways. It's always the company firing somebody. They never fire anybody on an even keel, it's always [based] on a grudge or something there.

SA:

You think that's because there's a big gap between labor and management?

RM:

There's a big gap between labor and management.

SA:

So, you think that the union people are upset at the management people and vice versa?

RM:

Vice versa. There's a big gap in there. They need to come together and talk more to each other as individuals. Now in my case, there was no talking. There was no communication in my case.

SA:

On two levels, right? The union people didn't help you and the management people didn't help you?

RM:

The management didn't help me either. Management needs to talk more. See, if my general foreman would have known then it would have never gotten that far. But by him [English] trying to go around the general foreman . . .

SA:

So do you feel like the management people don't respect the union policies? Like they're going to say, "Well, I'm not going to deal with that guy and they're gonna 'back door' him [seek to avoid union representation for the employee]?"

RM:

That's very true. They don't respect the union policies at all. They always look for ways to get around them. And they use force, power, and anger to satisfy their own taste.

SA:

Almost like a personal grudge?

RM:

A personal grudge, yeah.

SA:

Do you think James English had a grudge against you?

RM:

I think he had a grudge against me.

An August 1992 article in the local section of the *San Diego Union-Tribune* discussed the witnesses feelings of Post-Traumatic Stress Disorder in one of the witnesses to the Mack shootings. Mack comments on the piece:

SA:

When you look at this piece, they talk about the fact that there are a lot of people who are sort of on your side. There are people at General Dynamics who claim, "I'm not going to say that he did the right thing, but I can understand where he came from, and maybe if I had been in his spot, I'd have done it, too." How can this be possible?

RM:

That's right. There's that much tension in there.

SA:

Do you think that it's all just people who work on the line, or is it people in management, too, or how do you think it's broken down?

RM:

I think it's broken down to the people on the line, but then again, you must look at it like management has the same type of pressure we have put upon us. That's what makes management function in that particular way.

SA:

It says here in the article, "Employees at the Lindbergh Field GD plant, however, have been open about their views and they are mixed. 'There is a great deal of division within the plant,' said [Mack shooting eyewitness Arnold] Castro. 'There are people who are supportive of Mack and have been through the same frustration that Mack went through, and then there's a lot of people who feel it was a black issue.' "[1] Do you think it was a racial thing because of English?

RM:

It may have been a racial thing. At that time, I was too naive to look back on it as racial. I'm black, OKAY. If there was something to spark English in his ways, or if his old ways came about inside of him, then he would pursue the avenue that he pursued, because the union and management take things into their own hands on how to operate. If I didn't like you then I would find some way to terminate you. And that's how the company has its own forceful way of doing things. If they don't like what you do, they have a way of terminating you. It's been the old policy and the old system for the whole of my 25 years there. I've seen some guys get fired from General Dynamics for the way they walk or because of the way they talk. See what I'm saying? It's the way that the company have projected themselves all through this. Now, the time when people became aware of all this was when they started all the [employee] cutbacks. It used to be one, two people got laid off and that would be all right. Now you're talking about thousands of people getting laid off.

SA:

Right.

RM:

Thousands of people losing their jobs and their homes, and stuff like that. This is where the pressure comes in.

There is no evidence any of Mack's claims about "walking/ talking" terminations are true. His frustration with management treatment is obvious. As indicated in the following, his anger is also directed toward a widely publicized event where a number of top executives at GD received performance bonuses coming on the heels of another round of announced layoffs.

SA:

When you read in the newspaper and see that [GD leader] William Anders makes millions of dollars in salary and bonuses, and then they have all these layoffs, I'm sure that adds fuel to the fire?

RM:

Yeah, that adds fuel to the fire.

SA:

Do people talk about that on the line?

RM:

Yeah, they talk about that on the line. We can't get a nickel raise out of them but they [specially—compensated top GD executives] can make $25 million [bonuses]. If that million dollars would float down through the system, it would make everyone a little more comfortable. That's management. That's the way management operates.

SA:

Do you think that it widens the gap between labor and management?

RM:

Yeah. A lot of people were unhappy. A lot of people stood up and said they shouldn't have got those bonuses.

SA:

How do you think you're perceived now by the people on the assembly line? Are you sort of a hero to them, or do they distance themselves from you?

RM:

Some of them feel like that, "That's the man, that's the one that broke the camel's back. Now the pressure won't be on us as much." Because now they're [GD management] starting to change their ways.

SA:

So in what ways do you think anything positive came from this, besides the fact that there may be some new ways and, like you say, "the pressure's been taken off?" What positive might have come from all this?

RM:

Well, there's a lot of positive things that came out of it. It changed their ways. They looked back and now they're changing their policies. Union and management policies. They're going back and looking at them really strongly. But the company must know that their past history was rooted that way [with labor–management conflicts].

SA:

Yeah?

RM:

I'm sure that I'm not making any remarks for anyone to go out and do the same thing I did, but I'm sure that it's going to continue happening. Because the people, just like the man down there, the postal worker that shot and killed that lady . . .

SA:

The postal shooting incidents in Dana Point, California, and also in Dearborn, Michigan?

RM:

These were things that you can look back and see that there were incidents where the company uses their old policy ways, which have been imbedded in them. It'll take a lot to uproot those ways.

Mack mentions the two post office shootings in Michigan and California that took place on the same day together. He also criticizes GD for placing his fate in the hands of a 25-year-old manager (Konz) who, in effect, was an infant when Mack began at the company. His perception—right or wrong—is that the company handled his case in an insensitive manner, using a young man whom Mack could not see as a work peer.

SA:

If you were put in a position just to make as many changes as you could at General Dynamics, what would you start with?

RM:

I'd start with personnel and the way they treat people.

SA:

Is the industrial relations department and the union under personnel?

RM:

Yes. IR comes right up under personnel. Now I'm going to say this whether it's in context or out of context. It's just this one thought that I can never get out of my head. The union and the company knows what they're going to do about 5 to 10 years ahead of time. They think that far ahead.

SA:

Right, long-range planning.

RM:

It was the fact that they put that young kid [Michael Konz] in there in a position to terminate people. For the flow of people who come through there, they put that young kid in there, knowing he's going to try and do his best job to be a "company man." But there should have been something in his mind that day that said, "Hey wait a minute, I'm only 25 years old. This man has worked here for 25 years. How can I terminate a man that's spent 25 years working here on the job, and I'm only 25 years old?"

SA:

So you're saying that they failed to look at the larger picture of how things are? They didn't look at the big picture?

RM:

He doesn't have any idea what work is. He's only been there for three years. William Anders is saying that we are going to have to slash so many thousands of people. Let's start herding them through here. Let's get as many through here as we possibly can before something happens.

SA:

If you look at the whole management/labor issue side by side, would you say that 80 percent of labor doesn't get along with management or is it 95 percent, or is it a smaller amount? Or is it that some people say, "I don't have a problem" or do you think that everyone at General Dynamics is irritated at the way management is? I'm just trying to get a gauge on how the people feel . . .

RM:

I would say maybe 70 or 75 percent of the people [don't get along with management].

SA:

Do you think that the culture of General Dynamics—just the organization itself and how they treat everybody—has something wrong with it?

RM:

There's something wrong with it.

SA:

Even today?

RM:

Even today. You see, the company can't change their ways. And like I say, it's right back to business again.

SA:

Do you think that with the people—the management/labor split—things are going to get better or do both sides still have to give a little bit? Would that help? What's the best way to get them both to come together?

RM:

If you've got old ways imbedded in you, it's going to be very hard to change them.

SA:

But couldn't you say that goes for both sides?

RM:

Yes, that goes for both sides.

SA:

Labor has its old ways, and management has its old ways?

RM:

That's right.

Mack discusses other workplace violence–related incidents at General Dynamics:

SA:

What kind of problems have you seen at General Dynamics in terms of workplace violence? Have you seen guys punch their boss or have you seen sabotage or vandalism?

RM:

There have been many cases of vandalism and there have been many fights with supervisors.

SA:

Between supervisors and employees?

RM:

Supervisors and employees.

SA:

How about employee against employee?

RM:

There have been some—employee against employee. One trying to beat the other out of something, or one getting more than the other got.

SA:

So there's resentment?

RM:

Yeah.

SA:

Is it "employee hits boss" or "boss hits employee" or is it both?

RM:

It's "employee hits boss."

SA:

Because he's frustrated and feels like they're kicking him around?

RM:

Right. Supervisors know not to put hands on you, but we don't know how angry we get until they inflict something upon us. Then our anger runs the temperature gauge. If it gets up too high, something's going to explode.

SA:

Have you ever had any problems with a supervisor where you wanted to hit him or have you ever hit a supervisor?

RM:

No.

SA:

So prior to this, would you say you were a model employee?

RM:

I was a model employee, in fact I was the best employee of my division in what I was doing.

SA:

If you think about those incidents where a guy throws a punch at his supervisor, did he first exhibit certain signs that would have told the supervisor, "Hey, maybe I've got to back off. Or maybe I have to look at this guy a different way? Or maybe I have to do something that will bring everything down?"

RM:

Right. It's mostly [signs of] frustration and anger.

SA:

Which the supervisor should be able to read and doesn't or . . . ?

RM:

Well, in his old ways, he projected some type of discipline towards the individual, whether it was physical or mental.

SA:

So, either formal or informal discipline?

RM:

Yeah.

SA:

But is there a way the supervisor could say, "Hey, I need to look at this guy, what signs is he giving off, so that he doesn't take a punch at me?" or "What signs is he giving off so that something worse could happen?"

RM:

He's got to look at himself first. He's the one who is going to inflict the consequences. The person, the employee is gonna react; it's his natural reaction. If you start cussing at me, I'm going to cuss back at you. And by two people cussing, that leads to a level of misunderstanding. Now, you're at the level of violence. Then you're going up to where the [emotional] temperature changes on an individual and he strikes you.

SA:

Right.

RM:

Management can't see the things coming, but management can provoke those things that are coming.

SA:

What if you looked at it the other way and flipped it over? Would you say that people on the job and in the labor force have a certain responsibility to the company? And they have a certain responsibility to themselves to be able to just do their job like you did up to the point?

RM:

Right.

SA:

And just say, "Well, this will all pass over me. I'm just going to hang tough and do my job." Do you think they have their own responsibility that way?

This next passage fairly drips with irony. Mack admits that the company must terminate people who don't follow the work rules. And yet, he has spent much of the interview complaining that he was terminated for the same thing.

RM:

No, there's some people out there that do things. Management comes down with pressure to put on them. There's management's ways to put the pressure on them. So it's up to the supervisor to straighten that guy out. If you don't straighten him out, get rid of him.

SA:

Okay.

RM:

If a guy's doing something that he shouldn't be doing, it's like [the supervisor says], "OK now, if I catch you again, I'm going to fire you."

SA:

So, you think it's okay for management to do their job, but they just have to make their policies clearer so that people can understand exactly what they can do and can't do and also what their rights are?

RM:

The policy needs to be clear so that management and the people understand what the problem is or what the problems are.

SA:

So when you look at it, is it because the policies and procedure manual is too complicated, and nobody ever sat down and explained it to you?

RM:

Well, see in that case there, nobody sat down and explained the book to anybody.

SA:

When you first got hired, did they expect you to sit down and read it by yourself?

RM:

They expected you to read it by yourself. It's the same as the supervisors. They expect you to read it by yourself. Nobody sits down and helps you get the full extent of it.

Mack points to what he sees as organizational culture problems at General Dynamics.

SA:

The supervisors they hire, do they mostly come from the line? People get promoted up from the line?

RM:

People get promoted up from the line.

SA:

When they get promoted up from the line, do they stay in the same place, or do they go somewhere else?

RM:

They stay in the same place.

SA:

So there's a tendency that people may think that the wrong guy got promoted or he feels like he got this new power and he's going to abuse his old friends and people he doesn't like?

RM:

And abuse his old friends. They don't have friends then. They've got a policy there at General Dynamics where supervisors cannot eat with the employees.

SA:

Why?

RM:

They don't want them mingling.

SA:

Do you think that's another example of the gap between the two, and that leads to the problems?

RM:

That's another point where the gap is. They lose contact with the people.

SA:

The supervisors do?

RM:

Supervisors do, because they're not able to mingle with the employees.

SA:

And would you think that at the executive level it's even worse?

RM:

Right.

SA:

That they never come down to the assembly line?

RM:

Right!

SA:

They never have any idea what's going on?

RM:

It's their rooted ways. And it's going to take a lot to get that root out.

Mack discusses some of the symptoms exhibited by instigators of workplace violence.

SA:

Do you think that the supervisors need training in anything? Like a class that teaches them how to work with the people better, for better human relations? Or do they need some kind of training to teach them how people are in companies, and how to motivate them? Do you think that would help the employees at General Dynamics?

RM:

That can help some employees. That can be a big plus, but they already have courses like that there that they go through.

SA:

Do you think that it's a waste or . . . ?

RM:

It never sits because your own personal ways take over again.

SA:

So, you can't train somebody that's been doing that for their whole career? Retrain them?

RM:

You can't retrain them.

SA:

I want to create classes for supervisors to go to help them understand what kind of problems you have. So that they can say, "Look, here are the warning signs this guy is giving us. Here are some things we can do to intervene at the lowest levels." So when Robert Mack's upset, we can step in and say, "Okay, Robert, let's go to this grievance hearing, or let's go do this . . ."

RM:

Right.

SA:

Or, "Why don't we get a cup of coffee and we'll talk about what the problem is." What I see is that companies let things escalate and they let them get to the highest level. So they can't intervene before it's too late.

RM:

Right.

SA:

So managers have got to figure out how to step in when an employee is upset or where he's exhibiting the kinds of signs that lead to these kinds of problems? But it seems like they don't know how to intervene.

RM:

But when a supervisor chews out an employee, it's like a cancer, it grows on him. And it grows on him, and grows on him until this employee can explode.

SA:

If you were to look at other people, what kind of symptoms do they give off? What kind of signs? What physical signs do they see at work? If you were to watch some guy, you'd think, "Man, I bet he's going to hit the boss." What would you see?

RM:

Well, you can see those emotions.

SA:

He's upset, you can read it in his face, right?

RM:

Right. You can see those emotions in his face.

SA:

He's upset, his face is red, he clenches his fist . . .

RM:

His voice is stuttered, his balance is off, he curses, he doesn't look anyone in the eye. He mostly looks away from the boss and doesn't hear what the boss is saying. There are other symptoms where it can be that a person is quiet and not saying too much back to his boss. He's moody.

SA:

So, when you were home during the three weeks, did you get a lot of those feelings yourself? Did you feel like you were brooding, and did you feel like things were building and building?

RM:

Nothing was building, everything was exploding.

SA:

Every day?

RM:

Yeah, every day. Everything was exploding. The fire was exploding.

SA:

The fire was big in your eyes?

RM:

Yeah.

SA:

You hadn't had any problems at General Dynamics with anybody? No punchouts or anything like that?

RM:

No, no. I was a very happy person. I'm always smiling, happy, willing to help people. That was my job, to help people.

SA:

Did you have any kind of other problems? You've never been arrested before?

RM:

No, I've never been arrested.

SA:

Were you having any personal problems that you think were related, or were affected by this, or was your home life OK and it was all related to work?

RM:

Well, it affected my home life. And there were lies I had to keep putting out. I had to keep lying.

SA:

To your fiancée?

RM:

To my fiancée. Like I never told her I got terminated, that I was laid off, or even that I was going to be off a few days. There were lies that I had to tell each morning to cover up the days that I was off.

SA:

Do you think that if you had talked to her more, things might have been different?

RM:

Yeah, if I had talked more to her then they would have been different. She'd have been more understanding and probably would have been more supportive of me.

END OF INTERVIEW

The opinions expressed by Robert Mack in his interview are strictly his own. We have seen fit to point to some apparent discrepancies in his story and when appropriate, offer support or denial to his claims. Clearly, the last months of his employment with General Dynamics were a bad fit.

Problems with attendance, problems with his supervisors, and his inability to gauge the seriousness of his impending termination event caught up with Robert Mack.

It appears that neither side in this confrontation could step back and see the consequences of each other's actions. Mack certainly should have realized his job was in jeopardy; his union representatives may have misjudged management's frustration with Mack;

and the management officials, including his supervisor and the IR department, may not have realized how they were mishandling Mack's case from his emotional standpoint.

It also appears that Mack's suspension got lost in the sea of other personnel discipline cases at GD. He sat in unpaid limbo at his house for three weeks, hoping to hear when he could come back to the only real job he had ever held. And no one, especially a 25-year-employee of a company, would like to be told "You're Fired!" in a form letter sent home.

Prior to the shooting, Mack's whole life revolved around his job. Even after it, it's hard to listen to his obvious love for his work and not think that if both Mack and the people who employed him had made some adjustments in their perceptions of each other, he would still be a General Dynamics employee, along with James English and Michael Konz.

ENDNOTE

[1] "Workplace Traumatized by Slaying at Convair," *San Diego Union-Tribune*, August 11, 1992.

Chapter Six

Safe Discipline

The news accounts of many workplace violence incidents sound the same: "The disgruntled worker returned to the plant with a gun after being suspended . . ." or "Company officials had disciplined the worker only days before he came back and confronted the personnel manager . . ."

There's no question discipline is a necessary part of work life. Without it, the company would operate in a chaotic state. With it, managers and supervisors can correct problem behaviors at the lowest levels, before they flare into full-scale incidents.

Many companies have a hard time implementing a safe and successful discipline policy. Some edge more toward a punishment-based culture, where the employees are constantly being "dinged" for minor indiscretions. Others lean toward a more laissez-faire approach, where the employees are given freedom, or as one veteran personnel executive puts it, "Enough rope to hang themselves."

The ideal goal of any discipline program is to strike a balance between the too heavy-handed and austere approach and the too lax approach that gives employees the appearance there is no control in the organization.

In terms of violence in the workplace, the subject of discipline should give any manager pause. Now more than ever, the way we discipline our employees can have real consequences for the health and safety of the company, the other employees, and the person who must mete out the discipline.

In his book *Resolving Conflicts on the Job* (AMACOM), author Jerry Wisinski writes, "The best way to solve a conflict is with a win-win solution: nobody loses, everybody wins." He lists five basic methods for resolving conflicts in the workplace: competition, accommodation, avoidance, compromise, and collaboration.[1]

We endorse a model that relies on collaboration. By identifying areas of agreement and disagreement, looking for alternatives, thinking creatively, and eventually finding solutions that have the full support and commitment of all parties, a human resources manager is more likely to do his or her best to prevent the creation of tension that may spark the flame of workplace violence.

In their well-written training program, *Discipline without Punishment*,[2] authors Richard C. Grote and Eric L. Harvey have created a step-by-step plan for discipline at all levels of any organization. (Their five steps are discussed later in this chapter.) We like the concepts for our purposes because they fit with our own view of safe discipline, which should be the primary goal of any supervisor. The secondary goal, of course, should be to get the employee committed to make a change. But if you cannot safely tell an employee, "You need to change and here's why," then you are not in control of the situation and can't possibly create the necessary change.

Grote and Harvey's step-by-step plan offers a preventive, positive, adult-based method of discipline. We believe their method will work, regardless of who the employee is, what he or she does as a job, or the nature of the discipline problem.

If we think metaphorically for a moment, in many ways employees in your company are much like blades of grass that together make up a vast green lawn. Given the proper amount of attention, "care and feeding" if you will, nurturing, and exposure to warmth, this "lawn" will flourish. Left to grow unchecked, without careful supervision, control, and planning for the future, many parts of the lawn will wither and die or grow completely out of control. Think of the process of discipline as similar to weed control on your lawn. Allowed to fester and spread, the bad weeds can kill the good grass.

Many people who work as managers and supervisors find the whole subject of discipline distasteful. Frankly, it's hard to punish people, and if you were to take a poll among businesspeople, discipline would get ranked just above their other least-favorite activity, termination.

And for their part, some managers don't even see the process of discipline as something that should fall under their job description. "I'm an accounting manager," goes a typical complaint. "I don't have time to keep watch over every little thing my employees do. Besides, I hate all the tension and conflict discipline meetings create. It seems like everyone goes away mad."

While there is an air of truth to these statements, the bottom line is managers must manage and not just focus on incomes and outputs. Managers manage people first and goods and services second. Part of that process involves discipline for inappropriate actions, behaviors, or rule breaking. As a long-time executive puts it, "If you can't discipline people or terminate them when necessary, you shouldn't be in a leadership position. Other employees, besides the ones who need discipline, look to you for guidance and want to learn by your positive example."

In other words, you have to be able to walk the talk and model the right behavior yourself. If you can't or won't put any effort into the way you discipline problem employees, you're doing a major disservice to your company. Correcting problem behaviors, as we will see, has just as much to do with the good of the company as it does with the good of the employee.

WHAT'S WRONG WITH TRADITIONAL DISCIPLINE: A DIFFERENCE IN APPROACHES

For years, the western management mindset has seen the concept of employee discipline as one where the supervisor talks "to" the employee and not "with" him or her. The difference between the Grote–Harvey model and the "old school" of discipline starts and ends with treating the worker to be disciplined like an adult human being worthy of respect.

The Grote–Harvey approach asks managers and supervisors to hold back personal biases and judgments against the employee and keep the conduct on a professional level. Figure 6–1 points to the differences between "the way we've always done it" and what might work better today, especially in light of recent workplace violence tragedies.

As you can see by the comparisons, traditional discipline aims for employee compliance, or the "You will do it our way," approach. Historically, this often leads to anger, aggression, and low morale on the part of the receiver.

FIGURE 6–1
Traditional Discipline versus Discipline without Punishment

Element	Traditional Discipline	Discipline without Punishment
Goal	Compliance	Commitment
Focus	Employee	Problem
Responsibility	Supervisor	Employee
Time frame	Past	Future
Communication	*At* the employee	*With* the employee
Direction mode	Parent→child	Adult→adult
Process	Punishment	Coaching
Climate	Authoritarian	Collaborative

The old focus was on the employee (i.e., *"You're* the reason we have a discipline problem"). Grote and Harvey counsel that the problem—bad attendance, company rule breaking, not finishing work or doing it poorly, and so on—should be the issue of any discipline meeting. This helps to take personalities out of the encounter, which can eliminate the need for shouting matches, name-calling, and accusations thrown across the room like so many errant boomerangs.

Their approach also takes the responsibility for change off the supervisor's shoulder and places it back where it belongs, squarely onto the employee. This changes the conversation from, "Here's what I want you to do for me" to "Here's what you need to do to change."

And typically, traditional discipline tends to focus on the past (i.e., "Here's a list of all the things you've done wrong up until now"). The Grote–Harvey approach asks supervisors to look toward the future and say, "Here's what we can do to correct the problem. Here are some of the things I'd like you to change and here are some of the things you can expect from me in terms of follow-up, feedback, and encouragement."

When they want to be, people are amazingly perceptive observers. They can tell by just listening to the tone of someone's voice if that person is happy, sad, angry, sarcastic, apprehensive, or afraid. Nowhere is this verbal acuity more prevalent than during a discipline hearing. When you sit across your desk from an employee and begin to discuss a discipline problem that may affect that person's well-being at the company, you can bet he or she will be hanging on your every word, searching for the real meaning in everything you say and do.

In this respect, the differences between talking *at* someone, as the traditional discipline approach mandates, and talking *with* someone, as Grote and Harvey counsel, are significant. Most people know when you're doing one and not the other. Another common—and faulty—approach to discipline is the parent–child trap, where the manager takes on the role of the disapproving parent and expects the employee to take on the role of the subservient child. This only leads to a host of other problems related to morale, future work performance, and the complete erosion of the manager–employee relationship.

"Too often," say authors Grote and Harvey, "when a disciplinary problem comes up, we find ourselves acting in the role of a parent to a child who has misbehaved." This approach takes both parties and puts them into completely foreign roles. Employees certainly don't want their bosses to treat them like children, and supervisors shouldn't relish the chance, either. Grote and Harvey put it this way:

"If you treat a person with a problem as a child who must be punished for misbehavior, that person will respond as a child. But if you treat a person with a problem as an adult with a problem to solve, that person will respond as an adult."

To this we add that if you model appropriate adult behavior during the discipline meeting, you may find the employee will do the same. Keeping the emotional temperature down, allowing both sides to be heard, and remaining professional and unbiased can keep the encounter at an adult-to-adult level.

The process of discipline should evolve from one built on punishing to one built on coaching. As paradoxical as it sounds, an employee with an attendance problem can fully understand when you say, "When you come to work every day on time, you make things better for all of us on the job. Your co-workers will appreciate you more, and I'll appreciate your effort to be more of a team player. We're all in this business together."

Grote and Harvey ask supervisors to think of the process of discipline as a collaborative effort. Put aside feelings of anger, "one-upmanship," revenge for past problems, and the concept of punishment for punishment's sake. Using a positive, nonpunishing approach, you can discipline employees and make them feel like the process was beneficial in many ways. While they won't love you for it, they certainly will feel like you treated them like adults.

In organizations characterized by the Grote–Harvey model for discipline, we predict there is less chance that you will have a disgruntled employee based on the way he or she was disciplined. Organizations characterized by the traditional punishment-based discipline approach seem to be where many of the known workplace violence incidents have happened.

In our studies of the workplace violence problem, this approach can make all the difference for your safety when you need to discipline an otherwise marginal employee.

MANAGEMENT BY MOVEMENT

One of the reasons managers and supervisors find the subject of discipline distasteful is that in order to see problem behaviors, they actually have to leave their desks or work areas. While this sounds surprising, for the manager who abhors conflict and doesn't want to feel like he or she is "spying" on the other employees, it rings true.

There is a mindset for some supervisors that says, "If I can't see them doing it, it must not be happening." This keeps them chained to their own areas and away from the places where their people may be breaking the rules.

Only by getting out and moving around the organization can an effective manager see what is going well and what needs to be fixed, both for the company and its products and the people who do the work. While this concept is certainly not new—Ken Blanchard, Tom Peters, and other management writers have advised it for years—the lesson has still not always hit home, especially at the lowest levels of the organization.

What may be easy for the executive vice president of sales might not be so easy for his or her sales manager. Managers and supervisors, who are typically more obsessed with product (i.e., production, manufacturing, and the deadlines attached to each), may not have the personality or indeed the personnel skills to wander through the plant, observing people doing their work, and interacting with them as they do.

If we have learned any lessons from the violence incidents that have plagued our work force, it is that the people who usually engage in this kind of behavior come from the lower ranks of the organization. Ignoring these people and failing to deal with their work problems is often the first thing that leads them to their aggressive behavior. The troubled employee who thinks his always-absent boss doesn't care about what he does or who he is feels little sympathy for the rest of the organization.

In some instances where a problem employee has terrorized his co-workers for years, a conspiracy of silence can so firmly exist that the other people around this employee are afraid to speak out against him. Some problem employees have succeeded in creating such an atmosphere of fear that the others are just not willing to jeopardize their mental health or physical safety by telling the boss. In these cases, where the hidden cost of fear has so overpowered the other members of the organization, the supervisor must be able to spot the warning signs and act on them. The only way to do this is to get out and spend significant amounts of time among the employees.

Some supervisors can compound this problem in the worst possible way: by blaming the victim of the violent or threatening employee's abuse. In an attempt to rationalize the bad employee's behavior, some supervisors seek to pass the buck and avoid the subject of discipline by finding ways to explain away potentially distressing episodes. These supervisors say to victim-employees "What's the big deal?" or "You're overreacting," or the ever-popular, "I'll look into it and get back to you."

Blaming the victim for the aggressive employee's behavior is tantamount to accepting it. This type of avoidance can lead to expensive lawsuits and the kinds of workplace violence episodes that have become common in our work force.

Fortunately, for the managers and supervisors who decide to take action, identifying the instigators in most workplace violence situations is not difficult. These people rarely keep their emotions to themselves. As we have seen from the workplace violence profile characteristics in Chapter 4, even the most devout loner will give off warning signs just by his inability to interact with the others around him. The aggressive, intimidating employee lets everyone in the building know he's around.

In these cases, slight overreaction in terms of discipline may be more helpful than marked underreaction. The employee who feels as if the leaders of the organization have stepped in and set his or her work life back on track is bound to feel upset by the intervention. This is common and a natural human reaction. Few of us like to be told we need to fix a certain aspect relating to our behavior, but most of us will try to make the effort to change.

Studies of past workplace violence incidents related to discipline problems—meetings, hearings, and so on—seem to tell us that 95 percent of the work force will try to change once a supervisor points out a problem and the new behavior needed to make it right. Another 4 percent will go along, haltingly, with several backtracks that may lead either to positive results later or a termination. The remaining 1 percent are the potentially dangerous employees. They will not respond to any of your efforts to change their behavior through positive discipline. They may be so severely disturbed that anything you say will not affect them in a beneficial way.

The bad news is you may have one or more of these employees already working for you or for someone else in your organization. The good news is that using the process of discipline as created by Grote and Harvey, you can deal with the entire 100 percent safely and effectively.

BAD FROM THE START: THE WRONG APPROACH TO DISCIPLINE

Imagine the following conversation: Your boss stops you in the hallway one Friday afternoon. It's near the end of the work day and you think the conversation may have something to do with the weekend ahead. Instead, your boss hits you with the following:

Boss:
"I need to talk to you about a problem on Monday morning."

You:

"What about?" you reply puzzled.

Boss:

"It's about a problem with your job performance."

You:

"My performance?" you ask, as a chill runs down your spine. "What's it about?"

Boss:

"I'd rather not discuss it now," your boss says, turning to leave. "Just be ready to meet with me as soon as you get to work on Monday morning."

Now imagine how this conversation could ruin your entire weekend! Will you be able to spend it relaxing with your family and enjoying a nice time at home? Absolutely not.

Thanks to this kind of insensitive treatment, you'll probably spend your weekend sick with worry, talking on the telephone to other colleagues at your company about your work habits, or retyping your résumé out of fear you may not have a job come Monday night.

This kind of manipulation is common in some organizations and with some supervisors. The thinking here seems to be, "I don't feel comfortable with the subject of discipline, so I think I'll make the employee feel uncomfortable, too."

If this is typical of the way you prepare for discipline meetings, we suggest you make an immediate change in your approach to your employees. Putting them "on ice" over the span of a weekend is both cruel and counterproductive to your goals.

The key to success with discipline lies in your ability to treat employees like adult human beings with real feelings, sensitivities, and concerns.

So what's the best approach to scheduling a discipline meeting? Do it now! Why wait for the "best moment" in the workday, especially when it doesn't exist? Grab this tough problem by the neck and deal with it, the sooner the better. The employee will feel more secure and may even appreciate the discipline process more. An example:

Boss:

"Joe, I need to talk to you about something that's been on my mind."

You:

"What's that, boss?"

Boss:

"I want to talk to you about a work problem that I've seen with you. Can you come into my office and discuss it right now?"

You:

"OK, I guess. Let's do it."

See the difference? In the first scenario, both parties stew about the problem over a weekend. A two-day wait can generate plenty of discontent on both sides. The employee will wonder what he or she did wrong and feel resentful toward the supervisor. The supervisor frets over the problem and may feel resentful toward the employee for putting him or her into the unpleasant position of having to judge certain behaviors and hand out appropriate discipline. It's a lose-lose proposition, further compounded by the passing of time.

And the only thing worse than the manager who says, "See me on Monday" is the one who forgets the old people–management adage "Praise in public, criticize in private." You've probably seen some form of this scenario take place where you've worked:

The irate plant manager storms onto the assembly line and shuts everything down. Confronting an employee at a drill press, the manager begins a long tirade about some indiscretion. The employee can only stand there humiliated in front of his peers and co-workers as this harangue continues.

When this angry chewing-out is done, the manager stomps back to his desk, leaving the employee to feel like a wounded animal. The employee's co-workers may shake their heads and offer sympathy, secretly agree that the employee had it coming, or verbally or silently call the manager a dozen foul names.

The point is not whether the manager had a right to discipline the employee. The problem stems from *how* the manager went about it. By creating this tactless scene, the manager immediately destroys his own credibility and causes many people in the room to despise him. The targeted employee feels bad for the treatment, and the other employees now worry that they may be singled out for a similar tongue-lashing in the near future. This puts everyone on edge and completely defeats the purpose of positive discipline.

The rule is clear: Discipline meetings between an employee and a supervisor should always take place in private, behind closed doors. Give an employee hearty praise for a job well done in front of his or her co-workers and you'll make a friend for life. Heap mounds of abuse on an employee in public or seek to hold an entire discipline meeting in front of his or her colleagues and you'll make an enemy for life. And in these days of discipline-based workplace violence incidents, you could be putting yourself and others around you in jeopardy for your thoughtless actions.

Managers and supervisors should spend more time celebrating the small and large accomplishments of their people. The occasional verbal pat on the back can pay dividends for a long time.

DECIDE WHO SHOULD DISCIPLINE

Seeing the problem is only the first step in any discipline process. Deciding who will conduct the discipline meeting is quite another. Sometimes this decision is based on company policy. Firms with a strong infrastructure may delegate all discipline procedures to a company personnel representative. In these cases, the supervisor will submit a report and the personnel rep will follow through with the recommendations when meeting with the employee.

In strong union organizations, the subject of employee discipline can become quite involved. Labor will want its members to have union representation for even the most minor discipline episodes. For more advice about this, seek out the industrial relations managers at your facility.

But in the majority of cases, the person who will run the discipline meeting should be the direct supervisor of the employee involved. This process cuts to the heart of the matter and gets the two people most involved—the employee and his or her supervisor—talking immediately.

But what happens if the employee and his or her direct supervisor don't get along? Should the supervisor try to put aside personal differences and initiate the discipline meeting anyway? If this were a perfect world, we might say yes. But past feelings can lead to a host of problems not related to the actual discipline itself. If the supervisor holds a grudge from some previous encounter, it may be nearly impossible for him or her to squelch the desire to get back at the employee using an excessive punishment. The desire to revert to the negative parent–child mode can set the supervisor or the company up for a valid grievance complaint from the employee.

If the supervisor thinks the employee is a company troublemaker who works hard to make him or her look bad, the chances are good this feeling will contaminate the discipline process. Just as defense attorneys and prosecutors search hard for impartial jurors, so should you look for an unbiased supervisor to handle obvious or even not-so-obvious cases of employee–supervisor resentment. Letting a supervisor bent on revenge discipline an employee who clearly despises his or her boss is a bad mixture.

Often, all it takes is for the supervisor's boss to step in and handle the discipline process. This person may be well liked or respected by both parties and has the added value of seeing the discipline dispute as an interested third party. This helicopter view can lend an air of balance and fairness to any discipline proceeding.

After an initial meeting with the front-line supervisor to discuss the facts of the case, the higher level supervisor can intervene and meet with the employee, either alone or with the employee's supervisor present. Good sense, the degree of animosity, and the need for a witness to verify the procedure will dictate the right choices.

THE ROLE OF THE PSYCHOLOGIST AS A PRE– OR POSTDISCIPLINE CONSULTANT

But to move back to the problem of workplace violence, what happens if the supervisor is *afraid* of the employee? How do you handle a discipline problem when the supervisor feels physically threatened by the employee? This puts the subject of employee discipline in a whole new and frightening light.

In any situation where the employee exhibits or has exhibited a threatening type of behavior, the safety of the supervisor should be the primary concern of any discipline procedure.

The extent of your reaction will depend mostly on the circumstances, but as the workplace violence stories in this book have shown, it's far better to err on the side of caution than to take it for granted that a disturbed employee will comply with orders just because he's at work.

In some cases, just changing the roles of the discipliner from the employee's immediate supervisor to a manager or a higher-level supervisor will be enough to change the employee's behavior. But since gut instincts are often an excellent indicator of future problems, you shouldn't hesitate to make changes in your "standard" discipline procedures if the employee in question creates a fearful environment by his very presence.

If your firm has an on-site psychologist, bring him or her into the discipline meeting as either a facilitator or an intermediary who can guide the process in a safe manner. If you have access to psychologists through your company's employee assistance program (EAP), plan for one of them to attend the discipline meeting before you schedule it with the employee.

If it's clear at the onset that the employee in question is highly disturbed and volatile, don't continue the discipline meeting! End the meeting immediately and suggest that you reconvene at another time. Suggest that the employee may want to talk to "someone" to cope with the current anger or anxiety. For example:

"Joe, I can see you're very upset about this whole thing."

"You're damned right I am! This is unfair! I don't like the way I've been treated and I'm gonna do something about it!"

"I'd like for you to meet with someone from our EAP program. I'd like to have Dr. Smith come and talk with you about how you're feeling."

"You want me to talk to some shrink? Do you think I'm crazy?"

"No, Joe, I don't think that. It's just that you and I can't talk about what we need to until you feel less angry. Will you meet with Dr. Smith after lunch to tell him what you're feeling?"

"Yeah, I'll do it. I need to tell somebody what's going on around here."

Don't overlook the psychologist's role in any potentially difficult discipline meeting. By serving as a trained observer in distressed human behavior, the psychologist can intervene to lower the emotional temperature in the room and safely deal with the employee's conflicts, aggressive behavior, rage, or paranoia.

But what if, say the devil's advocates, we don't have an organizational psychologist on staff? What then?

Go to your phone book and call the mental health facility in your area. You may be able to arrange for a counselor to come to you, or at least, get the disturbed employee to speak with them by phone. If you explain the gravity of the situation—especially in light of all the workplace violence incidents—you may be able to get some outside help.

You cannot treat the disturbed employee like any other person working at your company. These people have special needs and don't always respond to "normal" behaviors on your part. Putting your arm around an employee as a gesture of friendship or conciliation may seem appropriate to you, but to the paranoid employee, inappropriate touching can trigger a violent response. Don't take chances. You can't always "follow the manual" in every discipline case.

If you think you should contact security in advance and have a guard posted in the room, by all means, do it. If you feel the discipline meeting will require the presence of two or three or five other supervisors in the room with the employee, do it.

If the employee asks you why these people are present, you can tell him directly that you want to avoid any unpleasant confrontations. Disturbed employees are not usually passive. Their actions, their words, and their personalities will help to tell everyone how they feel. They know it and in the vast number of cases, they know other people around them know it. The plant bully is not shy in his mistreatment of others. He wants to make other people feel uncomfortable. Sometimes if you meet force with "force presence," you can diffuse his behavior with a no-nonsense policy of your own.

By establishing a force presence of sorts, you aren't trying to start a fight. You're merely trying to tell the disturbed employee, in clear terms, that the purpose of your meeting is to talk about his behavior and how it will need to change if he wishes to remain employed at the company. Of course, if the tone of the meeting has taken on this degree of concern about the safety of others, you're probably ready to move on to the subject of the next chapter—safe employee termination.

As a manager or executive, don't hesitate to intervene if a supervisor comes to you with a discipline safety problem. These encounters have already established a dangerous history around them. Should the situation warrant extraordinary safety precautions, decide what to do to ensure a positive outcome for all concerned.

DISCIPLINING THE DISCIPLINER: COPING WITH THE PROBLEM SUPERVISOR

Perhaps the only thing worse than a problem employee who exhibits the potential for workplace violence is the problem *supervisor* who does the same. As much as we hate to think it, there are supervisors who, even though they are in a position of leadership, are just as damaging to an organization as a bad employee.

These kinds of supervisors tend to fall into two equally disturbing categories:

1. *The toxic supervisor.* This person goes about the organization creating hate and discontent wherever he or she roams. Employees hate these types for their terrible people skills, rude behavior, and their reputation for harassing behaviors—sexual, physical, or psychological. The toxic supervisor "wins" through intimidation, using various browbeating or put-down techniques to gain employee compliance. It's not uncommon for these kinds of supervisors to be the subject of violent attacks by disgruntled employees. Other upset employees may retaliate in other nonphysical ways, using vandalism, sabotage, or passive–aggressive work slowdowns or stoppages to get back at the hostile supervisor.

The cult-favorite 1992 book *Sabotage in the American Workplace,* edited by Martin Sprouse (Pressure Drop Press) is chock-full of these kinds of stories of the bad boss and how angry employees got back at him or her in particularly devious and destructive ways.

2. *The violent supervisor.* Although far more rare than the toxic supervisor, the violent supervisor is inherently dangerous. This person uses threats, physical intimidation, extortion, and actual physical violence to gain compliance. Employees fear this supervisor for the physical damage he may do to them. Worse yet, they may feel like they have very little recourse in the organization

if they speak up against a supervisor who makes them feel fearful. And the violent supervisor may be so good at covering his tracks or blaming other employees for their "overreaction" that he can get away with his crimes. In a large, heavily layered, bureaucratic organization, it may take a tragedy or a violent outburst of significant proportion to bring this person to the attention of senior management.

The role of the problem supervisor in the aftermath of any workplace violence situation can't be discounted. Although we never seek to blame the victim in these encounters, the fact that a supervisor may have indeed driven a borderline employee to violence is a real possibility. We've seen it in a number of the cases we've studied.

Taking a manufacturing plant as an example, the supervisor for the drill press operators was probably once a drill press operator himself. Over the course of his tenure at the plant, he may have formed several problem relationships with co-workers who regard him with great animosity. If the feeling is mutual, this employee may carry these grudges into his new role as their supervisor. With past history as his guide, he can set out to make his former co-workers' lives miserable. In the worst cases of this kind of abuse, it's no wonder violence arises in employees' minds as the only viable solution for relief.

This is not to say supervisors are to blame for all their employees' violent outbursts. But in any organization, the issue of how supervisors treat employees must be firmly attached to the specter of violence in the workplace. It is up to top management to be just as strict in their use of performance appraisals to judge supervisors as supervisors use them to judge employees.

The employee grapevine can become a useful tool in your evaluation of your supervisors. Along with all the other issues you rate supervisors on, their treatment of their people has to be near the top of the list.

Supervisors who violate our Golden Rule—"Treat others in the company as you would like to be treated yourself"—can cause just as many problems as so-called disgruntled employees. One of the reasons so many employees appear disgruntled may start and end with how they are treated by the people that supervise them.

What's good for the problem employee might be just as good for the problem supervisor. Discipline, as a tool for change and positive compliance, should know no boundaries in your organization. Supervisors should be subject to the same criteria and ramifications if they fail to make agreed changes as the employees who work for them.

THE GROTE–HARVEY MODEL FOR DISCIPLINE WITHOUT PUNISHMENT

In their training program workbook, Grote and Harvey offer a five-step approach to discipline without punishment:

Step One: **IDENTIFY**
Determine the DESIRED performance
Determine the ACTUAL performance
Focus on SPECIFICS

Step Two: **ANALYZE**
Determine the IMPACT of the problem
Determine the CONSEQUENCES the employee will face
Determine the appropriate ACTION STEP

Step Three: **DISCUSS**
Gain the EMPLOYEE'S AGREEMENT to change
Discuss the ALTERNATIVE SOLUTIONS
Decide what ACTION the employee will take

Step Four: **DOCUMENT**
Describe the PROBLEM
Describe the HISTORY
Describe the DISCUSSION

Step Five: **FOLLOW-UP**
Determine if the PROBLEM has been SOLVED
Reinforce IMPROVEMENT
Take required ACTION

Source: Richard C. Grote and Eric L. Harvey, *Discipline without Punishment* (New York: McGraw-Hill, 1993). © Performance Systems 1983. Used by permission.

In step one, *identify,* there are certain things you must do as a supervisor before you ask the employee to meet with you. Omitting any of these premeeting steps can leave you unprepared for what will take place during it. You must have already thought through the entire discipline process for the employee, be ready to ask questions, and more importantly, provide specifics to the employee about problem behaviors.

Some research beforehand will put you in a better position to respond to any situation that arises during the meeting. Further, just knowing that you have all your data in place should help to lower your stress level before the meeting begins.

So let's follow along as we watch a discipline meeting that is handled correctly:

"Dave, thanks for coming to my office. I wanted to talk with you about a problem that relates to your appearance here at work. I've given it some thought and since we're running a snack food business where we sell to stores and to individual customers, the appearance of our employees is important."

"Okay, so what's wrong with the way I look?"

"Well, Dave, you know we pride ourselves on the way we look. Our uniforms are always clean and pressed, our route trucks are always clean and polished, and our snack food boxes are always very clean." (You've just told the employee your *desired* performance.)

"And you have a problem with what?"

"I've noticed that for the past week, your shoes are dirty, your pants are not creased, and your shirt looks like you've been sleeping in it." (You've just told the employee his *actual* performance in a very specific way.)

And the way you get to this first step is by gathering your data. Take the time you need to collect your facts and organize them so that when you do meet with the employee, you know what you want to say and how you want to respond to his or her questions.

To gather information about any potential discipline problem, you can use a variety of sources. You may want to talk to other employees, meet with other supervisors who interact with your employee, review the employee's performance evaluations, review time cards, finished products, written reports, or observe the employee's behavior or job duties yourself. In most cases, it's always best to rely on your own observations. This protects you from having to say, "I didn't see it myself, but Mr. Jones said you did . . ."

To Grote and Harvey, all discipline boils down to three key areas:

1. *Attendance.* Does the employee show up on time? Does he or she come to work every day? Stay for the entire workday?
2. *Conduct.* Does the employee follow work rules pertaining to behavior on the job?
3. *Performance.* How well a job does the employee do? Does he or she know the policies and procedures? Can the employee complete tasks given?

These three categories need to be assessed individually. An employee could have a bad attendance record, follow the company work rules, and do an acceptable job. Or the employee could have a perfect attendance record, break company rules now and again, and do an excellent job. Lastly, the employee could have an average attendance record, follow the company rules, but do a poor job.

BASIC WORK PERFORMANCE FUNCTIONS

Of the three categories, attendance is the easiest to review. Unlike performance, which is much more subjective, attendance relates to the physical presence of the employee. Does he or she come to work on time, every day, and work for the entire day? Discipline problems relating to attendance typically revolve around employees who chronically come to work late, miss days, or leave early.

Conduct at work is a bit more difficult to document. While it's easy to see when an employee breaks a specific work rule, (e.g., no smoking in the office), sometimes employee conduct rules create gray areas. This can lead to differences of opinion between supervisors as to what is a rules violation and what is not. Sexual harassment issues lead the pack in this troubling area. Does the employee come back from lunch drunk? Mishandle inventory or equipment due to carelessness? Spill coffee on an expensive computer even when he or she knows not to keep beverages near it? "Borrow" tools from the assembly line?

Conduct is more than just what the company tells an employee he or she can or can't do while at work. It's more of a reflection of how the employee fits into the culture of the organization. Does the employee "fit" with the values, mores, ethics, and norms created by society and as these factors relate to compliance at the workplace?

This can be measured at an individual level—how well the employee complies with rules that pertain to individual conduct—and at a "team" level—how well the employee gets along with other people at work.

Performance may be the most difficult to assess accurately. Reams of material already exist on the subject of performance appraisal. Books and training programs fill the shelves of most managers and supervisors. Still, even with all the available material, rating the job performance of someone can be a hair-pulling experience. The following list of job duties may help you organize your thoughts, both in terms of appraisal and evaluation and for discipline purposes, too.

According to the way workers' compensation experts analyze worker performance, the following abilities are crucial to any employee's job performance:

1. The ability to comprehend and follow instructions.
2. The ability to perform simple and repetitive tasks.
3. The ability to maintain a work pace appropriate to the given workload.
4. The ability to perform complex or varied tasks.
5. The ability to relate to other people beyond giving and receiving instructions.
6. The ability to influence people.
7. The ability to make generalizations, evaluations, or decisions without the need for supervision.
8. The ability to accept and carry out responsibility for direction, control, and planning.

For your own purposes, you can take the tasks and duties of the employees that work for your specific organization and apply these abilities. If you work for a textile factory, the duties of a loom operator will be vastly different from a machinist at an aircraft assembly plant. But the key to this list is that these abilities are germane to all work.

If any of your employees have serious problems with any of these eight basic work functions, then you may need to schedule a discipline meeting to address one or more of them.

GAINING A COMMITMENT TO CHANGE

Step two in the process is to *analyze* the discipline problem itself. This starts with your decisions about what you want the employee to do once the meeting is over. You'll also need to think about the impact of the problem on the organization, the employee, and to a lesser extent, your relationship with that employee. Ask yourself, "What are the good business reasons why this problem has to be solved?"

Which of the three discipline categories—attendance, conduct, or performance—does the problem fall under, and how does it relate to the success or failure of the company as a whole?

From a personnel standpoint, what will happen to the employee if he or she fails to correct the discipline problem? What are the steps you are willing to take to solve this problem? Does your solution include placing a note in the employee's personnel file? Handing out a short or long suspension? Termination? How far are you willing to go to solve this problem? What boundaries have you set for yourself in terms of the employee's conduct at the discipline meeting? At what point will you be ready to make a difficult decision regarding this person's future with this company?

Lastly, what steps do you need to take and what steps does the employee need to take to solve this discipline problem? Will one action on his or her part solve the problem, or will you need to create a checklist of things?

According to Grote and Harvey, the reason most people continue with problem behavior is because they don't know what the consequences are and they overestimate their ability to avoid the consequences of that behavior.

If you know where the employee's problem lies—attendance, conduct, or work performance—what specific things you want him or her to do to correct this negative behavior, what the impact of this problem is on the organization, what consequences the employee will face if the behavior does not change, and what steps the employee will have to take to change, you're finally ready to call the person into your office for a meeting. If you don't have all this information at the ready, you'll cheat yourself, the company, and the employee.

Step three starts when you call the employee into your office or another private area and *discuss* the discipline problem.

Let's continue to use our snack foods route driver as the employee with the discipline problem:

"Dave," you start, "you know the quality and appearance of our snack foods is critical to our success. I wanted to talk to you today about some specific complaints I've been getting by supermarket managers." (Foreshadows the desired performance.)

"Oh yeah?" says Dave, as he leans forward in his chair. "Who?"

"I spoke to the managers at ABC Market, XYZ Market, and the Food Market. They told me that many of the bags of potato chips you've been leaving at their stores have been crushed and broken. This means the chips are not in good condition when the customer comes in to buy them." (Discusses the employee's actual performance by pointing to specifics.)

"C'mon boss! What's the big deal? So a couple of bags of chips get busted when I stock them. I've got a big route and I'm in a major hurry out there. I've gotta get that stuff off the truck and into the store and then get on to the next place."

"Dave, you may not realize this, but the impact of your actions on our company is tremendous. If people would rather buy another bag of chips from another company because ours looks damaged, then that's not good. When customers come into a store to buy chips and they see ours are broken, maybe they'll start to think something is wrong with the quality of our food. They may think that someone has tampered with the bag and it may not be safe to eat. If that happens, they start to lose confidence in our company." (Explains the impact on the business.)

"I'm trying my best out there but this is a tough job. I'm under a lot of time pressure to get those shelves stocked. You've never had a route sales job like this. You sit in your office all day while I'm out there." (Employee attempts to rationalize behavior.)

"Dave, you're right. I never have had a route sales job. But I do know what's important to this company and I do know that what you're doing has a significant impact on our business. Do you know what kind of message you send to our customers when you stock broken bags of chips? It affects their confidence in us. It makes them wonder about the quality of our food." (Steer the conversation back to the impact of the employee's behavior on the business.)

"But we have good products. Our snacks are the best in the business." (Employee starting to come around.)

"That's true, Dave. I want you to keep that in mind. If every one of our 100 route drivers broke 10 bags of chips per day, that's 1,000 bags of broken chips just in one day. Can you see where that would cause problems for us all here?"

"That sounds like it could affect my job. If we don't sell chips and snacks, I'm outta work." (Employee understands the consequences if his behavior continues.)

"You're right. It could affect your job."

"Okay, I think I better start being a lot more careful in how I handle our products." (Employee agrees to make change.)

"That's great. Let's talk about the specific things you can do to handle the products."

By now, the conversation has entered the third step—the *discuss* stage—where the supervisor and the employee focus on the solutions to the problem and decide what actions the employee will take.

As soon as the employee agrees to change his or her behavior, the discipline part of the meeting is, in effect, over. What remains is the discussion surrounding the steps the employee will need to take to actually make the changes.

But what if the employee refuses to make the commitment to change? What if you still get resistance, rationalizations, and excuses? You'll need to reinforce the consequences of his actions.

"Dave, do we agree that your behavior has a definite impact on our business?"

"Yeah, I suppose so."

"Then can we agree on the changes you'll need to make?"

"But what about the other guys out on the route? Have you talked to them?" (Rationalizing.)

"Dave, at this point, I'm only concerned with you. If I need to speak to the other drivers I will, but for now, let's focus on what you need to do to change the way you handle the products."

"I still think you're making a big deal outta nothing."

"Well, since you already know how our company wants you to handle our products safely and correctly, and we've discussed the impact your actions have on our business, we need to talk about the consequences if you don't meet your obligations as an employee."

"Like I could get fired?"

"You know from your employee manual that this company uses a range of discipline procedures. We start with counseling, then we put a written reprimand in your personnel file, then we suspend you without pay, and then we terminate you." (Consequences are spelled out.)

"I don't want any of that bad stuff to happen. Let's talk about what I need to do to keep my job." (Employee understands consequences, seeks to make a change.)

Now that you've explained to the employee what you want in terms of performance and what he or she has actually done, discussed the business impact of the employee's problem performance, emphasized the consequences the employee will face, and gained the employee's commitment to make a change, you'll need to walk the employee through the steps necessary to make that change.

"Dave, I'm glad you've agreed to make a change in the way you handle our products. Let's talk about the specific actions you can take to make those changes. Do you have any ideas?" (Focuses on alternative solutions and actions.)

"Well, I suppose I could come into the plant a little earlier and arrange my truck better."

"Good. That sounds like a fine idea. What else?"

"I could put pads in between the boxes of chips on my handcart so they don't bump each other. And I think the best thing I could do would be to slow down a bit and stock my shelves a little more carefully."

"Those all sound like fine ideas. I think you'll be able to get a better handle on this problem if you try those things."

FOLLOWING THROUGH

Once the third step is finished, move to step four, the *document* stage. Here, you'll need to make careful and complete notes that show what the problem was, how you came to recognize the problem, and what conversation took place between you and the employee. Some supervisors like to create a Memo of Understanding that covers what was said in the discipline meeting. They keep one copy and give one to the employee. This memo can also specifically indicate what the employee plans to do to change the incorrect behavior and the consequences (suspension, termination, etc.) the employee faces if he or she does not change the behavior.

The value of this record of the meeting is multifaceted. It protects you from legal action later; it prevents misunderstandings on either side; it gives you an accurate record of who said what and how the employee promised to change; and it gives both of you a written record of the potential consequences if the behavior goes unchanged.

The last stage, the *follow-up*, can cover two distinct areas. It helps you keep track of the employee's progress, and it gives you recourse should the employee regress or fail to make the changes discussed in the previous meeting.

It's always important to gain the employee's agreement to change. If he or she fails to make the change and you schedule another meeting, you can switch your focus from the prior problem to the employee's credibility. In this case, now the employee has failed to live up to an agreement you both entered into.

"Dave, the last time we spoke about this problem three weeks ago, you agreed to make changes, but you haven't. Your problem behavior is still continuing. But now, the problem is no longer about broken chips; it's about your credibility as an employee. I feel as though you violated an agreement between both of us. We need to discuss the consequences of this failure."

The onus for the change goes right back to the employee, who, in your previous meeting, agreed to make the required changes you both discussed. Should you need to increase the discipline level, you're now in a better position to do it. This shift from the original discipline problem to the new problem of failing to abide by the original agreement can serve as your strongest weapon in any hardcore discipline case.

Discipline is a fact of business life. Whether it pertains to an employee or a supervisor, a high-salary executive or a low-skill hourly worker, the goal should be the same: Seek a commitment from the person to change. With regard to violence in the workplace, the subject of discipline should force you to evaluate your own procedures for reaching this goal and doing it safely.

ENDNOTES

[1] Niki Scott, "Book Offers Ways to Solve Conflicts," *Orlando Sentinel*, August 21, 1993.

[2] Richard C. Grote and Eric L. Harvey, *Discipline without Punishment* (New York: McGraw-Hill, 1983).

Chapter Seven

Safe Termination

Now that we've motored through the often-dangerous waters surrounding discipline, the trip doesn't get much smoother. Whether it's from a euphemistic "downsizing event" involving a massive layoff, or a straight "you're fired," the process of termination—physically telling an employee not to return to work—can be an extremely stressful event for all participants.

This chapter tackles a provocative issue—how to terminate someone safely and effectively. We want to provide an approach to termination that can take employers through this difficult procedure in a logical, careful manner. The idea is to create a safe termination policy and maintain an atmosphere of compliance.

Past history now points to the same conclusion: If you have a problem employee, one whom you suspect has the potential to commit some kind of act of workplace violence, no matter how minor, chances are good the person will act out after a discipline or a termination meeting.

A quick scan of the daily newspaper headlines reminds us of the greater likelihood a disgruntled former employee will return with revenge on his mind. And an even more distressing scenario on the rise involves the disgruntled employee who leaves one job—for personal reasons or via a termination—and strikes back at the *next* employer who hires him.

The trouble is, since few of us have an accurate corporate crystal ball at our disposal, it's hard to tell exactly when this will occur.

Since we can't accurately make predictions about the *when* or *who* or *where* of workplace violence, let's focus on what we do know about termination and violence in the workplace—the *why*.

Thousands of people get laid off every business day and never return to cause problems for their previous employers. And as far as statistics and verifiable incidents are concerned, only a small percentage of terminated employees ever cause serious problems. But the ones that do return with death on their minds can create tremendous havoc in a short period of time.

You should not view the subject of violence after termination as a make-or-break issue; that is, whether you or someone in your company might be harmed by the employee in question should not determine whether or not you actually terminate the employee. Your decision to terminate someone should be based primarily upon two issues: (1) the availability of work for the person to do or (2) the person's performance, conduct, or attendance.

"Is there enough work in the company to justify the person's position?" and/or "Does this person follow the company rules, policies, and procedures in terms of his or her work performance, work behavior, and attendance?"

If you can't answer yes to either question, either because of a work slowdown, as is common in the automobile, airplane, or durable goods manufacturing industries, or because the employee has failed to respond to your attempts at discipline without punishment, then you probably will have to terminate someone.

It pains us to think that problem employees are being kept on the payroll because they have succeeded in intimidating the managers and supervisors who are too afraid to confront them, discipline them, or give them the boot. And yet, stories of this abound, especially in companies where strong labor union activists hold a deathlike grip on the management. The days of the "last hired, first fired" union shop still exist.

Many managers faced with the painful thought of a long and potentially violent work stoppage may bow to union pressure to keep borderline employees just because they have so much "time in grade." While they may privately curse the difficult, troublemaking employee, they will publicly do nothing, citing union troubles, labor laws stacked in favor of the worker over the employer, and the fear that one fired employee will become the martyr-like symbol for the others who remain.

And that leads us to another chilling and hard-to-answer question: Should it be possible for any manager or supervisor to terminate a problem employee because he or she feels that employee represents a workplace violence danger to the organization?

If this were a perfect world, we could quickly answer yes. But there are degrees to our assertion. The key to any workplace violence–related termination goes back to what we discussed in the last chapter on discipline. If you can safely say the employee in question violated the rules of either attendance, conduct, or work performance, has been duly warned about these issues, and has failed to make the prescribed changes, then you have the grounds for a termination.

The issue many story-seeking journalists or nervous managers want to raise is often tied to the existence of a workplace violence profile employee. We've addressed this carefully in Chapter 4.

People who don't or won't understand the purpose of a profile can confuse the issue even more. "Can a manager," goes this line of thinking, "terminate an employee who fits some or all the profile behaviors (see Chapters 4 and 5 for a review) associated with workplace violence?"

The answer here is a definite, absolute no. "You mean to tell me," says the worried plant manager, "that I can't fire a guy who seems obsessed with guns, had a bad military record, bitches to the people around him that he hates me and hates this job?"

Again, no, unless you want to get hit with a huge lawsuit based on wrongful termination and discrimination.

Here's the reason: We can look backwards and see that many of the instigators in homicidal workplace violence incidents fit a profile. But, the fact is, those people that fit the profile don't necessarily commit workplace violence. With hindsight, it's easy to use a workplace violence profile to try and retrofit potential problem employees into a list of subjective categories.

So what's the value of the profile at all? As we pointed out in Chapters 3 and 4 during our discussion of hiring precautions, the profile serves as a good indicator of warning signs for any potential new hires. From a purely background level, we suggest you be extremely leery of hiring any new employee who fits the majority of the profile and who reveals a substantial amount of problem areas during his background check.

So what is a manager or supervisor to do? How do you enforce company rules and maintain a safe, productive working environment filled with high-quality employees? You start by removing problem employees in a safe, legal manner.

If you can document the employee's workplace problem episodes (fighting, threats, vandalism, sabotage, intimidation, etc.) and see no other recourse (discipline, suspension), then you should be able to hand that employee his "walking papers."

This is not, sad to say, a perfect world. Managers who are not schooled in the latest, up-to-date personnel issues, labor laws, and equal employment opportunity commission (EEO) requirements may feel uncomfortable with their ability to make snap personnel decisions, even in the face of an employee with apparent violence-related problems.

So we'll ask the question again and then answer it:

> Should a manager or a supervisor have the right to fire an employee who engages in behavior that indicates a potential for workplace violence including fighting with other employees, threatening to assault other employees or supervisors, damaging equipment, or intimidating others into doing his work for him?

Are not these workplace violence indicators related to employee conduct?: Can't you use these specific criteria to document the employee's failure to follow conduct and work performance rules? Here, the answer is yes; you can terminate an employee who fails to fulfill his obligations to the three discipline issues we raised in Chapter 6.

If you establish a "zero tolerance" environment in your organization, you can say to the disruptive employee, "Your conduct is unacceptable. Your actions here disrupt the other people around you. We will not tolerate this behavior. You will either make changes in your behavior or you will not continue to work here."

By stressing to the problem employee the impact of potentially disruptive, antagonistic, threatening, or even violent behavior on the success or failure of the organization as a whole, you can remove much of the personality conflicts that impede most discipline or termination proceedings.

THE MEANING OF "MY JOB"

Deputy White House counsel Vincent W. Foster, Jr., who apparently shot himself to death on July 20, 1993, was long known as a workaholic who had been weighed down by the tremendous strain of his new job. Speaking to reporters at the funeral of his long-time friend and colleague, President Bill Clinton said, "Remember that we're all people and that we have to pay maybe a little more attention to our friends and our families and our co-workers. Try to remember that work cannot be the only thing in life."[1]

For some people, the job is more than just what they do, it becomes who they are; it gives them identity and purpose. To some rational, normal people, losing their job is just the same as losing their identity. Faced with the sudden prospect of no J-O-B, it's hard for even the most emotionally balanced worker to look up and say, "I'm no longer a (fill in the job title)."

By not "being" a lawyer, a cop, a salesperson, a store clerk, a welder, an engineer, or a computer builder, they feel like they no longer exist, at least on one important level that relates to their self-esteem.

Work, to most of us, is not just a place to earn a paycheck and leave. It gives us social interaction, satisfaction, and for some, a reason even to get out of bed in the morning. Faced with no job, or even the prospect of job loss, some people find their coping mechanisms sadly lacking. For those who see work as all they have, there is a sense of sudden disconnection from the rest of society if they lose their jobs. Their meaning of life, their sphere of existence, often starts and ends with work.

For those of us who see more to life than just work, this is hard to understand. These other people have confused working to live with living to work.

For the average person who sees work as just one part of the rest of his or her life, a termination, for whatever reason, is indeed traumatic, but only to a certain extent. For the unstable person, to whom work is everything, the trauma surrounding a termination—even if it did not occur because of disciplinary reasons—can be quite severe. The paranoid, delusional person already perceives "injustices" in the world. "They're out to get me. I've known it for years and now this (the termination) just proves it. If they take away my job, they take away my life."

During the 1960–70 heyday of space exploration, separation anxiety became a real factor in human space travel. In July 1969, Apollo 11 astronaut Michael Collins piloted *Columbia*, the Command Module, around the moon, while his partners Neil Armstrong and Buzz Aldrin worked out of the moon-based Eagle, the Lunar Module. Collins said that the only time he ever felt nervous about the entire mission was during the agonizing "dead air" time as he flew around the so-called "dark side" of the moon.

With his radio communications back to the Houston, Texas, Johnson Space Center interrupted by the blocking positions of the moon and the earth, Collins felt cut off from the rest of the universe. And indeed he was. If anything bad should have happened to Collins or his fragile spacecraft as he broke contact with the Earth, we would never have known about it.

Imagine this feeling in Collins as he floated along at 24,000 miles per hour, and then put yourself in the place of a disenfranchised, paranoid worker who has now been "cut off" from his own world.

CREATING SAFE TERMINATION PROCEDURES

It is the long-standing custom of our US armed forces to try and personally notify the next of kin any time a soldier, sailor, or marine is killed on duty. Typically, two representatives from the dead GI's branch of the service will go to the home of his or her parents or spouse and relay the bad news.

This visit takes place in all weather, day or night, and regardless of the distances involved. The Department of Defense believes this method offers the best way to tell surviving families that their loved one is now gone.

The reasons for this tradition are many: The government feels the traditional "bad news telegram" is impersonal and fails to reflect the collective sadness felt by the military; the personal visit helps the survivors to grieve with other members of the military; and it heightens the sense of importance the branch, company, or unit feels about this event.

The corporate world, on the other hand, can be unflinchingly cruel in its termination procedures. Within days of announcing an enormous round of job layoffs at its manufacturing plants, the aerospace giant General Dynamics came out with a press release trumpeting the news of huge bonus payments paid to top executives for their "performance."

As we have seen in Chapter 5 with an interview of former General Dynamics employee Robert Mack, the outrage from the rank and file was immediate and harsh. "You're paying million-dollar bonuses to these guys and I just got a pink slip?" was the common astonished response.

In any light, it's hard to see the logic in these separate but related incidents. The Virginia-based company tells its employees, "Uh, sorry. Times are tough and business is down. We'll have to lay you off." Then in the next breath, millions of bonus dollars get thrown out to the "deserving executives" who appeared to make all this supposed bad fortune possible.

Again, the Golden Rule should loom large here: "Treat your employees as you wish them to treat you." This applies to terminations just as it does to every other facet of business life.

Just as the military delivers bad news from "one of its own," so should business. In a normal situation, the best person to terminate an employee is the manager or supervisor who has the best relationship with that person. This is just good common sense.

In not-so-normal situations, you'll need to know when to use an authoritarian approach to termination, often by knowing when and how to turn the proceedings over to a person in a position of authority. Sometimes, it's the manager who has an arm's-length relationship with the employee—not directly supervising that person—who can initiate the termination in the most tactful manner—and in these days of growing workplace violence, maybe in the most "tactical" manner as well.

When a normal termination takes place, the company's own policies may dictate a variety of moves, including an opportunity for the employee to finish half-done work, receive severance pay, or get insurance benefit protection for a specific time period. These things typically occur when the termination is "friendly."

The "unfriendly" termination is a completely different event. Here, the disturbed or disgruntled employee should be asked to leave immediately. You should not allow the terminated employee time to stew, either by delaying the inevitable or allowing him or her to hang around the workplace and "poison" the other employees with negative talk or even dangerous behavior.

In general, if you suspect aggressive behavior, you'll want the employee to leave the premises immediately, but even if you don't, it's probably a good policy to ask the person not to return. Terminated employees may spend their remaining time on the job in a lame duck role, complaining about their fate and generally bringing everyone down.

And whether an employee leaves immediately also may depend on the person's tenure. The employee who has been with the company for three months probably doesn't have too many belongings to tote away. The 25-year employee may have years of memories, books, files, and related office paraphernalia to pack.

Some sensitivity is required in these cases. You can use good judgment and protect the company at the same time. If you have a gut feeling the terminated employee may cause problems if left unguarded, don't leave the room. If the employee says, "Well, what about this file or that case? Who's gonna do my work if I'm not here?" don't start an argument you can't win. When these questions—that are often harshly laced with guilt—arise, simply say, "Don't worry. We'll handle it from here."

Nothing wounds a long-time employee like being given the "bum's rush" by insensitive employers. One woman who had worked 19 years and eight months for a large cable satellite company was unceremoniously let go four months before her 20th anniversary. Someone from the personnel office walked in at lunchtime and said, "We're laying you off. Have your desk cleared out by 5:00."

The termination is not the issue in this case; the *way* it was handled is important. The woman in question was a hardworking middle manager with seniority, expertise, and unquestioned loyalty to the firm. Her treatment left her with bitter memories of a two-decade career with the same company.

Speaking on a 1993 Oprah Winfrey show, James Fox, a professor at Northeastern University and a noted author and speaker on the subject of violence, said, "We don't take enough time to fire people. We need to conduct our layoffs with more compassion. We spend a substantial amount of time and effort hiring these people, only to fire them in the middle of the week at the beginning of their shift. 'Clean out your desk by noon' has become the 'downsizing' model of today."

ALLOWING A TERMINATED EMPLOYEE TO RETURN

Some companies have a rather cavalier policy about letting terminated employees come back to the workplace—either immediately after the termination process or even weeks or months afterward. At some firms, it's not uncommon to see former employees eating lunch with their old co-workers in the company cafeteria, socializing at company parties, or mingling with the former supervisors who originally let them go.

Other firms take a much firmer stance. Once a terminated employee is let go, he or she must pack up and depart. Socializing with current employees at work is neither encouraged nor allowed. "If you want to talk to former employees," says one supervisor in no uncertain terms, "please do it on your own time and away from the workplace. Don't make your co-workers uncomfortable or force supervisors to put people on the spot."

While the difference between these two sides is clearly a matter of organizational choice, we suggest you take the latter approach. Allowing former employees to roam the building—even if they parted amicably—is bad for morale and creates an uneasy precedent for the future.

In the case of employees who leave in anger, it's even more dangerous to allow them easy access to the building. Better to set a firm, no exceptions policy early than risk a confrontation that will take more energy and resources to fix later.

This gives even more credence to the notion of a valid photo ID card for all current employees. The days of the organizational "one big happy family" are seemingly over. A company is not a public place; it is a private enterprise on private property. Not everyone belongs inside your building.

A strict badge policy protects the employees, the proprietary data inside the organization, and the integrity of the company. People without photo badges should be stopped and asked to state their business. Allowing former employees to come and go just adds to the confusion and can create security problems. Imagine the problems that will arise if a former employee spends some time with co-workers, leaves, and later someone discovers a missing purse or wallet. Wild accusations, hard-eyed suspicions, and new-found legal problems become the order of the day.

We'll touch on the definite security benefits of photo ID badges in the next chapter, but if you don't think you need to concern yourself with the validity of any employee's badge, keep the following story in mind.

On December 7, 1987, a terminated employee of a large California-based airline used his ID badge to go around the typical X-ray machines and metal detectors installed at an airport security checkpoint. He waved his badge at the security personnel and passed unchecked around them. Had they looked carefully, they would have noticed this man's employee badge had expired. Had they forced him to go through the metal detector and send his briefcase through the X-ray machine, they would have noticed he was carrying a large handgun.

Angry with his supervisors, this former employee boarded his flight and waited until the plane was 30,000-plus feet in the air before he made his move. Drawing his hidden gun, the man shot and killed several people on the plane, including most importantly, the pilot, the copilot, and other members of the flight crew. The plane crashed and 43 people lost their lives in this modern-day, large-scale workplace violence disaster.

HANDLING THE TERMINATED EMPLOYEE

Just as no one likes to be fired, no one likes to do the firing. We usually find it hard to reject people, and terminating someone is, in more than one sense, a way of rejecting them. Even if the employee in question is utterly despicable and should have been canned months ago, most managers and supervisors don't relish turning this person out.

In some respects, this instinct may actually help the person doing the terminating by forcing him or her to keep the humanity of the event in mind. *Humane termination* should not be a contradiction in terms. It should be possible to terminate someone—for whatever reason—in a safe, empathetic, and even compassionate way.

Our original Golden Rule for this book remains the same: "Treat others in your organization as you would like to be treated."

This should hold true for everyday work life events, discipline meetings, and terminations.

Termination of any employee should be a decision made after careful thought and study. We define it in terms of the person being terminated, fired, or laid off, rather than in terms of the person doing the terminating. If you are in the position to make these kinds of decisions over the health of other peoples' jobs, you need to ask, "What does this termination mean to this person? What will be the impact of this event?"

Companies can get into trouble when they fail to establish clear-cut guidelines for termination. The policies and procedures for any company must spell out the rules for the big three: attendance, behavior, and work performance.

The employee who is suspended and later fired for continuing to smoke in restricted areas inside the plant should have known beforehand that this violation of the written rules was unacceptable. Companies can end up in court when the fired employee says, "No one told me I couldn't come to work with beer on my breath or run a football betting pool for my co-workers."

If every employee knows the rules up front and knows the consequences for breaking the rules—discipline, suspension, or immediate termination—the personal side of the job-related issue is lessened. Like an easygoing parent who must discipline a bratty child, companies who allow a loose atmosphere will have a difficult time keeping order.

A common scenario attached to the pending termination of a manipulative employee is the "One More Chance" approach. Desperate employees may use guilt or even begging to keep their jobs. "C'mon boss, I promise this time I'll be better. I'll really work on this problem and you'll see a new me starting tomorrow. Can't you just give me another chance to make things right?"

Some supervisors may secretly admit that this ploy has worked before on them. In these difficult economic times, it's hard for some managers to be put into the "bad guy" position and give an employee "the axe." This "I'll be better" trap destroys any credibility a manager could ever have again with this employee or others who hear this lament. The should-have-been-fired worker tells a group of co-workers, "Yeah, I went into the boss's office and gave him the old sob story so I could keep my job."

This does little for morale and even less for the leadership reputation the manager should be trying to build.

The time for change in the employee's behavior should take place during the discipline stage. There should be no need to offer more than one second chance after that period. Don't commiserate with the employee, offer unnecessary sympathy, or waffle in your position. If you've made the original decision to terminate the employee, do it.

THE TERMINATION–REVENGE CYCLE

Work, for many of us, is more than just what we do; it's who we are. Some people have taken this to an even greater extreme and see the loss of their jobs as akin to the loss of their lives.

To the twisted person who suddenly believes he now has nothing to live for and thinks you or your firm is to blame, the value of human life—his, yours, or someone else's—rapidly decreases. Like a hungry lion released from a cage, this individual may be steeling himself to go on a rampage against the people and institutions who have "victimized" him.

One of the more terrifying facts linked to terminations and workplace violence is that the incidents follow no predictable time patterns. Angry ex-employees have returned with guns one hour, one week, one year, and in the case of the man who fired sniper rounds into a 16-story building, even seven years later.

On April 20, 1993, John Brian Jarvis, a 58-year-old former driver for Universal Studios, was arrested by Los Angeles police after he allegedly fired about 30 bullets from his 7-mm Remington sniper rifle into the MCA Motion Picture Group building, the parent company for Universal Studios. That morning, Jarvis parked his station wagon about 200 yards away from the well-known "Black Tower" building and began shooting. After five minutes of pumping rounds into every window he could see through his telescopic sight, Jarvis put down his rifle as the police arrived and waited to be handcuffed.

The responding officers said Jarvis made no statement to them as they seized his hunting rifle. They confiscated another 24 or so rounds from a vest on top of his car.

The fact that no one died in this case may be a testimonial to the safety of modern architecture or Jarvis's bad aim. Two people were hit by bullets and five or six others were injured by flying glass. Thankfully, none of the injuries were life-threatening, but the incident shook MCA/Universal employees deeply.

In a jailhouse interview, Jarvis admitted to firing 36 shots at the MCA tower and at an adjoining bank building in what he called "almost a political statement," adding, "The black castle, the wicked witch of the east, the ominous black tower that was almost untouchable—I blew that theory away."

He said "he had been considering the attack for years because he felt the entertainment giant (Universal) had blackballed him so that he couldn't work as a movie studio driver."[2]

Jarvis had worked as a full-time studio driver until 1982, when he was laid off and used as a temporary worker until he was ultimately let go in 1986. Detectives say Jarvis apparently owed money to the bank situated next door to the MCA building. The bank had been trying to collect the money from Jarvis, so it's thought that was why he fired a few rounds at their building as well.

Jarvis had lived with his mother in the years preceding this shooting incident. She died a few weeks before he opened fire on the building. Are the two events linked? Consider that Jarvis waited seven years before he returned to the scene of his "terminators." Our review of many workplace violence shootings points to another similarity: One seemingly catastrophic event, related to work or not, such as a death in the family, a suspension, or a termination, can trigger a violent response because the instigator now suddenly feels he has nothing to live for.

For the paranoid or delusional employee, getting laid off or fired is the proverbial straw that breaks the camel's back. It's the one, final "attack" that he feels he can no longer handle.

Ideally, any termination based on discipline reasons should come about only after repeated attempts by the manager or supervisor above this employee to communicate with him, meet with him, assist the person, discuss problem behaviors, and suggest alternatives or even mental health counseling.

The key to any termination proceeding for the borderline employee is to make it as clear as possible to the person that this move is for a specific reason (performance, conduct, or attendance), defining the termination as a result of one of those three factors and *not* as a result of some kind of injustice against the employee.

A few vignettes help to illustrate this point:

- To Joe, who believes his supervisor has been out to get him since the day he started, a termination means the final proof that he was right all along.
- To Henry, who believes there is a master plot against him, he sees a termination as all the evidence he needs to prove this conspiracy.
- To Phil, who feels he has no self-esteem left—his family has left him, he has no friends, he is on his last dime, he's turned down by every woman he meets, his car broke down that morning—the termination is the final insult to his life. "Why bother living anymore?" he asks himself. "And since I'm not going to bother living anymore, why not take the people who are responsible for this with me?"

The healthy response to a termination episode might be, "Well, this is definitely not good news. But I guess I saw it coming and bright and early tomorrow, I'm going to go out and look for another job" or "I'm not happy about this, but I'm going to start sending out my résumé and see if I can't land something better."

The employee whose response is unhealthy seeks to place the blame on others, wallows in depression, and may end up responding violently based on the need for retribution and revenge.

As the model in Figure 7–1 indicates, the comparisons between the two responses can help you better understand termination from the employee's point of view:

TERMINATING PROBLEM EMPLOYEES

Just as some organizations differ in their standard approach to discipline, the same holds true for terminations. In some compa-

FIGURE 7–1
The Response to Termination Model

Healthy Response	Unhealthy Response
Sees it as a life experience that must be dealt with	Sees it as the end of the world
Takes personal responsibility	Personalizes it; Projects the blame for it on others or the company
Shows short-term anxiety or depression; serves as a motivator to get another job	Full of long-term anxiety, depression, hostility, rage, and a deeply felt sense of injustice
Believes what happened; not in a denial mode	Refuses to believe it happened; in denial
Sees the big picture and is ready to move on	Can't see past the next day; refuses to look for another job
Has all the necessary coping mechanisms in place	Has a difficult time coping; Ruminates over fate
Uses adult problem-solving skills to handle it	Can't use problem-solving skills

nies, the employee's immediate supervisor is responsible for the termination process, while in others, the personnel manager delivers the news. Much of this depends on the reasons for the termination. Large-scale layoffs may be the responsibility of the personnel office, while individual terminations may be handled by the supervisor of that employee.

But no matter who is responsible for the termination, there is no way to safely "rubber-stamp" a terminated employee. Each situation is different, and each employee will respond differently. It won't be possible to make a tried-and-true generic "goodbye" speech that will fit all occasions.

And in no place is this more apparent than when you deal with a highly disturbed or significantly disgruntled employee. All the old rules don't apply, and it may not even be possible or advisable for you to take on the termination role.

If you think the person you're terminating is emotionally dysfunctional and has exhibited many of the following symptoms, coupled with what we've discussed in Chapter 4, it behooves you to use extreme caution during any termination encounters.

Be wary if you or others around you see an employee who:

- Displays intense envy for you or others.
- Has an unusually or grossly elevated sense of his worth, power, knowledge, or identity.
- Believes he is being treated badly or differently than anyone else in the organization.
- Has long been known for making complaint after complaint after complaint.
- Talks constantly about having many physical ailments or thinks that something bizarre is wrong with him.
- Is an overly suspicious person who sees many injustices related to him.

This is not a person you should terminate alone.

These symptoms indicate a person who *may* be the one guy who doesn't let go of the company. Like the terrifying movie of the same name, this employee has a *Fatal Attraction* syndrome regarding your organization.

In the worst case following a termination event, this person won't stop thinking about how "those bastards fired me. They took away my whole life. They ruined me. They took away my family. They ruined my reputation. I knew they would do this to me, and I've known it the whole time I've worked there. I was waiting for this, and I knew it would happen to me."

So how do you fire someone like this? Someone who is obviously disturbed and not able to function any longer as a normal employee?

The answer is *you* don't. In these rare but growing numbers of cases, you need to get immediate help from a qualified mental health professional. If you work in a medium- to large-sized organization, you may have a psychologist on staff. In most cases, your EAP department will be able to get you access to a mental health professional on retainer who can come to your facility and offer assistance. Your on-site medical facility personnel may also be able to offer advice and assistance.

In smaller corporations or small-business-type companies, you'll want to call your local mental health service agency and get a recommendation for help from them. They may be able to offer on-site counseling or refer you to a mental health professional in your area who specializes in behavior management. We don't advise you to just "wing it" with a disturbed employee. Seek qualified help first.

But there is one caveat here: The manager must truly believe he or she sees serious emotional dysfunction in the problem employee. It's too easy to cop out and say, "Pete looks pretty mad right now. Maybe I shouldn't be the one to terminate him."

If we looked at every terminated or soon-to-be terminated employee in the right light, lots of them could fall into these "disturbed employee" categories. We already know the act of being terminated is a distressing event. Some managers who aren't sure of their confidence may try to retrofit difficult (but not dangerous) employees into these categories, thereby seeking to pass the termination torch along to someone else.

What we're trying to get across is that the dangerous employee is significantly impaired, and people with severe emotional problems should be clearly visible to the average employer.

THE PSYCHOLOGIST'S ROLE IN
DISTURBED–EMPLOYEE TERMINATIONS

Witness the following disturbing scenario:

"You can't discipline me," says the about-to-be terminated employee. "I'm not crazy! These other people who work here are the crazy ones! Look at all these secret files I've kept on every one around here!"

So what's a supervisor to do when a seriously disturbed employee won't accept a discipline order? At this point, it's legitimate for you to ask the employee to accept a mandatory referral to a psychologist or other mental health professional for an evaluation.

In these highly charged events, you want to see if this employee is dangerous to himself or others or if he can successfully return to work. At this point, it's not your job to make an evaluation about this employee's sanity. Get professional help.

Using the psychologist as a buffer between the supervisor and the disturbed employee may enable you to identify the root of the problems.

In some cases, when the employee is uncooperative and termination looks like the only alternative, the psychologist may work as your agent and assist you by explaining the risk of termination to the employee. He or she may explain the choices the employee must make—that is, take a drug test, accept a short- or long-term suspension, make significant behavioral changes, or be fired.

"Think about these choices and these things you're being asked to do," says the psychologist to the angry employee. "Call me tonight or in the morning or meet me for another meeting and tell me what you've decided to do."

This meeting with the mental health professional—be it a psychologist, a social worker, a counselor, or a psychiatrist—can take place on the company grounds or at an office away from the company. By foreshadowing the coming events, the psychologist can lessen the impact, prepare the employee for what is to come, and deal with feelings of rage or anger right there on the spot.

In a worse-case scenario, the highly disturbed employee will tell the psychologist to take a flying leap and will out and out refuse to cooperate with any suggestions. In these cases, where termination is the only answer, you or the mental health professional should request that your company security guards—or if danger seems imminent, the local police—escort the employee off the premises forever.

In these gone-to-hell events, you need to take extraordinary safety and security steps to protect yourself and the other employees. While we'd like to say that following safe termination procedures can protect you or others from harm, we just can't. Sadly, history tells us the well-known "disgruntled employee" could possibly return one hour, one day, one week, or 100 weeks later and try to seek revenge for some past inequity.

While we can't offer guaranties about safety, we can say if you make good business decisions, treat people in a humane fashion no matter how hard it may be for you personally, and keep your overall welfare in mind, you can better handle any termination episode.

THE RIPPLE EFFECT OF ANY TERMINATION

When someone gets terminated, many employers don't realize the effect the action has on the remaining workers. At issue is the fact that if you draw concentric circles around terminated employees who have been let go for any reason, you will see a potentially large number of current employees who are affected by this move.

Let's use an example of Joe, a male office worker whom you had to fire because of his constant sexual remarks, gestures, innuendos, and even threats against female employees. You and he may be the only ones in the office who know the reason for his firing, or he may have told a select group of co-workers. After you finish your termination meeting with him at the end of the workday, he gathers his belongings and leaves.

When his now-former co-workers arrive the next day, they notice he is gone and ask you why. You explain that he won't be returning to work. Now let's look at the people who feel the impact of this move. There may be:

- One person who is really upset with you because you fired him.
- Three people in the office who thought he was a great guy.
- Three people who don't care either way that he is gone.
- Three people in the office who couldn't stand him and thought he should've been fired years ago.
- One person who is really upset with you because you took too long to fire him.

Those people who worked around the terminated employee are, whether they will admit it to you or not, affected by his absence. Some may feel relieved, some may feel outraged, and some just won't express themselves.

Some may think, "Am I next on the chopping block? Have I done anything that could get me fired?"

Or they may say, to themselves or others, "Our boss is a real jerk. That guy was treated unfairly!" If other employees side with the terminated worker, they may buy into his story that he was being unfairly victimized by you.

It's your job to pay attention to these feelings and act on them. You just can't file the whole episode away and move on. As odd as it may sound, other people in your office may have been "victimized" by the process and manner by which that person was terminated.

So how do you "debrief" the remaining employees? What do you tell the people about what just happened? More importantly, in the context of violence in the workplace, how do you deal with the post-termination feelings of that employee's "victims"? What do you say to the woman who has been sexually touched by this person or the man who was intimidated or threatened or even assaulted by the employee?

First, is it right to tell another employee that you have fired someone? From a confidentiality, legal, or even ethical standpoint, we counsel that this is not wise. On an individual basis, you should make yourself available to anyone who would like to sit down and discuss why the terminated employee is no longer with the company.

If a terminated employee wants to tell everyone about being fired, that is certainly his or her prerogative. We suggest that you take the time to listen to any employee who wants to talk to you about the incident. Do some "organizational sensing" to see what you need to do to assuage the fears or concerns of others.

It's not your job to explain why or if someone was fired. Don't feel as if you have to offer rationalizations or justifications as to why an employee was let go.

Here's a typical conversation from an upset employee:

"Look, I know you just fired Joe. He came out and told me before he left. I'm really upset about it. I'd like to know what's going on around here."

"Well, I can understand that you'd be upset, but as far as that goes, I'm not in a position to discuss Joe's work record or his performance with the company. Those are confidential matters and it wouldn't be ethical for me to discuss it with you. But I would like to hear why you're upset and what we can do about it."

"I don't like the way things are going around here."

"Look, I can see you're obviously angry. It's clear that you're very upset. I don't want to have you be upset because you work here. And if you're angry when you're working here, you're not going to be as effective. So let's talk about what we can do to help you put away some of this anger."

"Well, you can give Joe his job back!"

"Obviously I'm not going to be able to give Joe his job back, for whatever reasons Joe might have already discussed with you. Short of that, is there anything else I can do to help you get over your anger today, so that you can go back to being productive?"

"Look, boss, I'm angry today but it's not gonna affect my job performance."

"You know, when people are angry, sometimes it affects the way they work, the way they concentrate, what they do, and how they think. If you want to talk about what we can do for you, I'd be happy to help, but I just can't discuss Joe's situation with anyone but him."

Like it or not, this approach serves to tell the employee one thing loud and clear: You are not about to break another employee's confidentiality about a personnel matter. You are not there to gossip about the terminated employee.

What about the victims of Joe's assaults and abuse? How do you respond to their needs?

"I'd like to know how you feel about the fact that Joe, someone you've been having a lot of problems with over the last few months, is no longer working here."

"I appreciate that he's gone, but you know, boss, he should have been put out of here several months ago."

"I can understand how you feel. Sometimes these issues relating to personnel can take time. And it may seem like we're not doing anything, but we have to handle things legally and properly. If you want, let's talk about your feelings now that he is gone."

And how about the employee who seems not to care either way about Joe's dismissal—until you bring that person into your office for a chat.

"You know, I'm really glad Joe is finally out of here. You should have seen the things he did around here. He brought guns to work, he threatened several people with them, and he made us all nervous with the way he talked about hurting people."

"I'm glad you've come to me, but I wish you would have told me about some of these things earlier so I could've acted faster. What is it about our relationship or the way you and I communicate that could be improved so that you feel like you can come and talk to me at anytime?"

"Well, I didn't want to get myself or anyone else in trouble, and I didn't feel like I could come right to you with these things."

"Do you feel now that you can always come to me with any problem that affects your work or the work of others?"

These short conversations help us illustrate a simple point: Build on the future with your employees. Tomorrow, after the terminated employee is long gone, you and your people will all have to go back to work, both individually and as a team. By managing these feelings and these relationships as they relate to the termination of another employee, you lay the groundwork for more effective communication in the future.

In the context of workplace violence, you want your employees to know, rain or shine, if they have a problem with another employee, they can come and talk to you about it. The unapproachable manager who always seemed to be too busy to talk with the employee being threatened or harassed by an abusive co-worker will certainly have to find the time to appear in court for the civil suit that names the manager as a defendant.

We hear a similar complaint from managers and supervisors who work for large bureaucracies, government agencies with strict civil service regulations, and other large organizations stifled by a plethora of discipline or termination rules. "I knew he was harassing the other employees and I wanted to fire this guy, but it takes a pile of paperwork and approval from umpteen supervisors to get rid of someone, even if they make threats or intimidate other employees."

If this sounds like the policy in your organization, it's time to ask for or make real changes in the way you deal with these significant personnel issues. Help create new discipline and termination policies and set up different mechanisms to implement them immediately if necessary. If you don't have them, help establish new written guidelines for conduct and behavior at work.

Supervisors and organizations who fail to act quickly when dealing with employees with a potential for violence will find themselves in deep legal waters. If you cannot be swift and decisive in your decisions to discipline or terminate a potentially hazardous or outright dangerous employee, you can expect to see the victim of his abuse in a court of law.

Don't wait for the problem to go beyond the point of no return—either with an injury, or death, or an expensive trial that can drain the organization of its finances. The case law about failing to act against potentially dangerous employees is there; the precedent has already been set.

ENDNOTES

[1] "Clinton Attends Funeral of Friend," *New York Times*, July 22, 1993.

[2] "MCA Shooting Figure Alleges Conspiracy," *San Diego Union-Tribune*, Associated Press story, April 22, 1993.

Chapter Eight

Protecting Your Assets: Human and Otherwise

The day of the destructive, vindictive, violent employee is here. In addition to the threat of a workplace assault or homicide, stories of computer sabotage and data destruction, theft, arson, burglary, and vandalism are real. Knowing how and why to safely protect all the company's assets—physical, intangible, psychological, and human—is one of the cornerstones of providing a safe working environment.

If you haven't thought about it before, now is the time to consider the level of security where you work. Is it just adequate? Nonexistent? Overwhelming? Prisonlike? Or does it offer a blend of professionalism, reassurance, and protection?

YOUR SECURITY FORCE: PROBLEMS OR PROFESSIONALS?

Ask many executives about the security guards at their facilities and the following story will surface:

> Yes, we have a security staff, but they're not exactly a crack force of highly effective protectors. We've got Petey and Jake, who retired from the military about 1975. They spend their time checking ID badges at the front door, drinking coffee, and telling sea stories. And we've got a couple of kids who're working their way through college, so they spend most of their time reading textbooks. We do have a director of security, but he's usually stretched pretty thin and can't watch these people too well.

In *Dress for Success*, his well-known book on proper business attire, John T. Molloy recounts an example where one company's

security force was used to run errands, fetch lunch for the executives, and generally act like everything but a security staff. Molloy
observed the guards roaming the plant in their ill-fitting baggy blue
uniforms, and when he had seen enough, he called for changes:

> You dress your guards to look like nobodies who should be sent for
> coffee; you do send them for coffee; and everyone else in the plant,
> even if they don't send him, looks upon a guard as someone who
> could and should be sent. He couldn't protect anything because of
> his image; he's not a guard but a gofer and everyone knows it.[1]

Since the plant was having a difficult time with employee thiev-
ery, Molloy made some suggestions to help combat the problem.
He told the owner to change the job title for guards to Security
Officer, to prohibit them from running errands, and to take them
out of their baggy uniforms and put them into suits and ties. The
message around the plant became more clear: These guys mean
business now. Plant shrinkage went down immediately.

DOES THE COMPANY HAVE A DUTY TO PROTECT EMPLOYEES?

The short answer is yes. Case law already exists that says building
owners and employers can be held liable for failing to provide
proper security precautions. In 1982, the husband of a worker in
a San Francisco, California, office building killed three people and
injured eight after arriving on the 18th floor where his wife worked
and shooting her in the legs.

At the civil trial, a jury held that the building's landlords and
the woman's employer failed to offer proper security and awarded
a $5 million judgment to the employees involved in the shooting.

In La Mesa, California, a woman was shot and killed by her
estranged husband as she worked at a branch office of the Southern California auto club (AAA). The surviving minor child of the
woman sued the well-known travel-related company for failing
to protect the woman. The suit was later settled out of court.

According to AAA attorney Alice Bisnow, at issue in the case
was the company's duty to protect the woman from known harm.
In its argument, the AAA said that the woman failed to notify
them of the dangerous nature of her marital discord.

Had she told her supervisors and other company officials of her husband's threats, Bisnow says the company would have taken a number of steps to protect her. "In these cases, it's not uncommon for us to immediately transfer the employee to an office in a new location. When employees tell us of restraining orders and the like, we keep track of that information and work with them to change their situation."

In this case, the woman failed to notify her supervisors or ask the company for assistance. Bisnow also says the AAA club offers employees access to counseling programs, legal help, and other family services if they need them.

It appears this tragedy might have been averted if the woman in question had looked more to her employer for the protection she needed.

GOOD RULES TO LIVE AND WORK BY

If Willard Cushman, director of security for San Diego's Titan Corporation, could make a wish list of security measures to limit a company's exposure to violence in the workplace, he would suggest the following:

1. Be a good employer, and be good managers. Supervise your people and the plant properly. Treat people with respect, and don't alienate your employees with harsh or uneven treatment.

2. Be a selective employer. Screen potential new hires carefully, interview thoroughly, and above all, do background checks on any new employees before you bring them into your facility. Be especially careful if a background check or interview reveals overzealousness when it comes to the person's interest in weapons. Use caution if the person openly displays an unnatural amount of religious fervor during an interview. People who appear clearly obsessed with either or both categories need careful scrutiny before they are hired.

3. Provide a secure facility for the people who work there. Set up systems to restrict access to areas where people don't need to go. And develop ways to protect the people

inside from intruders outside. If you have the resources and need to protect people and property, you may want to invest in closed-circuit TV monitors, ID badges, badge-activated key locks, uniformed guards, plainclothes officers, or whatever fits your company environment.

4. Assess ongoing problems with employees. Keep a careful finger on the pulse of the company and its workers. If you see employees with clear emotional or psychological problems, don't let it go. Have a plan to get these people to the right EAP program for counseling.

5. If you're a smaller company, get professional security and psychological consultants to help your human resources and security people develop plans to prevent workplace violence.

Cushman warns worried employers about overreacting with expensive, overblown security schemes and systems that do more harm than good. There needs to be a careful balance between the company that is set up to look like a prison and the one with no security measures at all.

Ron Davis, the director of security for General Dynamics, Space Systems Division, echoes many of the same concerns as his colleague Willard Cushman. One of the first steps he suggests is to raise the awareness level of your supervisors. They need to be more cognizant of their employees' performance, attitudes, value systems, and behavior.

Says Davis, "Security techniques to deter workplace violence should begin with some form of prevention training. We give classes, seminars, and briefings to supervisors, HR people, labor representatives, and personnel department officials. In these sessions, we teach people to heighten their security awareness."

Davis uses a common occurrence to illustrate this need to pay attention to real or perceived threats.

It's just like those signs you see at the airport security checkpoints—"We take all remarks or jokes about guns or bombs very seriously." This also should be the policy on the job. Anything related to violence on the job gets our attention. If we hear of bomb jokes, talk about using guns against people, or other threats of violence, we investigate those things immediately. These kinds of remarks are totally inappropriate for the workplace and we act on them right away.

Incidents that involve potential precursors to workplace violence—arguing employees, shouting matches, vandalism, sabotage, and anonymous threats—also get Ron Davis's full attention.

During our investigation, we talk first to the person's supervisor, and then the witnesses to the incident or threats, and lastly, we talk firsthand to the instigator. We try to get a quick evaluation about the situation to see if it's serious or not.   .

Davis says that in most cases, it's just inappropriate remarks, jokes, or misunderstandings that bring out his investigators. Nevertheless, they take all incidents seriously and work hard to get the details sorted out and then speak to the employee and the direct supervisor about changing the behavior.

In light of the Robert Mack shootings at General Dynamics (see Chapter 5), Davis says his firm has made some significant changes in its discipline and termination procedures. "We've upgraded our sensitivity and awareness to the potentially volatile circumstances surrounding these events, especially for those people we may have some concern about."

So concerned has General Dynamics become that it has taken the unusual step of installing metal detectors at the entrance to the interview rooms where discipline and termination hearings take place. All participants in these actions—employees, union people, management, supervisors, and so on—must pass through the detectors, which are similar to those used at airports.

Davis is quick to note that the presence of the metal detectors does not indicate that anyone in the company might be a potential killer, but it helps with the general peace of mind for the people involved in these employment actions.

Davis admits this additional "force presence" inside the organization is one of the obvious fallouts of their particular workplace violence episode. "There is also an enhanced sensitivity," he says, "to the people who have to run these meetings." After the Mack incident, it was not uncommon to hear personnel and human resource supervisors ask themselves, "With these potential hazards and the dangers relating to workplace violence, do I want to be in this business?"

Davis answers this by saying, "As security professionals, we owe it to these people. We have a duty to help them do their jobs safely. Just as the airport metal detectors act like a good deterrent, we like to have our own deterrents."

During discipline and termination hearings, GD will keep a security officer nearby, not in the room but close at hand in a nonintrusive position.

Ron Davis also agrees that companies have a duty to protect their employees. For their part, his security people and the company as a whole try to meet this duty. "We try to exercise due diligence and provide as safe a working environment as possible. We do a number of things to reach this goal. We can't make guaranties, but on the other hand, we try to take prudent, realistic measures to provide a safe environment."

For all the media portrayals, Davis feels the likelihood of workplace violence is low. Still, the problem does exist and he urges employers to balance a commonsense approach to security with what impact it has on their businesses.

In investigating workplace violence threats or incidents, Davis and his staff try to look at the big picture before they take action.

Our intervention is immediate. If we recognize high-risk people, we look at them right away. We try to identify specific instances where a problem may or has already occurred. We get feedback from the supervisors, and this may include things they saw or heard directly, or had told to them by other employees. We review the statements from the victims, any witnesses, and finally, we get a statement from the employee. Most times, the problem ends right there, after we've talked to the instigator directly and he gets counseling from his supervisor. We are there to make a professional evaluation of the employee from a security standpoint.

While he does see the need for basic security controls, Davis says he is not an advocate of ID badge access cards as a method to prevent workplace violence. "Security equipment is fine, but it's better to try and identify the causes and the people who may commit these crimes first, and then have good EAP programs for them as an outlet for help."

Davis warns employers to get expert, professional advice before installing any security systems in the facility. "Some of the programs sold by people who aren't security professionals end up being overblown and very expensive. Nobody profits when a security program or system is unpopular, excessive, or exorbitantly priced."

Further, even with an elaborate security system in place, Davis sees some companies spend the money, only to use the security system for a few months and then stop using it, thinking it's a waste of time and money.

"Be realistic," he says, "and find something you can live with and work with right away."

According to Willard Cushman of Titan, preventing access to places and people depends on the culture of the corporation. "In some high-tech software firms," he says, "the computer people see each other as one big family. Their togetherness is part of their culture. It's how they work and generate ideas and solve problems."

Firms with an open-door policy take a risk of theft, or in the worst cases, workplace violence. Tom Erickson, vice president of human resources for the San Diego Elgar Corporation, admits that following their workplace violence shooting, which left the general manager and the sales manager dead, the company had to make significant changes in access policies.

> Before, we worked together as one big, happy family. We had a more or less . . "open door" policy where our employees would bring their kids or other family members by to visit. It wasn't unusual for former employees to drop by and say hello.

Since the Larry Hansel shooting incident, Elgar initiated immediate changes in its security system. Instead of easy and uncontrolled access to all areas of the plant and the offices, all employees must use a security badge key code card to get access to various parts of the building.

Most employees carry these credit-card–sized "keys" in their pockets or pinned to their outer clothing. One "swipe" of the digitally encoded card is all it takes to get into a locked area. This type of controlled access offers higher safety and relative convenience for the people at Elgar.

Elgar had no established security force in place before the Hansel shootings. "Immediately after the incident," says Erickson, "we brought in a group of armed security guards who were on the premises 24 hours per day for a period of a few weeks. We wanted to send a message to our employees that we cared about their safety and wanted them to feel secure."

After the key code door locks were installed, Elgar initiated a more "closed door" policy with regards to access. With the new security procedures in place, Elgar went back to business as usual, as best as it could.

Erickson also says that his firm took immediate steps to protect its greatest psychological asset—its employees.

"Our incident took place on a Tuesday, and we were back in business by Thursday." This was not an easy task and forced many of the company's top people to deal with issues they had never experienced before.

"We immediately put our EAP team into action. We brought in a group of counselors and psychologists for our employees. We started counseling with the managers and executives, and they, in turn, called in each of our employees and explained what had happened and what would go on over the coming weeks."

Elgar offered individual and group counseling to all employees for one month following the shootings. On the one-year anniversary of the incident, the firm held a brief memorial service in the cafeteria. "It was strictly voluntary and at the discretion of each person. One of our employees is a lay minister and he said a few words. We also brought in the psychologist who had helped us before and he spoke to the group too."

PSYCHOLOGICAL CLEARANCES FOR SECURITY REASONS

Another key to security in any company where employees have access to valuable data—information, financial assets, database lists, software, and so on—is the use of psychological clearances. For key employees who have their "hands on the button," this early testing is crucial to reveal potential problem areas. By screening workers who have access to restricted data, you lessen the risk that a disgruntled or emotionally disturbed employee will take your company down in flames by erasing, destroying, or misappropriating data.

If you run a bank and you employ several people who operate the software that controls all of the computer operations, can you trust them?

For these key jobs, you'll need to give them psychological screenings. The employees who have access to the most important systems have tremendous hidden power over your company. One act of sabotage or vandalism could ruin you, shut down your entire operation, and put your shareholders and customers in jeopardy.

"Be careful in your assumptions," warns a security expert. "Don't underestimate the power of your lowest level employees. And don't underestimate the actual influence of what seems like your least influential employee. They can shut you down in a hurry with one keystroke."

With the potential economic costs of violence in the workplace at sky-high levels, you need to give plenty of thought to your need for security professionals on the job site, proper insurance, loss prevention controls, and the safety and security equipment necessary to protect your people from inside or outside harm.

A SECURITY PROFESSIONAL'S RESPONSE TO VIOLENCE IN THE WORKPLACE BY IRA A. LIPMAN, CHAIRMAN AND PRESIDENT OF GUARDSMARK, INC.

Thirty years ago, the typical image of a private security officer was that of a pensioner who was supplementing his social security income by spending a few nights a week patrolling a warehouse or keeping watch over a panel of closed-circuit television displays. Unfortunately, this stereotype was often not far off the mark. Since that time, however, the changing nature of business and society as a whole has led to a radical change in attitudes. Business owners and managers have come to see professional security services not simply as a way to prevent trespassers or thieves from entering company property after hours but as a critical component of their daily business operations.

First, more and more employers are realizing that one of their foremost responsibilities is to protect the lives and property of their employees while they are on company premises. These employers refuse to allow fear in their workplace.

Furthermore, the change in attitude can be attributed to the fact that maintaining strong security measures simply makes good business sense. The productivity of a company as a whole is dependent on the productivity of its individual employees. Employees who do not feel safe at work, who feel that their employers have not taken adequate measures to ensure their protection while they are on company premises, who are anxious about the mental stability of their fellow workers, or who have witnessed a former employee make threats of violence and believe that those threats have not been taken seriously will be more anxious and less able to concentrate on their work. As a result, overall productivity may fall, stockholders may lose confidence as their shares decrease in value, and the company as a whole may suffer financially—even if an incident of violence never occurs. The very fear of violence in the workplace is enough to do harm to the stability of a company.

Security, however, is no longer simply a matter of hiring a few uniformed guards to stand watch at the entrance to a facility. Business security needs are as varied as places of business themselves. A myriad of factors—the size and physical layout of the place of work, the type of business conducted there, even a business's management philosophy—determines the type and amount of security protection needed to make a site as safe as possible. The security needs of a large industrial complex, for example, are going to be vastly different from those of a high-rise office building or of a retail establishment in a busy shopping mall. Thus, there is no one, "right" way to set up a security program, and the only wrong way to do so is to take someone else's security plan and try to make it work for your company. The purpose of this chapter is to provide overall guidelines to the basics of security measures to help protect executives, facilities, and employees from crimes by disgruntled co-workers or anyone else intent on making your company the scene of violence.

HOW TO PICK THE RIGHT
SECURITY COMPANY

It is a sad irony that many companies hiring a security force to protect them from the actions of violent criminals are, in many cases, actually hiring violent criminals. The security industry in the United States is woefully lacking in meaningful, uniform standards for the screening, hiring, and training of security officers. Eleven states currently have no licensing requirements for individuals hired as security officers. Unbelievable as it may seem, in some states it is possible for a convicted felon to be released from prison in the morning and be working as an armed security guard by the end of the day. The consequences of such a lack of standards are indeed grave. Each year, hundreds of individuals hired as security officers are arrested for crimes that they commit on duty—ranging from theft to assault, rape, even murder. Thus, choosing a security company is a decision that must be taken seriously and made carefully.

The first step in finding a security company that meets your needs and your demand for quality is to determine what those needs are and to set guidelines for your search. Know what led you to the decision to hire the services of a security company, and determine what you want to protect: buildings, information, personnel, equipment, valuables, perishable commodities, or the continuity of the manufacturing process, among others.

Once these goals have been determined, the next step is to interview security companies and evaluate them.

- Check into each security company's reputation by consulting with security managers or directors at sites whose security needs are similar to your own, and learn what accounts similar to your own the security company serves nationwide.
- Learn if the security company offers a quality assurance program that is not merely a marketing concept; find out who administers the program, how it works, and how long it has been in place.
- Ask about the security company's annual client retention rate.
- Perhaps most importantly, do not simply eliminate a security company from your search on the basis of price. A low bid from a security company often means a correspondingly lower quality of service.

Once you have narrowed the field, continue with a more detailed investigation of each security company and its claims.

- With any service, customer satisfaction is one of the best indications of the quality of the service provided. Thus, request the name and phone number of the client contact at each of the security company's accounts in your area. When interviewing the client contacts, compare your perceived needs with those of the client, and base your questions on this comparison. For example, if a vendor client was required to employ the lowest bidder, and you intend to base your decision on other factors as well as price, you may conclude that the comparison of your company to the vendor client is an invalid one.
- Next, visit a facility served by the prospective security company. Arrange the visit through a third party such as a business associate of the security manager of that facility. Do not arrange the visit through the vendor's sales representative—an unscheduled visit can tell you much more about the quality of service provided on a daily basis than a special, prearranged visit can.
- Ask about the security company's insurance coverage. The vendor's insurance company should carry a rating from the A. M. Best Company of "A" or higher, which indicates a level of

financial solvency great enough to cover the vendor's contractual obligations.

• Verify the vendor's workers' compensation interstate Experience Modification Factor (EMF). The EMF is determined by the National Council of Compensation Insurance and is based on the vendor's three years of workers' compensation experience prior to the year just ended. This rate is an objective measurement by an external agency of the vendor's success in preventing workers' compensation claims. Check the EMF rate for a 5- to 10-year period in order to get a long-term picture of the vendor's performance. An EMF significantly lower than 1.00 means that claims have been far less than industry norms and the vendor pays lower than normal workers' compensation premiums. But for those companies with higher EMF ratings, to remain competitive while paying for their higher premiums they, of necessity, will be forced to cut costs somewhere—cuts that could have disastrous consequences for your company. New employees may be screened less effectively, the number of supervisors may be reduced, or training courses could be shortened. Such measures often result in placement of an unsatisfactory individual on post, a higher turnover rate, and, ultimately, decreased security.

• Learn whether the security company is involved in major litigation with clients who have suffered losses as a result of its service.

Perhaps what is most important to remember when choosing a security company is that the quality of a service is only as good as the quality of the individuals providing it. Security officers should, of course, be honest, courageous, and responsible. They should also maintain a neat appearance, since the image they present reflects on your company. While in the past security jobs were often considered moonlighting positions, in today's security environment career officers provide the best protection. Career officers will be more alert on duty and will not be able to use having another job as an excuse for tardiness or absenteeism. In short, the best security officer is one who is thoroughly professional. Therefore, learning about a security company's policies in regards to personnel selection, training, and supervision is vital in judging the quality of individuals who will be providing security at your facility.

Personnel Selection

The security company truly dedicated to providing the highest possible quality of services will perform the following steps in screening potential security officers:

- Conduct investigations into potential criminal histories of its personnel.
- Unless prohibited by law, polygraph all applicants to determine whether an applicant has stolen from a previous employer or has used or sold illegal drugs.
- Interview former employers for the last 10 years to verify the applicant's work record.
- Require a notarized explanation of any gap of 30 days in an applicant's work record.
- Conduct a Motor Vehicle Report search for every applicant to ensure a safe driving record.
- Interview all neighborhood references to establish stability and character.
- Obtain a statement of medical history and, in total compliance with the Americans with Disabilities Act, screen for illnesses or medical conditions that could impair job performance.
- Test applicants for illegal drug use. The vendor should require a full 10-panel drug screen, and tests should be conducted only in labs accredited and certified by the Substances Abuse and Mental Health Services Administration (SAMHSA). All positive results should be further verified by gas chromatography/mass spectrometry (BC/MS), the most reliable and acceptable confirmation method.
- Require financial references to ensure that the applicant is not in financial difficulty.
- Give new employees a psychological inventory, such as the Minnesota Multi-Phasic Inventory-2 TM, to facilitate placement. This test should be evaluated and validated by fully licensed and qualified psychological professionals.
- Verify all education references, including high school, college, or trade schools.

Such screening procedures may seem excessive at first, but they are necessary to ensure that a security service does not actually increase a facility's security risks by employing people of questionable character and ability. Any selection process that is less comprehensive than the one described above may be a sign that the vendor has traded high quality for lower costs.

Personnel Supervision

Supervision and a desire to respond quickly and effectively to your security needs are crucial to maintaining high morale and effective service. Skilled supervision also reduces turnover. Ask the following questions to evaluate a vendor's policies on supervision:

- Who supervises the security officers at the site? Are security officers supervised by other security officers? Are they supervised by experienced field officers? Are they supervised by local management? How have the supervisors been trained? What is their educational level?
- Will you receive a range of regular inspection documentation from the vendor? Are security officers inspected each day? Will the vendor provide a daily report for each security officer and special reports that document each unusual incident witnessed by a security officer?
- How frequently are on-site inspections conducted by regional or executive management?
- If a service problem occurs, will a response team from the vendor provide you with access to a complete chain of command ranging from the on-site supervisor to corporate headquarters?

Additional Services

Your security firm should also be able to provide the following services.

- General investigations (overt or covert).
- Background screening of potential new employees.
- Kidnap or ransom insurance.

- Security coverage for computers.
- Preparation of a comprehensive security manual.
- Electronic audio countermeasures sweeps.
- Special publications informing you of the latest loss prevention techniques.
- Monthly security diaries for all security personnel.
- Specialized training videotapes (produced on-site when requested).
- Rapid deployment of strike or emergency personnel.
- Antiterrorist consulting.
- Safety consulting.
- Specialized personnel to support a broad range of security management activities.

WHY PROPRIETARY SECURITY IS NOT THE ANSWER

In light of the extensive amount of research that must be completed in the search for a security company, it is no surprise that many companies decide to use proprietary—or in-house—security forces. However, recent studies of trends in the security field have found that there has been a substantial shift from the use of proprietary security forces to the use of private security firms. Because of the many advantages of contracting with a private security firm, it is likely that this trend will continue in the coming years. For example, when both direct and indirect costs are tallied, contract security costs 20 to 40 percent less than proprietary security. These services will also assume the responsibilities for screening, hiring, training, and supervising the security force and tending to other administrative duties such as payroll and benefits.

Private security firms can also offer the services of highly trained officers who see security as a career rather than as a secondary or temporary source of income. This attitude also helps private security officers maintain morale because their positions can have great opportunities for growth and advancement. Contract security also offers the flexibility of adjusting the size of the security force to suit special needs or to staff jobs of limited scope or duration, to increase or decrease the number of hours worked, and to alter the expertise of personnel as the needs of the client change. Finally, there are also screening and training tools that are exclusive to the private security industry, such as the polygraph. In states where the use of the polygraph is not prohibited by law, the security industry is one of the few permitted to polygraph applicants.

THE ROLE OF THE SECURITY DIRECTOR

Once a security company has been chosen, the next choice to be made is how to fill the position of security director. Many companies prefer to provide their own director, while others instruct the security company to provide a security director or manager for the facility. However the position is filled, it is essential that the security director be on a level equal to other company managers and that he or she be a security professional. Ideally, the sole responsibility of the director will be overseeing the security program; if at all possible, the security director should not have numerous other management responsibilities. Finally, the role of the security director should be a proactive one of deterring losses rather than one of investigating losses or disturbances after they occur.

SECURITY BASICS

Since no two facilities are alike, a detailed guide to the physical security of any place of work must, of course, be determined on site by a professional security survey. However, there are a few basic guidelines to security measures used at any site, many of which can prevent a disturbed individual, disgruntled employee, or ordinary troublemaker from gaining access to the facility.

Access Control

First, there should be a minimal number of available peripheral entry points to a building or facility, and all entry points should be attended by a security officer or a receptionist. All employees should have an identification card to present to the security officer or receptionist as they enter the building. Many businesses, especially those with a large number of workers on site, also require employees to wear this identification card as a tag at all times they are on company premises. The identification card should be laminated in plastic to prevent alteration and should include:

- A color photograph.
- The employee's name, signature, social security number, and title or department.
- The employee's address, height, weight, hair and eye color, and gender.
- The card serial number.
- The name of the facility.
- The signature of the person authorized to authenticate and issue cards.

Entry points could also be electronically controlled with a card access security system controlling a turnstile or a revolving door. The success of a controlled entry policy is dependent on the uniform, consistent administration of access control procedures. Strict guidelines for admitting employees who have lost or forgotten their ID should be established ahead of time and be well publicized.

Whatever the form of access control, it is essential that the identification or access control medium be recovered immediately whenever an employee resigns or is suspended or terminated. If an employee leaves under less than satisfactory circumstances, especially if that employee has made direct threats to the company or has exhibited any of the other warning signs of potential violence, all people within the facility, not just security personnel, should be instructed to contact a supervisor or a member of the security force if that individual appears on company property or attempts to enter the facility. It is essential that you not assume that all employees at a facility will know by word of mouth if one of their co-workers is no longer on the payroll. For example, a receptionist or even a security officer returning from several days of sick leave or vacation may not be aware of an employee's dismissal and may not do anything to prevent him or her from entering the premises. Official communication is key.

Likewise, strict access control of visitors should also be maintained, particularly in large facilities where a former employee could easily pose as a visitor without being recognized. All visitors should be screened at the reception point to verify that they have a legitimate business need to be in the building and that they are expected. Where permitted by law, purses, briefcases, and packages of visitors should be checked at this point. All visitors should be issued a temporary identification badge and should be escorted back into the private areas of the facility, either by a security officer or a designated employee. It is also possible for visitors to be divided into two clearance groups: those who should be escorted whenever they are within the protected areas of the building, and those who do not require an escort while they are in protected areas.

Outside vendors and solicitors should also be subject to identification badges and escorts. Employees in departments through which contractor personnel may have to pass or work should be advised that these outsiders will be in their areas and that company proprietary materials, theft-vulnerable company assets, and personal possessions should be protected while these outsiders are in their work area.

Within the facility itself, access control may be equally important in keeping the harm done by a violent intruder to a minimum. All interior office doors to public corridors should be attended or locked against uncontrolled entry. Keys and access codes to these doors should be strictly limited and, if deemed necessary, changed to prevent a former employee from gaining access. An intrusion detection alarm system should be used, especially on ground level peripheral doors and stairwell doors opening to critical areas within the building. Silent duress alarm switches—"panic buttons"—should be installed at reception points and in offices of executives and their secretaries. Closed circuit television (CCTV) cameras can be installed in the building, either to be monitored at all times or to be activated when a silent alarm is triggered.

Facility Design

Regardless of the type of the facility, a few commonsense rules govern in planning the location of two critical areas: the executive offices and the human resources offices. Executive offices, especially those of the top executive, should be located on the highest possible floor within a high-rise building or, in other types of structures, in an area with limited access. These offices should be accessible only after someone enters an initial reception lobby and then a second control point at the executive suite itself. A ground or lower level office with large windows overlooking an immaculately landscaped courtyard might be the location preferred by an executive for aesthetic reasons, but security basics dictate otherwise. The harder an intruder has to work to reach a potential executive target, the safer that executive will be.

Placement of the human resources offices is a little more complicated. These offices must be accessible in order to accommodate job applicants, but this accessibility must not be allowed to compromise the security of the facility as a whole. Ideally, these offices should be located in a separate building so that individuals who may be caught wandering through the building cannot claim to be applicants looking for the human resources department. If there is no separate building, these offices can be located on the first floor and have access from the main lobby. This location is also the most logical one in the case of employee terminations, as the last stop for terminated employees who are being escorted from the building is generally the human resources department. Furthermore, in spite of its need for accessibility, the human resources department can still maintain security measures with physical barriers that prevent access to other areas of the building and with silent duress alarm switches at critical locations within the area.

PERSONNEL MANAGEMENT

Supervisor Responsibilities

Even the best facility layout plans will fail if employers fail to follow a few basic rules in the handling of employees, especially those who may be inclined to violence. Company and security force supervisors cannot be expected to be experts in all forms of human behavior, but they can be trained to recognize the most common warning signs of violence by employees, such as chronic complaining, insubordination, stress, depression, and especially direct threats. These supervisors must be the eyes and ears of the company, constantly alert for signs that an unhappy employee may attempt to resolve conflicts or problems at work with violence.

It is not enough, however, simply to watch for these signs; supervisors must be encouraged to take their concerns and observations to the appropriate members of management who may be receiving other information regarding the individual's behavior from other sources within the company. Employees must be convinced that the confidential, responsible reporting of a co-worker's odd behavior is essential to the well-being of everyone who works at the facility. At the very least, the information they provide can enable an employer to help a stressed or depressed employee receive help. In a worst case scenario, such reports could prevent a troubled employee from inflicting harm on him- or herself or on company employees.

Disciplinary Procedures

When it becomes necessary to discipline employees, disciplinary procedures should be consistent and fair. All employees should be made aware of the disciplinary procedures established for offenses against company policy. Each time an employee is disciplined, the nature of the offense and the punishment levied should be carefully documented and placed on record in the employee's personnel file. Thus, if the employee is eventually terminated and an unemployment benefits hearing results, the company will have a complete record of the steps that led to that termination.

Terminations

Should company officials determine that an employee must be terminated, the termination process should be fast and objective. Ideally, the termination will take place in the human resources department, and a security officer should be standing by in an adjacent office in case the terminated employee becomes violent. If the employee must return to the workplace to clean out a desk or office, he or she should be accompanied by a supervisor, a member of the human resources department, or a security officer. If the terminated employee has access to a data processing system, the system password security administrator should be instructed to immediately delete the individual's access privilege from the system. All keys or access cards should be retrieved from the employee before he or she leaves the premises. If there is a legitimate reason for the terminated employee to return to company property, he or she should be accompanied by a security officer at all times.

PERSONAL SECURITY FOR EXECUTIVES

The type of violent employee who receives the most media attention is generally the lone gunman—the angry and unstable employee or former employee who suddenly "snaps" and opens fire on employers and co-workers. Unfortunately, violence in the workplace—or violence connected to the workplace—can take many other forms. Executives and their relatives are increasingly becoming victims of a variety of criminal actions, including forced entry, office occupation, sabotage, hostage taking, kidnapping, murder, and even assassination. Many of these crimes are committed by the very people who would know best what their vulnerabilities are: their employees. While shootings in the workplace are often impulsive, spur-of-the-moment actions, the kidnapping or murder of an executive is generally a well-planned activity, often practiced many times before its execution. Preventive measures, thus, are key to avoiding these tragedies.

In recent years, many executives and their companies have learned this lesson the hard way. On April 29, 1992, Sidney Reso, a high-ranking executive with Exxon Corporation, was kidnapped as he left his home in New Jersey to go to work. Almost two months later, Arthur Seale—a former policeman and an Exxon security official from 1977 to 1987—and his wife were arrested for Reso's kidnapping. As a police officer in Hillside, New Jersey, Seale was reportedly disciplined numerous times on charges that included striking the mother of a suspect in the face with his gun. For one reason or another, these charges apparently went unnoticed by Exxon officials. Following the kidnapping arrests,

Mrs. Seale confessed and led police to Reso's body. The executive had apparently been killed shortly after his abduction.

The kidnapping of another executive by one of his own employees ended on a happier note. In August 1993, Harvey Weinstein, the CEO of a large men's formal clothing company, was kidnapped and held in a small underground pit for almost two weeks. A creature of habit, Weinstein ate the same breakfast in the same diner every day for years. This habit was apparently well known, since Weinstein was abducted in his car as he was leaving the diner. Law enforcement officials became convinced that an employee or former employee was involved when the kidnapper making a ransom call referred to the victim as "Mr. Harvey," as Weinstein was often referred to by his employees. Shortly after the ransom drop was made, police arrested Fermin Rodriguez, an employee at Weinstein's factory for over eight years, and his brother. A short time later, police found Weinstein, exhausted and hungry but in relatively good health, in the well-camouflaged pit off a Manhattan highway. At a press conference a few days after his release, Weinstein stated that what was most horrible about his ordeal was that one of his own employees had instigated the entire incident.

Prevention

Many executives may resist taking security measures to protect themselves from such crimes because they feel that they would never be the target for a kidnapping or because they refuse to let fear rule their lives. There is, however, a difference between being paranoid and being careful. The following measures could be instrumental in preventing you or your family members from being abducted:

- Vary your schedule. The easiest way to become a victim of kidnappers is to become predictable in your habits.
- Do not use vanity license plates or put your name on the mailbox or your address in the phone book.
- When at all possible, avoid ostentatious displays of wealth or status. Wearing the best jewelry, staying at the finest hotels, or riding in stretch limousines only suggests to

potential kidnappers that you have easy access to large amounts of money.

- Consider the use of bodyguards for yourself or your family, especially when traveling. For a lower profile, bodyguards can be disguised as lower-level executives or administrative assistants. Some executives may wish to consider protection for children in school.
- Take any threats against you or your family seriously. Detailed records of the content of the threat and any information that might indicate who was making it should be kept for reference if an attack or kidnapping occurs.
- Screen the backgrounds of all employees carefully, using the guidelines similar to those suggested for the screening of security officers.

In addition, use the following general precautions while traveling by car:

- Vary your routes to and from work. Analysis of most of the major kidnappings over the past three decades reveals that the majority of victims—by one estimate, up to 90 percent—were abducted while they were going to or from work or to another official function.
- If possible, vary your vehicles.
- Keep the car locked at all times, and do not lower windows more than two or three inches, especially while you are driving through unsafe areas.
- Avoid parking in areas that are largely deserted or where visibility is poor.
- Park in a lighted area at night or near sunset.
- Be alert at garages where attendants park and return cars.
- Be especially alert in parking lots. Glance between, around, and under cars you pass and be aware of people in or around cars near yours. Always check the back seat of your car before entering it.
- Carry a cellular phone so that you can quickly summon help if you have car trouble or report that you have safely arrived at your destination.
- Be careful of strangers who offer to help you if you cannot start your car; they may have sabotaged the car in order to

make you more vulnerable. Be alert without letting it show.

- Keep a map of the area within reach.
- Beware of staged accidents, and be cautious of stopping to help apparently stranded motorists, especially at night. If you feel you must stop to help someone having car trouble, stay in the car with the engine running and do not roll your windows down more than a few inches. If the driver does indeed need assistance, leave the scene and send a mechanic back to help, or summon a tow truck on your cellular phone. Do *not* get out of the car or offer to let someone in the car with you.
- Consider taking an evasive driving course, which can offer executives or their chauffeurs training in such evasive maneuvers as skid turns, high-speed backing, and crashing through road blocks. For higher-risk executives, cars can also be protected with such equipment as bullet-resistant glass or armor or high-intensity taillights that can blind pursuers during a nighttime chase.

Preparation

Even once such measures have been taken, however, it is important to be prepared to respond to a kidnapping should one take place in spite of your efforts. With the help of your security manager, design a form containing precise instructions for responding to a kidnapping phone call and the phone numbers of the police, FBI, and your security offices. This form should also have adequate room for taking notes on the details of a call. (The bomb threat phone checklist in the forthcoming section on explosive devices can be modified to meet your needs.)

Place copies of the form in specially coded file folders—for example, reserve a special color of file folder for this purpose only—and distribute the folders to personnel who would be most likely to receive a ransom call if an executive is kidnapped. Instruct those staff members to wave the folder as a signal if they are receiving a threatening call. This signal should trigger your planned response.

It is also advisable to assemble special, confidential personnel files on those employees who would make likely targets for kidnappers. These files should be kept in a secure location but should be accessible to security directors and other designated company officers at all times, even on nights and weekends. Employee files should include the following information, which should be updated annually:

- Employee name and nickname.
- Home address and phone number.
- Names and nicknames of the employee's spouse and children.
- Names, addresses, and phone numbers of all family members' schools, of the spouse's employer, and of neighbors on all sides.
- The year, make, color, and license number of all family cars and the names of the people who usually drive each car.
- Regular social activities of each family member.
- Color photo of each family member.
- Descriptions of the type of clothing usually worn by each family member.
- Other essential identification information such as birthmarks, scars, or other distinguishing features.
- Medication requirements.
- The names, addresses, phone numbers, and work schedules of domestic employees.

Threats Received by Phone

A telephone call relaying the message that employees or their family have been taken hostage should be handled in the following manner:

- Remain calm. Losing your composure can push a nervous caller into rash action.
- If at all possible, record the conversation, even if the only equipment available is a dictation unit. Keep such equipment close to your phone at all times.
- If taping the call is impossible, take detailed notes on the call, including the exact time the call was received, the

exact words of the caller, the caller's speech characteristics, and any background noises.

- Alert your secretary or other personnel to start a phone trace. Make sure that these employees know how to do so by requesting this information from the phone company now, before a crisis occurs. Or ask the phone company if instant caller identification systems are available in your area.
- Regardless of the demands, tell the caller that you will cooperate fully.
- Since tracing a call takes time, try to keep the caller on the line by asking questions: Who is calling? Is this a hoax? Why have you been singled out for attack? When will you receive further instructions? What is the hostage wearing? Has the hostage been hurt? What bill denominations does the kidnapper want? Where should the ransom be delivered? How do you get to the drop-off point? How will you recognize the drop-off person?
- During the first phone call, try to arrange a simultaneous exchange of ransom and hostage. Tactfully suggest a person-to-person exchange by pointing out the risk of someone else intercepting the money at a drop-off point.

Ransom Money

Any ransom payment should include a minimum of 5 to 10 percent "bait money." The safest way to do so is to record serial numbers, including series year, from selected bills.

How to Deal with the Press

Once the police are notified of the kidnapping, the press may learn of the crime and contact you for further information. It is vital that the information you release to the press, if you choose to do so at all, not hamper the investigation or put hostages or witnesses in further danger. Guidelines for dealing with the press include:

- Consult the police or FBI before releasing any information.
- Only you or a designated spokesperson should release information.

- Request politely but firmly that reporters protect the identities of witnesses.
- Do not allow members of the media to enter the home or office of the victim or to examine the scene of the crime.
- If police approve, you may consider releasing the following information: name, age, and relationship of the victim to family; time and method of the kidnapping; descriptions of the kidnappers; items stolen during the kidnapping; and the victim's medical needs.
- Information that is generally *not* appropriate for release to the press includes names, addresses, and photographs of witnesses; serial numbers and denominations of ransom money; cash or other valuables overlooked by the kidnappers; and details of any security measures in use at the scene of the crime.

Two recent cases confirm the value of preparation for violence against executives. In the first, an employee of one company had served as an informant to his employers on several criminal matters, although the reliability of his information was questionable. Mistakenly convinced that he was an expert investigator, the employee requested a transfer to the company's security department so that he could carry a gun and flash a badge—a request that was quickly rejected. Incensed at the rejection, the employee continued to harass one company executive to overrule the job transfer decision. Eventually, his deteriorating mental and emotional condition caused the employee to lose his job, a loss that he immediately blamed on the executive whose help he had sought.

Meanwhile, this same executive had accepted a job with another company in a different city. Before the executive could sell his home and move his family, the former employee reappeared and threatened to kill the executive and his entire family. The executive's original employer was rightfully convinced that these threats presented a very real danger and assigned a team of bodyguards to their former executive and his family. Shortly thereafter, the disgruntled employee took his own life while on the property of his former employers. Preventive action, thus, very likely prevented the former employee from involving the executive and his family in this tragic incident.

In the second case, preventive measures succeeded in averting a tragedy as well. Shortly after voting large pay increases for its top executives, another corporation found it necessary to borrow money to pay an annual dividend to stockholders. There were also allegations of insider trading when large blocks of stock were sold at inflated prices. After the company later declared bankruptcy, there were literally thousands of stockholders and employees left angry and disgruntled. After the chairman of the company received a threatening letter, the company made arrangements for special bodyguards and around-the-clock security for the chairman and his family. No unusual incidents developed.

BOMB THREATS

While bomb threats are not generally thought of in connection with violence by employees, it is an employee or former employee who could potentially do the most damage to your company should he or she choose an explosion as a form of revenge. Employees or former employees will know the best places to hide an explosive device—those places where a bomb would be most difficult to find and where even a small explosion could do the most damage to the company, such as computer centers, classified document storage areas, and proprietary information centers. These individuals will also have much easier access to the facility than an outsider would, especially if security measures are lax. Even if there is no real bomb, the very threat of a bombing can be an enormously satisfactory weapon for a disgruntled employee who gains his or her revenge on the company by disrupting daily business and instilling fear in current or former employers and co-workers.

Again, the best protection against a bomb threat is to be prepared. An extensive company bomb threat response plan can not only help you be better prepared for a potential bombing but it may also reduce the threat of a hoax bomb threat by a dissatisfied employee. The more prepared a company is for a bomb threat, the less chaotic—and less satisfying for a prankster—the response will be.

In addition to the basic security measures outlined throughout this chapter, the points below should be incorporated into a bomb threat response plan:

- Create an evacuation plan. Designate one person authorized to evaluate a threat and to order an evacuation if a threat is received. Depending on the circumstances, the evacuation can take place immediately after the call is received or near the time the caller says the bomb will explode. Make sure all personnel know who are the one or more persons authorized to order an evacuation.
- Establish a specific signal for the evacuation. This signal must be different from the fire-warning signal because the response to a bomb threat differs from that of a fire emergency. For example, doors and windows should be opened in response to a bomb threat in order to allow the pressure of the blast to escape if a bomb goes off. However, doors and windows should be closed in case of fire in order to smother the flames and to prevent smoke from coming back into the building from the outside.
- Install closed circuit television cameras to maintain surveillance on all vulnerable areas.
- Know at all times who holds keys to the premises. If any set of keys cannot be accounted for, or if a dissatisfied employee is allowed to leave without turning in keys, change the locks immediately.
- Keep the phone numbers of the police, fire department, your security forces, the FBI, and any other relevant emergency numbers nearby.
- Establish strict control and inspection of packages going in and out of the premises. Be especially aware of any mail that looks suspicious.
- Ask local police or fire department officials to go over your facility architectural plans to determine potential hiding places for explosive devices. Some departments may even be willing to conduct on-site inspections for these purposes.
- Storage closets, workrooms, vacant offices, boiler rooms, stairwells, elevator shafts, false ceilings, plumbing and electrical access areas, and trash receptacles (among others)

are common hiding places for bombs. Instruct maintenance personnel to conduct routine inspections of these areas, or consider installing closed circuit television cameras in those areas that are considered to be the most vulnerable.

- Assign a sufficient number of managers to scan the area during an evacuation. If a former employee is responsible for the threat, he or she may actually wish to witness first-hand the disturbance created by a bomb threat.

Responding to a Bomb Threat

Generally, it is the switchboard operator who receives a bomb threat message. However, all employees should be instructed in the basics of responding to these threats, particularly if outside calls can go directly to extensions:

- All threats should be considered serious until a thorough investigation proves otherwise.
- Make notes on a form similar to the one provided (see accompanying example) or on any paper available.
- Ask the caller to tell you the exact time the bomb is supposed to explode. Note whether the caller uses the 24-hour time system.
- If possible, determine whether the call is coming from inside or outside the building.
- Ask questions that may help locate the bomb or determine if the call is a hoax. An employee or former employee will obviously be able, if he or she is willing, to provide a precise description of the bomb's location.
- Make note of background noises such as running motors, music, voices, or other sounds that may reveal the location of the caller.
- As soon as the caller hangs up, report the information obtained to the appropriate manager, who should then immediately notify the police, fire department, and any other appropriate agency.

BOMB THREAT CHECKLIST
GENERAL TELEPHONE INSTRUCTIONS

BE CALM. BE COURTEOUS. LISTEN. DO NOT INTERRUPT CALLER. NOTIFY SUPERVISOR/ SECURITY OFFICER BY PREARRANGED SIGNAL WHILE CALLER IS ON THE LINE. TAPE RECORD CONVERSATION IF POSSIBLE. TRY TO WRITE OUT COMPLETE MESSAGE. PROLONG CONVERSATION. DETERMINE AND NOTE AS MUCH OF THE FOLLOWING INFORMATION AS YOU CAN.

BASIC INFORMATION

NAME OF PERSON RECEIVING CALL _____ Time _____ Date _____

CALLER'S IDENTITY   Male ___ Female ___ Adult ___ Juvenile ___ Approximate age ___

ORIGIN OF CALL   Local _____ Long distance _____ Booth _____ Within building _____

EXACT WORDS OF CALLER. Use extra paper if necessary. _____

BOMB FACTS

PRETEND DIFFICULTY WITH HEARING. KEEP CALLER TALKING. IF CALLER SEEMS AGREEABLE TO FURTHER CONVERSATION. ASK QUESTIONS LIKE:

When will the bomb go off? Hour _____ Time remaining _____
Where is it located? Building _____ Area _____
What kind of bomb is it? _____
Where are you now? _____
How do you know so much about the bomb? _____
What is your name and address? _____
If building is occupied, inform caller that detonation could cause injury or death.

CHARACTERISTICS OF CALLER

VOICE		MANNER	
___ Loud	___ Nasal	___ Calm	___ Office machines
___ High pitched	___ Lisp	___ Rational	___ Mixed
___ Raspy	___ Other	___ Coherent	___ Street traffic
___ Intoxicated	**ACCENT**	___ Deliberate	___ Trains
___ Soft	___ Local	___ Righteous	___ Animals
___ Deep	___ Foreign	___ Angry	___ Quiet
___ Pleasant	___ Race	___ Irrational	___ Voices
___ Other	___ Not local	___ Incoherent	___ Airplanes
	___ Region	___ Emotional	___ Party atmosphere
SPEECH		___ Laughing	
___ Fast	**LANGUAGE**		**FAMILIARITY WITH**
___ Distinct	___ Excellent		**THREATENED**
___ Stutter	___ Fair	**BACKGROUND**	**FACILITY**
___ Slurred	___ Foul	**NOISE**	
___ Slow	___ Good	___ Factory machines	___ Much
___ Distorted	___ Poor	___ Bedlam	___ Some
	___ Other	___ Music	___ None

ACTIONS TO TAKE IMMEDIATELY AFTER CALL

Notify your supervisor or security officer as instructed.
Talk to no one other than as instructed by your supervisor or security officer.

Consider reprinting the above form in the front or back of your company telephone directory so that it is always available at all phone locations.

Evacuating the Premises

The evacuation unit should consist of key management personnel trained in the details of the evacuation, such as the designation of a rendezvous point, the deployment of elevators, and the establishment of priorities by department and floor. Police and fire departments and your private security service can also offer instructions on evacuation procedures. In a multitenant facility, the evacuation efforts must be coordinated with the other tenants of the building. Inform all employees of evacuation procedures, as well as procedures for reentering the building once authorities have given clearance to do so. The following guidelines are suggested components of an evacuation procedure:

- Security controls should ensure that no unauthorized persons enter or reenter the building once it has been evacuated.
- Establish routes of evacuation. Floors above and immediately below the danger point should be evacuated first.
- Move personnel at least 300 feet away from the building to protect them from flying glass and other debris if a bomb explodes.
- Cut off all electricity, gas, and fuel lines at the main switches. Use flashlights and battery-powered lanterns for illumination.

Searching the Premises

While search procedures are generally conducted by police or fire fighters, it is important to provide as much assistance to these officials as possible, since they may not be familiar with the layout of your building. A floor plan of the building should always be available for immediate reference. Furthermore, if personnel from your facility are asked to help in the search, the designated search unit should follow these guidelines:

- Use only telephone lines to establish a two-way communication system between search units and a central control point. Do *not* use a radio system, because radio signals are capable of detonating an electrical blasting cap.

- If officials have decided that an immediate evacuation of the premises is not necessary, have office personnel search private and semiprivate areas while the designated search unit inspects public areas.
- If a suspicious object or suspected incendiary device is found, do not touch it. Report its location and description to the appropriate official.
- Once an explosive device is discovered, the police will contact the nearest Explosive Ordnance Disposal (EOD) detachment, which will remove the object or render it harmless while at the site.
- If a bomb explodes before police or fire officials can arrive, do not allow personnel in the area to tamper with debris. Investigators will search the debris to obtain evidence for forensic analysis.

STRIKES

The one event that is perhaps most likely to give rise to violence in the workplace is a strike. Dissatisfied employees who as individuals may never pose a physical threat to employers or co-workers can, when organized as a group, intentionally or unintentionally create an atmosphere conducive to violence. The best advice for avoiding violence stemming from labor disputes is to be prepared; most strikes do not come as a surprise but at the end of protracted and often heated labor negotiations.

Before such a situation even arises, an emergency planning committee composed of a cross section of personnel from management, security, labor relations, public relations, and transportation should be formed to prepare for a potential emergency. When it becomes evident that a strike will occur, management officials should advise all company personnel of company policies on the following:

- Access to company property during a strike.
- Crossing the picket lines.
- Unauthorized absences.

- Participation in demonstrations.
- Special work hours.

Vendors, suppliers, service personnel, and transporters should also be notified about the impending emergency situation. While vendors or suppliers may attempt to fulfill contractual agreements, their truck drivers may decide not to cross a picket line after reaching a facility. Salaried personnel trained and licensed to drive various vehicles should be available to drive these vehicles across picket lines.

In the event of violent confrontations on the picket lines, the company safety and training director should ensure that adequate first aid equipment and qualified personnel are on hand to treat the injured. Salaried personnel should also be trained in the use of video and still photography equipment and in taking signed statements from individuals who suffer personal injury or property damage as a result of the strike.

In the event of a wildcat strike, follow the guidelines below to keep personal injury and damage to company property to a minimum:

- Immediately inform the security director of the strike. The director should then inform the rest of the security force and the emergency planning committee.
- Instruct the security director to investigate the scope and purpose of the strike and to report findings to the emergency planning committee, which must then meet in emergency session to evaluate the findings and prepare a response.
- Instruct the director to prevent strikers from gathering or demonstrating on company property. Security officers should identify and record the names of all employees who reenter company premises after the strike has begun. If necessary, deploy additional security officers for the duration of the strike.
- Limit access to company facilities by closing all gates and exits not controlled by security officers.
- Issue special identification cards during strikes so that security officers know who is authorized to enter the facility.

- If necessary, require management personnel trained in fire fighting to go on 24-hour duty for the duration of the strike.
- Inform company supervisors of all management decisions. All employees should receive written copies of company policy and special instructions in effect during the strike.

CONCLUSION

In preparing a security program, many business owners or employers make the mistake of merely focusing on how to protect themselves and their interests from criminals who are strangers—vandals, burglars, shoplifters, and armed robbers. And their concerns about such individuals are legitimate; watching a five-minute segment of any news broadcast would convince anyone that taking protective measures is simply a matter of common sense. However, in a world where violence is no longer limited to the streets outside the workplace, ignoring the potential for violence by individuals within your company could be a deadly misjudgment. Whether you are the owner of a small retail store, a plant manager, or the CEO of a major corporation, the worst security mistake you can make is thinking that problems with employees will simply work themselves out and are not a legitimate cause for company concern.

What is the answer? Prevention. Carefully evaluate your place of work, your employee policies, and your other security needs. If you decide that you need the services of a security company, choose that company carefully and demand that your security program be specifically tailored to fit your needs; a ready-made, standard security package will benefit neither you nor the employees and customers you are trying to protect. With the help of security professionals, review the overall security measures provided throughout this chapter to decide which ones are appropriate for your facility and ask for additional suggestions or instructions. Finally, educate yourself and your employees to the danger signs for violent behavior. When combined with a comprehensive security program, finely tuned observation skills and a philosophy of aggressively resolving potential problems without delay can make your workplace a safer environment for all.

ENDNOTE

[1] John T. Molloy, *Dress for Success* (New York: Warner Books, 1975), pp. 213–14.

Chapter Nine

Managing Critical Workplace Violence Incidents

Crisis management is a learned skill. Many executives, business owners, and managers have not given much thought to how they would handle a catastrophic workplace violence incident like a homicide or a serious assault.

The reason for this is evident: Significant changes or the development of plans may appear only *after* a highly unpleasant experience such as a worksite murder, and it often requires a tremendous use of company dollars, assets, and time to create a workable plan.

And yet, with no action plan in place to handle small or large workplace violence incidents, many organizations can be caught flatfooted if one occurs. The lessons these poorly managed episodes teach can be expensive, both in financial and human terms.

This chapter illustrates the dynamics of a traumatic incident, all the way from an assault in the workplace to a homicide. Businesspeople at all levels can and should learn what to do and what not to do before, during, and after one of these stressful encounters.

THE NEED FOR A PLAN

As we have pointed out in our Workplace Violence Spectrum in Figure 1–1, Chapter 1, there is no worse example of the disgruntled employee, angry customer, or outside interloper gone bad than the one who commits murder. The trauma associated with this event flows in an outword circle like a stone dropped into a lake, touching nearly everyone associated with the organization.

And any real trauma moves the majority of people out of their respective "comfort zones" and into a state of highly stressful disequilibrium. The surviving victims of workplace violence, the eyewitnesses to the event, the people related to the victims, witnesses, or suspects, and the company as a living entity all get thrown off balance. How they come back to a positive state of equilibrium and, in effect, "recover" their balance after what has happened to or around them largely depends on what kind of psychological care they get from the people who respond to their need for help.

The best provider for short- and long-term mental health care, in addition to qualified psychologists and counselors and a healthy family unit, comes from the people in the company itself. Using the "greater good" philosophy that tells employees "We are all in this organization together and we will sink or swim together" is one important key for a rapid and healthy recovery.

But this recovery doesn't happen by accident. Like it or not, your organization must prepare itself to handle the emotional needs of its employees. People who have lived through traumatic events frequently look to an "outside authority" to help them restore their own sense of internal and external order. The problem of violence in the workplace makes the company's need to provide for its employees even stronger.

Just as every company should have a set of emergency guidelines to follow in the case of a catastrophic event like a fire, a natural gas leak, a tornado, a hurricane, or an earthquake, so should they have a similar plan to initiate after any significant workplace violence event.

But what's the definition of a "significant" workplace violence event? Certainly, a homicide in your building would qualify. But what about other events? What other violence-related work-related incidents should cause you to put your company's "recovery steps" into motion?

- Any event involving one or more murders on or near the grounds, between employees, customers, or a homicide that does not necessarily involve an employee or someone related to the company (e.g., a delivery driver who is slain in a robbery attempt near the front door of the plant).

- Any event where an employee, customer, or related person is seriously injured in a workplace violence gun attack (e.g., shot and wounded but not killed).
- Any event where an employee, customer, or related person is seriously injured in a fight or some other intentional act of assault involving weapons, motor vehicles, or force.
- Any employee-related suicide on or near the company grounds.

This last example seems to be growing at an alarming rate. An employee suicide on company property can be a horrifying workplace violence event. Even if the dead employee was long known as a disturbed or unhappy individual, the act itself serves to send out distressing signals to other employees about their own mental health and the potential work-related reasons for the death.

Employees of a southern California electronics firm came to work one morning to find one of their co-workers had shot himself right inside the doorway. His body lay slumped near the threshold, requiring horrified co-workers to step across him to get inside the office.

Other cases of depressed workers hanging themselves on company grounds or shooting themselves in their cars while parked in the employee lot are equally disturbing. They are another example of workplace violence events and require the same type of emotional care as would a homicide or serious assault.

We believe you should similarly respond to any workplace violence incident or altercation where an employee is injured, and here we define the nature of the injury as either physical or psychological. We now offer a plan for meeting the needs of your organization and your employees, regardless of the nature of the workplace violence incident.

Working with the National Organization for Victim Assistance (NOVA), Dr. Mantell helped other Oklahoma mental health professionals to develop a critical incident response program after the August 1986 Edmond post office shootings, which left 14 people dead.

The group developed a working definition of a "community-wide trauma-inducing event" that certainly encompasses many factors that make workplace violence so difficult to deal with:

"A community-wide traumatic event is one that causes life-threatening injury or death. A community may be 'natural,' as in a neighborhood or a school, or 'artificial,' as in the passengers on a train. It may include natural disasters, incidents of crime, man-made disasters, and certain types of accidents. Criteria to consider when determining whether the event may cause widespread trauma include the following nonexclusive attributes:

- Incidents that occur within communities in which people are strongly affiliated with each other.

[The employees who work for a company certainly apply here.]

- Incidents in which there are multiple eyewitnesses.

[Many workplace violence homicides, serious assaults, or even suicides occur in front of co-workers of both the victim and the instigator.]

- Incidents in which the direct victims have a special significance to the community affected, as may happen with the assassination of a public figure or the killing of a child in a daycare center.

[Post office shootings or workplace murders in public places such as supermarkets affect the community at large around these public entities.]

- Incidents in which the community is subjected to exposure to carnage or misery.

[Here, the community made up of the employees of a company may have to see dead bodies, blood, or weapons.]

- Incidents that call for numerous rescue workers.

[The subsequent arrival of police, fire, and ambulance personnel who must take action can create tremendous anxiety for the eyewitnesses to any serious workplace violence incident.]

- Incidents that attract a great deal of attention.[1]

[The seemingly large number of post office shootings makes headlines across the nation. The remaining postal employees must continue to work through the incredible public and media scrutiny. Any time some deranged person shoots several people with an assault rifle, the headlines scream of workplace chaos for days.]

Clearly, a serious workplace violence incident involving the death or significant injury of one or more employees, customers, suspects, or "outside" people reflects many of the above factors.

Here's hoping you never need to initiate any part of the forthcoming plan, but in these times of rising violence, the need for a set of real, written, and even rehearsed guidelines is no longer a luxury; it's a requirement.

"Do you mean to tell me, Mr. Vice President of Personnel," says the plaintiff's attorney, homing in like a guided missile, "that your firm employs 200 people from all walks of life and you have no written policy about responding to a workplace violence event similar to the one where my client was killed?"

Failing to establish some kind of action plan can leave you open to civil suits for failing to respond to either previously documented employee problems or traumatic incidents of any kind involving employees. And since history tells us such lawsuits rarely just involve the participants—the lawyers will go after the well-known "deepest pocket," which means the company and its insurance carriers.

If you run a small business, you'll probably have a small plan. If you run or work for a large business, the size and scope of your plan will need to match the size of your operation, the number of employees, and the company's collective access to various employee assistance program (EAP) resources. Whatever the size of the plan, it should get a thorough update and review each year, so that new executives are familiar with it and long-time personnel continue to know their roles in it.

And speaking of EAP, if your firm has a specific EAP department, it makes good sense to give the manager in charge a copy of any workplace violence plan you develop. Thanks to budgetary cutbacks and a sense of "we'll cross that bridge when we come to it," many EAP departments are underfunded, understaffed, and because of that, underutilized. Employees in need may look to their EAP for help only to receive some outdated brochures and the toll-free phone number for a counseling service in another city.

To avoid the risk of being criticized as gloom-and-doomers, let us first say that we don't expect you to spend every waking moment worried about workplace violence. We're only asking you to take a healthy dose of concern for your company and the people who work there, not to go looking for trouble behind every corner or to treat your employees as if they were potential suspects.

Any tactical action plan dealing with violence in the workplace should, at the very least, (1) identify the people in charge of safely managing all parts related to the incident during and after its occurrence, and (2) offer written guidelines to put these people into action. In the event someone in senior management or even the business owner, president, or CEO, is incapacitated in some way by the incident, the people at the next levels in the organization should be able to step forward and initiate the plan.

Our discussion of these two must-haves will cover three distinct areas related to the company's responses to workplace violence incidents:

1. What to do before things have gone bad.
2. What to do when things are over.
3. How to get back to work and keep the company running.

This chapter and Chapter 10 will address these concerns. We start by focusing on what to do *before* any significant workplace violence incident.

THE FIRST STEP: LEARN STRESS MANAGEMENT BEFOREHAND

In his book *Making Work Fun: Doing Business with a Sense of Humor*, Ron Garland succeeds in doing something difficult. He teaches people how to actually enjoy the time they spend at work. Using everything from meetings at the beach to costume parties to singalongs to T-shirt contests, Garland shows organizations and employees how to lighten up just a bit.

In justifying his brand of humor management and stress relief, Garland first asks employers a critical, albeit rhetorical question: "What should be an employer's primary objective?"

To this he gets all the usual answers: To make money, to increase profits and productivity, and to provide job security and a decent wage for employees.

Garland, while agreeing that each of the above is certainly true, thinks that these answers are means toward an end and not the end itself. "I maintain," says the author," that the primary objective of most employers should be to provide the members of the organization (including managers and employees at all levels) a high-quality work environment."[2] To us, this ties neatly back into our running definition of the Golden Rule; "Do unto your employees as you would have them do unto you."

Studies of employee satisfaction reveal an obvious yet often ignored fact: The work environment *is* critical to employee morale. People enjoy their work for a variety of reasons, but the *atmosphere* of their workplace has to rank near the top. Average pay and excellent working conditions are much preferred to great pay coupled with horrific working conditions. People want to enjoy their work, their co-workers, and their supervisors.

An old joke illustrates this best:

A man is sent to Hell, and at his first meeting with the Devil he is given a choice as to where he would like to spend all of eternity. Taking the man to the first room, the Devil opens the door to reveal a huge steam engine. Dozens of sweaty workers are shoveling huge piles of coal into the machine as it fills the air with heat, noise, and gas. The man quickly decides he doesn't want to spend his remaining days there.

The Devil takes the man to a second room and opens the door to reveal a lake full of crocodiles and alligators. The water is filled with people swimming desperately out of the range of these angry reptiles. The man tells the Devil he's not interested and they move on.

Coming to the third room, the Devil opens the door and the man sees a group of well-dressed businesspeople standing around talking and drinking coffee. The entire room is filled waist-deep with sewage and as much as the man hates the smell and the slime, he reasons that this punishment is not so bad. He tells the Devil this is his choice and enters the room to greet the people.

Later, before the man can finish his first cup, the Devil opens the door and yells, "Okay! Coffee break is over! Everybody back to standing on your heads!"

The business bookstores are filled with good books on stress and stress management. There are a number of reputable companies and training consultants who offer full and half-day stress-management training seminars for all levels of an organization.

In the past, the typical company-offered stress management class was often a voluntary event, filled with a mixture of employees who really found the information extremely useful (i.e., job and life-specific); those who learned a few small things quickly forgotten; and those who only came for the donuts.

Some companies have changed this "come if you like" offering to a mandatory class for every employee, and not just the so-called "high-stress" executives, managers, or supervisors. We applaud this use of stress-management training as a positive intervention into all employees' lives.

THE SECOND STEP: RETAINING THE ON–BOARD PSYCHOLOGIST

You need to establish an ongoing relationship with a mental health professional who has some experience handling violence in the workplace. This could be with your own in-house psychologist, a private-practice psychologist or psychiatrist in your local community, or a social services counselor affiliated with your local mental health agency.

Experience in the field, on-the-job training, and real, practical experience with actual incidents is a must for anyone you choose.

Ideally, the psychologist or mental health professional who does the preemployment screening and helps with the hiring practices for your firm should be the same person who establishes an ongoing relationship with the people working there. He or she also should be involved in the human resource training programs for the first-line supervisors, middle managers, and top executives.

And ultimately, this person should also be the one who is involved with all of the employee counseling, so that if something bad should happen at the company—a workplace violence incident of any magnitude—he or she will be there to help everyone involved pick up the pieces.

The reasoning behind this is based on the hope that the psychologist has built a close working relationship with the company and its people. In effect, he or she has helped to hire these people, offered training sessions to deal with personnel, supervisory, and human resource issues, and provided individual or group counseling at all levels throughout the organization. This bond with the firm makes it easier for the psychologist to intervene before, during, or after potential workplace violence episodes.

PSYCHOLOGICAL SERVICES ON A BUDGET

Firms with a thriving EAP department and that are large enough to justify the expense of in-house psychological services have a valuable and even life-saving resource right at their collective fingertips. Midsize firms may be able to contract with a mental health professional on a monthly retainer or an ad hoc, as-needed, basis.

But what about the small-business owner, who may not know how to get in touch with qualified mental health counselors? How about the small manufacturing plant owner, the convenience store owner, or the small-business person who owns a number of stores in different locations? How do they protect themselves and their employees with the power of properly aimed psychological services? The lament is a familiar one in these cost-conscious times:

"I'm just a small-business owner," says the woman who runs a commercial dry cleaning plant. "How do I prescreen my new job applicants?"

"I don't have the resources to hire a full-time psychologist," says the owner of a payroll check processing company. "How do I offer counseling to the employees who need it?"

"How do I take advantage of the variety of mental health 'wellness services' a psychologist can offer to me and my 20 employees?" asks the owner of an office supply store.

"Who do I turn to if one of my employees is killed or injured on the job? Either by another employee or an angry spouse?" asks the owner of a large realty company.

If you're a small-business owner, manager, or employee, you are not without resources when it comes to procuring qualified psychological services. Just as there is often safety in numbers, there is power in them, too.

Here's an example of how to start at the grass-roots level and still provide for your needs and the needs of your employees, and even your customers. Put yourself into the following scenario, and if you're a small-business owner, see how you could apply it to your situation:

Let's say there are 15 businesses on your block. Besides the drug store, the stationery store, the gift shop, the liquor store, and the pet shop, there are also two small restaurants, an insurance company, a dry cleaning shop, a fast-food outlet, a sporting goods store, a shoe store, a bookkeeping firm, and two banks. You're all part of the Main Street Business Association, and you hold monthly luncheon meetings to talk about problems or opportunities that pertain to your stores and businesses.

One month, the lunch topic could be a nagging graffiti problem on some of the buildings, while another month you might meet to discuss the impact of a new state sales tax proposal.

Your association collects dues from the merchants and businesspeople to keep in a general fund. This helps pay for lunches at your meetings, and it exists to pay for large and small expenses that relate to the healthy operation of your group.

As one of the many business owners on this street, your task is to go to the next meeting and raise the issue of violence in the workplace. Certainly everyone at your meeting will have stories to tell of problem employees who have worked for them, or traumatic events and significant workplace violence episodes they've either heard or seen.

By now, you've all agreed that a workplace violence problem could erupt on your street. And once you've agreed that the problem both exists and would require the help of a qualified mental health professional, what now?

Why not contact your local social service agency as a group and ask them for a referral? Call the referred psychologist or mental health counselor and ask him or her to speak to your association and offer an on-call relationship. With sliding-fee scales and group buying power, you can get him or her to help you with preemployment screening on one day, supervisor training on another, or employee counseling on another.

"But why do I need preemployment screening for my clerk who only makes $6 per hour?" asks the shoe store owner.

"But what happens," counters the psychologist, "if someone is killed outside the front door of your store, or your clerk is assaulted by another employee and can't return to work without tremendous fear? Aren't you leaving yourself open for a civil suit if the employee says that you failed to offer him the counseling he needs to return to work?"

"You're right," admits the shoe store owner. "If I can have these mental health counseling services available, I can offer them to my employees on an as-needed basis."

THE THIRD STEP: IN CASE OF A REAL EMERGENCY—BREAK GLASS AND REMOVE WORKPLACE VIOLENCE ACTION PLAN

In situations of extreme stress, we tend to revert back to what we know—in essence, how we have been trained to respond. This is why soldiers spend years shooting from their tanks even during peacetime, fighter pilots make thousands of landings on aircraft carriers at night, and police officers spend so much time on the firing range. This is also why we have fire drills at elementary schools and lifeboat drills on cruise ships. Practice, especially in times of great stress and chaos, makes perfect.

So are we suggesting you have "violence in the workplace" drills? No, but in the words of an old plumber, "The time to look for the water supply cutoff valve is before the pipes break at midnight."

- If you follow your postincident plan as closely as possible, it will help get your organization back on track and back to business as efficiently, safely, and humanely as possible.
- If you don't follow a preconceived, rehearsed plan, you will do a disservice to those employees who look to top management for leadership, guidance, and as often happens in these cases, physical and psychological protection.
- Lastly, your company leaves itself open to litigation for failing to provide what are sure to be classified by plaintiff attorneys as the "basic minimums" in these cases:

Prompt notification of law enforcement agencies and rescue personnel.

Protection of the workplace violence scene for investigators.

On-scene employee counseling immediately following a significant event.

Media relations to explain the situation accurately.

Grief and trauma recovery time for victims and related witnesses, bystanders, and employees.

Company sanctions and/or punishment for the instigators in lesser cases.

Access to appropriate EAP and psychological counseling programs to help employees cope with postincident trauma problems.

Sympathy and aid to victims' families.

Psychological follow-ups and debriefing sessions for any employee who desires them, at intervals of one month, three months, six months, and one year following the incident. These will be aimed at helping survivors cope with long-term traumatic stress reactions and to help prevent the onset of Post-Traumatic Stress Disorder (PTSD).

THE KEY ELEMENTS OF ANY POSTWORKPLACE VIOLENCE PLAN

It is our hope that the workplace violence response plan created by your firm is actually just a part of an ongoing review of the mental health of the organization. This involves the use of pre-screening for potential new hires, the creation of a humane working environment, safe and legal discipline and termination procedures, and the offer of counseling for any employee who requests it.

Your plan should be filed in the CEO's office, the personnel office, the human resources office, the EAP office, and the security office under the heading "Our Plan for the Worst, Although We Hope It Never Happens."

The top executives, the senior managers, and the people who are in charge of the well-being of the employees should meet to give their selected input and help prepare this plan as a group. The health and survival of the company is at stake; it's that important.

Just as the president of the United States has a chain of command who will initiate his orders in the event of his death or other incapacitation, your firm should create a list of people who will be empowered to put your workplace violence plan into action if the situation dictates it.

Starting at the top and moving down, make sure that each person knows what is required should the need arise. It's no secret that many disgruntled employees and other workplace violence instigators aim their fury at the leaders of the organization that has "wronged" them. Stories abound of CEOs shot dead in their offices, plant managers killed on the factory floor, and high-level executives, managers, and supervisors slain where they stood. Your plan must take this frightening but possible reality into account.

Even strong, well-known organizations who have lost their company presidents—for example, Exxon (executive kidnapping) and Volkswagen USA (executives killed in an airline crash)—foundered for a time until the surviving leaders could take over. Don't leave this chain of command decision to chance.

Here are the areas and actions your workplace violence plan should cover:

WORKPLACE VIOLENCE
INCIDENT CHECKLIST

- Know who and how to contact your designated mental health professional immediately. This should happen no later than 24 hours after the incident.
- Arrange for this psychologist or counselor to meet first at the top levels of the organization for executive debriefings and then to schedule meetings with anyone in the firm who wants to talk about what happened.

These first meetings with the senior management should be a mandatory requirement. Attendance and participation at this meeting should not be an "I'll get to it later" event.

The psychologist or other mental health professional who presides over this meeting will have many specific questions about the workplace violence episode, and senior management should cooperate fully. Sometimes, it will just be necessary to bare the corporate soul, warts and all, and tell the psychologist what happened and why.

Now is not the time to sugarcoat things. If you're having problems with specific employees and for specific reasons, make that information known. Hiding key facts, attempting to make things seem better than they are, or trying to shield key witnesses, victims, or even the instigators will only make matters worse.

The second-level meetings with the other employees are equally as important. Studies of these traumatic incidents reveal the same thing: immediate, on-site crisis counseling and intervention can make a tremendous difference in the mental health and the recovery time of the people involved. The faster the counselors can get to work, the better for the survivors.

- Establish a critical incident debriefing area for the responding mental health professionals.

This can be a conference room, a cafeteria, a training room, and so forth. Just make sure it's private, accessible to all employees, and near a restroom facility. Be ready to stock this room with chairs, tables, tissues, coffee, water, snacks, and other amenities to make everyone who comes in as comfortable as possible. You may want to coordinate these activities with your EAP department.

- Designate a representative to work with local law enforcement.

This person should be ready with answers to important questions. Now is not the time to hide anything or be uncooperative in the hopes the cops will just go away.

The May 1993 post office shooting case involving Dana Point, California, suspect Mark Hilbun did not end at the post office. Law enforcement officers had to organize a large manhunt to capture the assailant. Vital information about the suspect in your incident can help the police work more effectively.

- Designate someone to notify the victims' families of the incident. Be ready to offer them immediate support, counseling, and debriefing services.

Above all else, try hard to make sure the victims' families do not learn of the tragedy from the media. Hearing that your loved one was murdered at work is bad enough; hearing about it from a reporter and not someone from the company is even worse.

Ask your psychologist or mental health professional to schedule immediate counseling meetings with grieving relatives.

- Designate a media spokesperson to brief the media and, more importantly, to keep them away from grieving employees, family members, or eyewitnesses.

This person should already be well qualified to give statements to the press and handle the harsh glare of the media spotlight. This is not a job for the meek; it takes guts, poise, and the ability to stay cool under tremendous pressure.

Good media coverage at a serious workplace violence incident can have a positive impact on the victims, survivors, families, well-wishers, customers, and the curious. But if it's not handled well, it can have a negative impact. While it's not necessary or even advisable to tell all, you don't want the media to get the impression that you're covering something up.

The primary goal of the media relations person is to tell the media what happened and ask them to correctly inform the public as to what occurred and why. Now is also the time to tell everyone who will listen that your company has already brought in mental health professionals to help with on-site crisis counseling.

The media liaison should also prepare all press releases with the consent and approval of senior management; give all official statements; arrange interviews as appropriate; and try to answer questions only in a controlled environment such as a press briefing or press conference. Giving other than basic information over the telephone can be risky. Get your facts straight before you speak.

- Be prepared to offer optional "debriefing" services for all potential workplace violence victims outside the immediate survivors or employees.

Whether they were physically injured or not, eyewitnesses, innocent bystanders, family members, and nearby neighbors may also be psychologically injured. If they know the participants and grieve for them, they may need counseling.

This is not to say that you should establish a "free psychologist's clinic" for people off the street, just that you may need to be more sensitive to the needs of the people on the periphery of the event. An offer of counseling can serve as a "siphon" for their anger and grief.

- Notify in-house legal counsel or your outside law firm of the incident, and ask them to respond to the scene.

Your legal counsel may be able to help with the media inquiries and prepare for the postincident legal actions that may come from several sides. They also can notify the company's insurance representatives, who also may want to respond.

- If necessary, appoint a qualified public relations spokesperson or an outside firm to handle the media and questions from customers and the public.

This person or group should give some thought as to how the public perceives the way your company handles a workplace violence incident, including your firm's credibility, the perception of danger or safety at the company, and the perception of callousness or concern on the part of the company and its leaders.

For all the good work it's trying to do to prevent future outbreaks of violence in the workplace, the US Postal Service has suffered tremendously from bad public relations. Some of the reading and news-viewing public tends to perceive the post office leadership as a group of Draconian slave-drivers who feel no sensitivity to their employees. While this is clearly not true, the perception is there. Making your company the butt of jokes, insults, or half-truths spread nationwide is obviously not advisable. You need to create positive perceptions of the work you are doing to handle this event.

When violence of any kind occurs in your facility, you have an opportunity to actually improve your standing in the business community by being sensitive to the needs of those involved. What you do to help your employees recover can show the public, the media, your customers, and your competitors, "We've had something bad happen in this place. Here's what we're doing right now and for the future, to help those who were involved, and to prevent it from happening again."

The concept of service management demonstrates the role the employee plays as the customer's agent or advocate. In conversation, the subject of the workplace violence event is bound to come up. It's only natural for human beings to want to hear the details and offer their own degree of comfort.

When the customer asks, "So, what's going on over there?" and the employee says, "You know, I need a couple of days off to cope with this but they're not letting me take any. It's like nothing happened around here. They wouldn't even let us do . . ."

You can fill in the blank here. By not following through with your employees, you run the risk of not only alienating them, but the lifeblood of your company as well—the customers.

At every company where Dr. Mantell has counseled people after a workplace violence incident, the media always wants to know, "What is this firm doing for the survivors?" You had better be prepared to offer an answer that shows your concern.

- Notify the personnel managers to arrange for time off for grieving employees as appropriate.

With rotating shifts and a large enough number of employees who are willing to make schedule changes, you can still get coverage to avoid a complete work shutdown.

- After the initial stages of the incident, brief managers and supervisors as to the ways employees may memorialize the victims.

They will need to know why compassion is the key to any response and why employees will need time for grief, mourning, and memorial services.

People who are not necessarily involved in a trauma often feel a strong need to grieve with the living victims and mourn the dead in their own way. On July 5, 1993, San Francisco gunman Gian Luigi Ferri opened fire at the law offices of Pettit & Martin, killing eight and wounding six.

Later, over 650 people attended the funeral for one of the slain lawyers. For several weeks afterward, people from all over came to the entrance of the high-rise building in the city's financial district to lay flowers, memorial wreaths, and notes of sympathy. Even though they may not have known any of the dead or wounded personally, the residents of San Francisco still wanted to show support and offer silent remembrance to the dead.

- Designate someone to immediately check, protect, or restore the integrity of your data systems, computers, and files.

This person can come from the department of information services, the security department, or the financial side of the company. Some workplace violence episodes involve sabotage, vandalism, or the destruction of key assets prior to or following a murder or assault. It's just as important to protect the company's data resources as it is to protect and provide for the human resources.

- Designate a clean-up crew for the site of the attack.

As grisly as this sounds, it needs to be done. Pending approval from the law enforcement representatives on scene, one approach is to try to clean up the site immediately and correctly. Patch bullet holes, remove blood, and gather belongings. It's highly disconcerting for grief-ridden employees to return to the worksite and see gaping reminders of the horror that occurred.

When postal workers returned to work after the Edmond, Oklahoma, massacre, they found bullet holes still in the walls and their workstations moved or rearranged. For those people who wanted some security or familiarity, this did little to help.

Since most of us hate disorder, we all have a need to put everything back the way it was. In the aftermath of a workplace violence episode, don't be in such a hurry to make drastic changes to other areas near the death or injury scene. Moving someone's desk from one location to another is disconcerting and even rude on a good day. Imagine how you would feel if someone disturbed your personal belongings, especially in light of a tragedy.

We understand this all may appear insensitive. "It's like nothing happened. Joe's dead and now everything is back to normal.

Where's the sensitivity around this place?" Make a decision to clean up the worksite immediately or not, depending on how the company's leadership feels at the time. There are no hard and fast rules. Do what seems best. Is it better to clean up the area and try to maintain some semblance of relative normalcy, or is it more fitting to leave the area alone for a few days? This choice probably will be made by circumstances.

What the police want to do, what the employees want to do, and what the surviving victims want to do should all be taken under consideration. There's a very thin line between scouring the area with industrial-strength bleach to make it look like nothing ever happened and leaving bloodstains on the floor so that co-workers are constantly reminded of the incident. Mix compassion and empathy into any decision involving the site of the violence.

- Arrange a follow-up schedule for the psychologist or mental health counselors to return at intervals for further debriefings.

In the heat of the moment, it's hard to remember this last step, but it may be one of the most important. The healing process begins at the end of the traumatic event, but it will take time to work. Ongoing counseling offers the best hope for the recovery of those people who suffered, directly or indirectly, in this tragedy.

Now that the worst has happened, it's time to pick up the pieces and focus all efforts toward protecting the company's most valuable resource—its employees.

THE AFTERMATH: THREE STAGES OF SHOCK FOLLOWING WORKPLACE VIOLENCE

In any traumatic incident, the participants, surviving victims, eyewitnesses, and associated bystanders may pass through three distinct stages as they react to what has taken place. While there are certainly no absolutes when dealing with the fragilities of the human psyche, these stages have been well documented in interviews and counseling sessions with grief-stricken people.

Survivors of violence in the workplace—a highly traumatic event in itself—may spend time passing through these stages.

How long or how short depends on the person, the availability of quality counseling and psychological care, and the support the person receives from family, friends, co-workers, and others who can offer a clear view of stability.

STAGE ONE: SHOCK, DISBELIEF, AND DENIAL

This stage begins immediately after the incident and may last anywhere from many minutes to many months. In severe trauma cases, people act like "walking wounded," where they feel they are in a daze about the event they saw or experienced.

"I can't believe what I saw" or "I don't believe what happened" are common statements.

This stage may occur strongly at first and then begin to dissipate over time. It also may work in conjunction with the remaining stages.

STAGE TWO: A CATACLYSM OF EMOTIONS

Here, the victims may run a gauntlet of different emotions as they try to cope with their experience. This stage can last for a short time or linger for years, and it includes:

- *Anger or rage.* This is often directed at the instigator of the violence, as is the case in many workplace violence episodes where a disgruntled employee has shot and killed a popular co-worker. Rage and feelings of revenge are often mixed with the anger as the victims seek to place blame on the person responsible. Sometimes, the anger is turned inward, as the victims try to blame themselves, God, society, the criminal justice system, other family members, or friends of the victim or the suspect.

- *Fear or terror.* The survivors may suffer from extreme panic attacks where they are literally unable to function in any capacity. This is quite common in cases where employees have returned to the worksite following a workplace violence incident. They may be unable to work or even speak without tears or other wracking emotions. Often, the death of a co-worker brings on their own fears of death.

- *Frustration.* This is often linked to the survivors' feelings of utter helplessness as to what happened. "If I had only . . ." is a common statement, especially in workplace violence incidents where the suspect made threats or otherwise revealed himself to others before an attack.
- *Confusion.* This is the "Why did this happen?" and "Why did it happen near me?" emotion, where the survivors look to themselves for reasons why someone was killed and why it wasn't them. As the victims look inward, they often blame themselves for the new disorder around them. They don't know why this has happened to themselves personally or to their loved ones. "This happens to people on TV, not to people like me," said one.
- *Guilt or self-blame.* The concept of survivor guilt is common here, as the victim tries to find some reason for the event and why he or she survived and the co-worker didn't.
- *Grief or sorrow.* This stage may last for a long time, especially if the feelings rekindle themselves every time the survivors are reminded of the victim. In a workplace, this trigger of an inner "grief anchor" could occur when the survivor passes the dead colleague's workstation, desk, locker, and so on; sees a photo or hears the name of the assailant; reads or hears about the incident on the nightly news; or passes an "anniversary" date for the event.

STAGE THREE: RECONSTRUCTION OF EQUILIBRIUM

Here, the surviving victims have finally started to regain their emotional and mental balance. They have a new outlook, not only about what happened, but also for themselves and how they have coped and will continue to cope. While this stage is not without its good days and bad days, it does tend to signify the presence of recovery.

The journey from stage one to stage three may be amazingly brief or agonizingly long. Again, the time it takes to complete the process depends on the severity of the event; the physical proximity of the survivor to the actual trauma (i.e., did he or she witness a workplace homicide, hold the victim as he or she died, or only hear of the event and see its aftermath later); the length of the traumatic event (i.e., a long hostage standoff in a factory, a brief shooting, or a rampage involving many victims); and lastly, the mental stability of the surviving victim prior to the incident itself. While we never get used to trauma, some people are better equipped to handle extremely stressful events than others.

Psychologists and other mental health professionals trained in on-site crisis intervention and counseling are well aware of these stages and aim their efforts at listening to the survivors talk about their feelings. They strive to provide a highly supportive environment and offer a sense of efficacy of the experience to the survivors. Using the techniques of "ventilation" and "validation," they help victims identify their feelings, release stress by talking to an uninvolved third-party about the event, and offer coping mechanisms: "This happened and I'm sorry it did. You survived and will continue to survive. Let's talk about what you're feeling now and what you can expect to feel later on."

History and experience with many thousands of trauma victims tells us that with quality counseling and support from friends, family, and co-workers, the recovery is usually complete within six months or less.

ENDNOTES

[1] *Crisis Response Training Program Manual* (Washington, DC: NOVA, 1986).

[2] Ron Garland, *Making Work Fun: Doing Business with a Sense of Humor* (San Diego, CA: Shamrock Press, 1991).

Chapter Ten

Back to Business: Can It Be Done?

YOU STILL HAVE TO BUY STAMPS

"Neither rain, nor sleet, nor gloom of night will stay these carriers from their appointed rounds" So goes the motto for the US Postal Service. Bad weather, mean dogs, or icy roads don't stop the mail from going through, and apparently, neither does murder.

The US Postal Service, like many businesses, must continue in the face of adversity. And it does. We talk about the Postal Service as a model for a company that does in fact continue to do business even in the face of violence in the workplace. Its ability to deal successfully with the aftershock of a workplace homicide should serve as a standard for other companies around the country to follow.

As an entity, the Postal Service holds a unique position as a "public trust" business. Like police and fire departments, the "show must go on" regardless of the turmoil around them. When a police officer is killed, his or her colleagues don't all call in sick for the week and stay home to grieve; they put on their uniforms the next day and go right back to the streets. If the fire department loses a firefighter in a blaze, other firefighters don't take a week-long break and stop answering fire calls.

Does, or more specifically, should, business continue as usual after a workplace homicide? Absolutely.

After the 1992 Los Angeles riots, when most of the South Central area of the city was in ruins, the mail got through. Many thousands of dedicated postal workers moved the physical and psychological rubble out of the way and delivered the mail.

When Hurricane Andrew cleared a wide path of homes and buildings along most of coastal south Florida, the mail still got through.

Following what is now called the Great Floods of 1993 that ruined many houses and farms, not to mention hopes and dreams, in cities and towns along the Mississippi River, the mail still got through.

There have been workplace homicides or shootings at the post offices in Johnston, South Carolina; Anniston, Alabama; Atlanta, Georgia; New York City; Edmond, Oklahoma; New Orleans, Louisiana; Escondido, California; Ridgewood, New Jersey; Royal Oak, Michigan; and Dana Point, California.

In all, 29 postal employees have been slain in the past 10 years (14 of these in the Edmond incident alone). One of the common threads running through all of the incidents is this: The survivors grieved for the victims, comforted each other in a wide range of ways, and got back to the job at hand—delivering the US mail.

So how do we address the critics, many of them in the media, who say, "That's their problem. They go right back to work as if nothing happened."

First, everyone, from the public, to other postal workers in other states, to the people assigned to that specific post office, knows *something* happened. To their own personal extent, everyone associated with the Postal Service is affected by any violent death on the job there or at any other postal station.

But remember that the Postal Service is mandated by law to deliver the mail. That's why you see them out in blowing snowstorms, drenching rains, floods, and stifling heat doing what they're directed to do—continue to deliver the mail. If it was up to you, would you go out in an Alaska blizzard, fly a seaplane across a vast snow-covered continent in the dead of a cold winter's night, just to deliver mail? Probably not, given a choice. But for the men and women who do these kinds of activities all in the name of the US Postal Service, there is no question. They do it. They just go on.

And what about other public trust organizations? Shootings at hospitals are now more common than ever. Some of these involve crazy people looking for drugs, and still others involve grief-stricken family members who blame the doctors and staff for the death of a loved one.

What happens after a hospital employee is shot and killed in the emergency room, as has happened many times? Does the whole hospital shut down and nurse their collective wounds? Do they put a "Closed for Repairs" sign on the door and turn away sick or dying patients? Absolutely not.

There are just certain businesses that don't have the luxury of shutting down after a tragedy. As much as they would like to stop and grieve and mourn and recover, a hospital organization has made an unbreakable commitment to the public. Regardless of the events going on around us, we will treat your injuries and diseases.

Someone might say, "Our business is to make rubber gaskets for car engines. We don't see ourselves as that kind of 'public trust' business. Our only mandate is to ourselves."

Our answer is perhaps you only make rubber gaskets, but you still have a number of responsibilities and commitments to a whole list of people associated with your firm. You have employees who need to earn a living, you have customers who need your products to successfully run their own businesses, and you may even have shareholders who demand value for their investment.

The point is, as brutal as this may sound, you truly cannot afford to let a workplace violence incident close you down. There is too much riding on your success as a firm to grind to a halt and wait for the "proper time" to resume operations.

THE CORRECT RESPONSE TO EMOTIONAL TRAUMA

Having said all of this, we certainly recognize that ordinary people respond to traumatic incidents in many different ways. From the stoic, "I'll deal with it later" response to the people who wear their emotions on their sleeves, everyone is different and will require their own time and space to deal with what has happened near or in front of them.

Not everyone will be affected in the same manner. But those who need to take time off should be able to do so, and those who need additional counseling should be able to take time off to get it. Those that need psychiatric medicines should be able to take them to help their recovery. And those that will go on long-term disability should be helped through that process.

We want to clarify a myth about this healing process. The company owner or executive who says, "If we 'give in' to our employees like this, our business will fail" is more than just a little wrong. This will not happen. Maybe it will slow down, maybe things won't get done with the same speed, but this is not to say you will cease to function if you reach out and help those people who work for you.

There is a big difference between closing down an entire plant for one week and giving selected employees grief time off as needed. If your organization has suffered through some significant workplace violence incident, you have a duty to your employees to make sure you do the right things—in the right way—to help them recover from the ordeal. And it should be possible, if your organization is large enough, to schedule appropriate "grief days" for those employees who need time to deal with these kinds of events.

A metaphor may help here: Some businesses are made of stiff plastic; if you put pressure on them, if you try to bend them, and if you try to force them into a position where they cannot go, they will break. These firms cannot adjust to the needs of their employees, their customers, or the world around them. If you force them, they will crack.

Some businesses are made of cotton; you can bend them, change their shape to a degree, shift their coverage, and even apply a few "wrinkles" to their collective fabric. With some care and washing and a few passes with a steam iron, they rebound to their original size, shape, and durability.

It all comes down to the leadership of the organization. Do the people who run the organization see the trauma surrounding a workplace violence incident of any magnitude as something that is real? People who go through these circumstances have experienced a real and compelling trauma. It's not make-believe, and they aren't trying to milk the system for a few extra days off. They have psychological needs that may require counseling. Giving them access to these programs will call for your guidance and sensitive leadership.

If you still have doubts about the differences between physical injuries and psychological ones, consider the following story:

Let's say you're at home one night after a long day at the office. The phone rings and it's your daughter-in-law calling to tell you some good news. She and her husband have just won $1,000 in the lottery. They're clearly excited and have spent the day discussing what to do with the money. Under the rules of the lottery contest, they can only spend the money on one item, so no splitting it.

Her husband, your son, is taking college classes part time and, although he doesn't need them immediately, wants to buy school books so he can get a head start for the next school year. Your daughter-in-law has told her husband, "I'm here all day raising the kids and trying to take care of this house. I've been going crazy in this tiny kitchen of ours for the last five years. It's far too small and I can't work in it for very much longer. It makes me tense just to go in and clean it everyday. You know I want to spend the money on remodeling this kitchen so I can feel better about this house."

What's the right thing to do?

What if your daughter-in-law had severe migraine headaches that made her unable to even move for several hours? And what if she and her husband found a doctor who could guarantee to cure her, but it would cost $1,000 for the special machines, prescriptions, and therapy needed to relieve her pain? Now how would your son spend the same money?

"There's no question," he would say. "I'd spend the money on my wife's migraine treatment." And therein lies the answer to this riddle.

Every piece of ethical, philosophical, and moral writing over the last century dictates that the $1,000 should be spent fixing up the kitchen. Your daughter-in-law's emotional turmoil surrounding her environment is just as real as if she had migraine headaches.

Her husband is just like the CEO of a major company who says to a physically stricken employee, "Migraine headaches? No question about it. You're physically sick. Take time off."

But at the same time, the leader also may say, "Emotional sickness? That's a lot of head shrinker mumbo-jumbo. There's nothing wrong with you. I need you to get back to work and produce for me."

If it was *your* daughter-in-law and she told you this story about the books versus the kitchen debate, how would you respond?

If you tell your son to buy the books because they're more important, then you may need to look at how you respond to the emotional needs of others.

If your answer is, "I'm sympathetic to the fact that my daughter-in-law's emotional needs are just as important as her physical needs," then reward yourself for your understanding and sensitivity.

CRISIS LEADERSHIP

In truth, certain corporate leaders and top executives will be better equipped to deal with the many intricacies surrounding a workplace violence incident than others. While some of this has to do with a take-charge personality or the ability to adapt in a crisis and even thrive on the pressure, we believe more of it has to do with the existence of a plan of action. As we discussed in detail in the last chapter, you have to be prepared for something that may never arrive.

The aftermath of any workplace violence incident, whether it's from an assault, a shooting, or a similar act of destruction against people or things, has a way of revealing glaring errors, omissions, or bonehead policies in the victim organization.

While it may be unavoidable at the time it's discovered, part of any after-action plan should include a careful review of what went wrong and what went right. Don't worry if the wrong seems to overshadow the right. Part of real maturity is the ability to admit mistakes and learn from them. This is especially critical of the life-and-death potential surrounding workplace violence.

Admitting to problems in your organization takes the skills of strong, introspective leadership. While we can almost always learn from our mistakes, that doesn't make them any easier to confess, especially when lives were lost as a result.

RESTORING CONFIDENCE

In terms of creating, maintaining, or restoring confidence in the company in light of workplace violence issues, two strategies are necessary:

1. *Create and maintain confidence.* This starts at an almost subconscious level, with a message from the top that says to all employees:

We've taken a hard look at the way we do business, the way we treat our people, the way we hire, counsel, discipline, or terminate employees, the way our policies and procedures interact with our goals, plans, and mission statements, and the way we offer support to everyone in the organization who needs it. We aim for unity of purpose in what we say and what we do. This is a team-built company that thrives when we all do our best in our work and in our relationships with each other.

With this message of strength and purpose in place, it's possible to generate a sense of unshaken faith and trust among the work force as a whole. While there will always be naysayers and people who go around with buckets of cold water to throw on enthusiasm, it's far better to exude confidence in the face of crisis rather than search about for it when times get tough.

2. *Restore confidence.* This becomes an addendum to the first statement.

While we still strive to do everything in our power to protect the people who work here from all types of workplace violence, we know from reality that these events, although rare, may occur. Besides our built-in strategies to deal with these problems at the lowest levels, we have an entire plan ready to put into effect should the unthinkable occur. Our chain of command has been fully trained and briefed and is ready to put this plan into operation should the need ever arise.

We will offer counseling to those who need it, long-term medical and psychological services to all who request them, and we will support law enforcement and all related government, labor, safe working, and human resource agencies in their efforts to combat this problem.

Both of these workplace violence mission statements do the same thing: They serve to create employee confidence: "This is a safe place to work now and we will strive to make it even safer." And they serve to create customer confidence: "This is a safe place to do business because we look after our employees and our customers."

We're not saying it's ever easy to deal with a significant workplace violence event like a homicide. You can't just wash your hands and believe everything is suddenly back to normal. Just as your employees need time to recuperate and recover, so does your company. And unless you follow the trauma and grief steps we suggest, you'll have a hard time operating as a business entity.

You need to have the same realistic expectations about your company's ability to bounce back from a serious workplace violence incident as you have for your employees.

If you own, manage, or work for a large organization in one city and one of your branch offices in another state has a significant workplace violence problem such as a homicide, you'll have to temper your expectations with the realities of the situation. It's easy for the tremendously insensitive CEO to say, "Hey, what's going on out there? That incident happened four days ago. Why can't we get the show back on the road over there? How come those people aren't all back to work?"

It's just not that simple. People respond to these kinds of traumas in different ways. The best we can say is that if it didn't happen to you or near you, you can't possibly understand the feelings involved.

Just as many police officers are more sensitive to crime victims if they have been crime victims themselves, people in an organization should strive to walk a mile in the shoes of their co-workers who have experienced workplace violence trauma.

As an executive or a leader in any company who has experienced this kind of problem, you should be ready and willing to give employees the time they need to grieve, mourn, and recover.

Your job is to bring in the mental health professionals and stand back and let them work. Give them space and time to hold private and group counseling sessions.

Further, besides a facilitator role, the CEO or the COO should be the one who goes from meeting to meeting, making announcements to the employees. People want to see signs that the leadership has not caved in and that there is still a steady hand at the company helm.

If you don't allow this healing process to take place, you will certainly anger your employees and the people who care about them, your customers, who will hear how you are treating the people they do business with, and thanks to media exposure, the public.

Being perceived as an insensitive and uncaring company can lead to more animosity from people inside the organization—the employees—as well as from those outside it. By failing to address carefully the needs of all concerned with this traumatic event, you run the risk of setting the stage for more animosity aimed at the company—and in the worst case, another workplace violence incident.

A PROBLEM THAT WON'T GO AWAY

The end of a business book is usually where the author or authors try to offer some hope for the future about the topic that has spanned the last several hundred pages. While we'd like to offer a glowing forecast about workplace violence prevention, it's hard to be totally optimistic.

The workplace violence problem is here to stay. The best we can offer in terms of hope is that with the proper energy and commitment devoted to the problem, business leaders and their companies and political leaders and their resources will be able to see the future problems leading to workplace violence and plan against them.

Neither can we offer any guaranties about prediction or control of the problem. The Robert Earl Macks of the world are out there—the 25-year employee who does his job day after day until something snaps and people are killed where they stand.

Ultimately, society will have to start the change process. The way we have little respect for the value of human life; the way we mistreat each other; the prevalence of death and violence on television; our culture's long-time fascination with guns and their easy availability; the prevalence of drugs and alcohol and the numbers of people who abuse them; and finally, the way some unsophisticated people seek to solve their problems—real or otherwise—by violence have all been mixed together by time into a deadly witch's brew.

While there are no easy or off-the-shelf solutions, we'd like to offer some strategies that may help business, society, law enforcement, and the government to combat this problem.

These involve three main ideas that ask the different entities in the private and public sector to:

1. Change the way most companies treat employee lawbreakers of all types.
2. Modify the way law enforcement treats the problem.
3. Change the way the statistical information about workplace violence is gathered, analyzed, and reported.

THE COMPANY AS "POLICEMAN"

Most companies are not used to enforcing the laws of the "real world." The people who work in most firms are used to seeing the outside world as separate from the business world. The problem of violence in the workplace has changed all that. But organizations in the private sector or even in government still find it difficult to prosecute employees who actually break the law. This is an odd paradox and one that must change at the lowest levels of crime (theft, vandalism, minor assaults) so the punitive process may later serve as a partial deterrent for the more serious offenses (aggravated assaults and homicides).

Some cases in point:

If you went into the Nordstrom department store and stole a pair of shoes and the store security officers caught you, what would be the likely result?

They would call the police, who would come and either arrest you and take you to jail or arrest you, write you a citation with a court appearance date, and release you outside the store. Later, you would have to appear in court or accept some plea bargain arrangement for your crime. You would now have a criminal record for a misdemeanor offense.

Now, let us keep everything the same in this small crime drama save for one—the participant.

If you *worked* at the Nordstrom department store and stole a pair of shoes and the store security officers caught you, what would be the likely result?

You probably would be told to return the merchandise, then you would be fired and asked never to darken their doors again. Wait a minute! Where are the police? Where is the arrest process? The citation or the handcuff-clad trip to jail? The court appearance? The criminal record for your conviction?

None of that seems to exist in the business world. We tend to handle employee crimes like theft, euphemistically called *"shrink-age"* by industrial security experts, with relative velvet gloves. "Don't make waves" seems to be the slogan, followed by "Let's handle this in-house and avoid any unnecessary exposure or problems with our reputation. After all, we wouldn't want our customers or our competitors, or least of all the police, to hear about this matter."

Let's change the scenario again to include the specter of violence in the workplace.

Suppose you walked into a McDonald's fast-food restaurant and got into a confrontation with the manager. Things get ugly and you hit him right in the nose, breaking it. The police arrive on the scene within minutes and you find yourself in handcuffs en route to jail on a battery charge.

Same scene, different *participant*.

Suppose you *work* at a McDonald's fast-food restaurant and you get into a confrontation with your manager. Things get ugly and you hit him in the nose, breaking it. What happens next? Please see the second department store scenario for your answer.

Typically, you will be summarily fired, given your last pay-check, and escorted off the premises. No police and no criminal prosecution, although the manager may attempt to sue you for civil damages for his injuries.

In effect, you've committed a crime—it says so in the penal code in your state—and gotten away with it. The sanctions against you are so faint as to be almost microscopic.

"You know," says the fuming factory worker, "I've had it up to here with my boss. The next time he smarts off to me I'm gonna pop him right in the mouth."

Regardless of the fact that the disturbed employee–supervisor relationship has deteriorated to this level, what's the worst thing that could happen to this employee if he follows through with his threat? He could get fired? Not much doubt about it. He could get arrested? Hardly seems likely.

"If I'm making six bucks an hour," he reasons, "and I take a swing at my boss, so what if they fire me? I can always go out and get another six-buck-an-hour job."

We know these kinds of internal conversations take place all the time among disgruntled or disturbed workers. And why shouldn't they? There really is very little consequence for their actions, short of a significant assault or a murder.

A colleague tells us a story he overheard in a crowded coffee shop one night. Two construction workers were sitting nearby, bemoaning the fact they were about to get laid off for lack of work.

"I'm gonna take some power tools before I go," says one worker, grinning smugly.

"But that would be stealing," says the other, puzzled.

"Yeah, I know, but they owe it to me for laying me off. And besides, what are they gonna do, call the cops on me?"

How true. This sense of employee "entitlement" is common enough. But when it gets coupled with the possibility of workplace violence and no punishment, it's even more dangerous.

There is very little sense of consequence in our society. Law enforcement intervention into company problems is rare. Many companies prefer to handle things "internally," which really means doing very little at all in terms of punishment, enforcement, or restitution.

And for workplace violence incidents, the response is generally the same. Except in those rare cases where someone is killed or badly injured, we rarely think of calling the police to intervene.

It's time for this mindset to change and the sooner the better.

We're not asking firms to become police agencies; *that's what we have police agencies for* in the first place. But if you look at a large organization as if it were a small town, you can see the need for—lacking a better phrase—the company "police department."

An organization with a 5,000-employee work force functions on a systems level like a city. There are services of various types to care for the members' needs and in turn, the "occupants" of the city who help keep it running with their work contributions.

And like any city filled with a diverse population of adults, there are going to be problems of every size and shape that need solutions. This is where a highly trained security staff can pay enormous dividends in safety and peace of mind. As we have already pointed out in this book, the problems people tend to have at home get carried to their "home away from home"— the job.

Writing in *The Lipman Report*, Guardsmark Chairman and President Ira Lipman says, "Sometimes the violence perpetrated by an employee is generated by personal problems entirely unrelated to his or her job. A rancorous divorce, the effects of substance abuse, the demands of an ill or disabled relative, or any number of other personal conflicts cause tensions which can spill over into the workplace."[1]

Alcohol or drug abuse at home, the potential for it at work; constant arguments and foul language at home, the same at work; and so on. Home life mirrors worklife, and vice versa. A total lack of regard or the theft of other people's property growing up can lead to similar behaviors at work.

It's time businesses started holding bad employees accountable for what they do. This starts by seeing that the laws of the state and the nation are properly enforced.

What is the impact of ignoring criminal behavior on the other people in the organization? Do you think this sends a positive message to the employees who see someone get off the hook? Guess again. Normal, hardworking employees will be shocked, angered, and no doubt outraged the company allows this behavior to go unpunished.

Borderline employees who witness these kinds of criminal activities—stealing, vandalism and sabotage, assaults, threats, blatant drug use, and so on—may file that information away in their minds under the "Look What I Can Get Away With" category.

So what's the solution to this prosecution problem? How do you get employees to take your organization's response to crime of any type more seriously?

Start by treating crimes like what they are—violations of societal rules and norms. If an employee steals an $800 copy machine, don't just expect the guilty party to return the goods and be gone after you fire him or her. If someone punches a supervisor, a termination for violating the work conduct rules should be only one of many steps to follow. Immediately call the police or sheriff's office in your community and ask them to take a report of a crime case. That is what these events really are—crime cases with bonafide victims and real suspects.

If you don't feel like taking these steps—and they are often tedious, time-consuming, paper-intensive, and even intimidating—think of the consequences down the road. The employee you fire for stealing those shoes from your department store can just go do it again at the next place he or she works.

The employee who punches his fast-food restaurant manager and storms off the property untouched may do it again, or worse, at some other unsuspecting manager's place of business.

Law enforcement intervention into disturbed employees' lives is a powerful tool against such serious issues as violence in the workplace. Follow through against any employee who chooses to victimize your company and the people who work there. Sending a thief, vandal, or batterer away with that shopworn threat of "You'll never get a job reference from us!" is hardly much of a deterrent to him or anyone else watching the scene.

It's time we started treating company-based crimes like regular "street" crimes, regardless of our connection to the person committing them. Employee or otherwise, call the police, get a report of the incident, ask police investigators to follow up with an arrest, go to court, and fight for the rights of your company. Your lives or the lives of other workers may be at stake if you fail to do your part to help stop this kind of behavior.

RETHINKING THE LAW ENFORCEMENT RESPONSE TO VIOLENCE IN THE WORKPLACE

One of the primary reasons why so many companies fail to notify their local police departments of workplace violence incidents or related crimes is because it's quite possible they were burned in the past. "We called the cops the last time we had a big office equipment theft," says one irritated company owner. "They came out and took a report and that was the last we ever heard from them. We gave them some information about the people we thought had committed the crime and they never bothered to follow up with us. Our equipment and the people who took it are now long gone."

This is a valid complaint and one that most report-laden street cops or investigators will sadly admit is true. The maxim "Do more with less" has hit the law enforcement sector hard in recent years. With wafer-thin budgets and short staffing, many small police agencies (and even some larger ones) can barely keep their officers in police cars that run.

But while this may be true, it should not deter you or your organization from pressing for more police involvement in workplace violence and other company crime cases.

One of the reasons why police departments don't devote much enthusiasm to workplace crime cases of any sort is because they, too, have been burned themselves. No officer, detective, or prosecutor likes to work hard on a crime case involving a current or former employee only to have the company owners or managers say, "Sorry, we changed our mind about pressing charges. Let's just let the whole thing drop."

The time for unity of purpose with workplace crimes is now. Violence on the job incidents offer the best place for companies and police agencies to join together in a united front. Ask your local law enforcement agency for help with workplace violence. They may offer security suggestions, some safety procedures for dealing with potentially dangerous employees, and liaison help with federal or state agencies, or they may even supply undercover operatives to verify, document, and prevent these workplace crimes.

A major sporting goods manufacturer was having a number of problems involving employee theft and threats made to those who dared to report it. The police department put an undercover officer into the plant posing as a new employee. He managed to interrupt the thefts and catch the guilty parties.

We need to make changes in law enforcement, in the policies and procedures our police officers use in their response to workplace violence issues. Intervention for this kind of crime should begin far earlier than it does now.

We need to start proactive intervention into cases at the earliest stages, before the trouble escalates. Studies with domestic violence suspects who have been arrested and vigorously prosecuted by the legal system point to improvement in their behavior. It only makes sense. If you know that if you beat your wife the cops will come to your house and unceremoniously haul you off to jail each time you do, you will certainly think harder about it before you do it again.

If you make threats or assault people at work and then the cops come and unceremoniously haul you off to jail and you will be in definite jeopardy of prosecution besides losing your job, perhaps you will think twice before raising your fists or a gun in anger.

These initiatives will help law enforcement go after the problem employees hard, send a message to the borderline employees, and help to protect the innocent from becoming new victims.

Further, before it can offer the most successful kinds of help, law enforcement itself needs to look at the way it documents workplace violence incidents of any kind. We'll discuss this in the next section.

NEW REPORTS, BETTER DATA, MORE FOCUS

An old maxim in law enforcement says, "It usually takes a tragedy before we make changes that prevent future tragedies."

In no other area did we see this come true as with domestic violence, or spousal abuse. Thanks to some landmark civil court cases where battered women (or their survivors) sued several police departments for failing to protect them from known batterers, the way these cases are now handled has changed for the better.

With these civil cases paying some whopping judgments against law enforcement agencies and their host municipalities, the days of doing nothing to the perpetrators at domestic violence crime scenes or taking yet another wife-beating report and filing it away untouched are becoming less and less common.

Former US Surgeon General C. Everrett Koop called domestic violence one of our nation's worst family problems. Our legislators, to their credit, have tried to take steps to put an end to the cycle of home-front violence.

Today, most states demand that law enforcement take a new position with domestic violence. If the parties are involved in a cohabitation relationship, or have children together, or are or were married, and there are visible injuries (usually to the female), then the abuser is going to jail.

In the times before these new laws, street cops tried to separate the parties, keep the peace while they were there, and then get out of the area and hope the problem would solve itself. All too often it did, and they would return to find someone dead on the kitchen floor.

We believe workplace violence cases are at the same relative do-nothing stage as domestic violence was several years ago. Police department agencies are often reluctant to intercede in areas that have typically been handled informally or even secretly at the company level. Companies have been hesitant to prosecute, thereby stifling any worthwhile police response. The victim gets no satisfaction, and the perpetrator, the guy who did the punching, threatening, or extorting, feels little discomfort.

One of the reasons the response to domestic violence took a turn for the better is because law enforcement officials, prosecutors, and legislators from across the nation banded together to change the way these incidents were reported. Using state-mandated guidelines, it is now necessary for officers to document even so-called "minor" domestic violence incidents. The theory here is that small problems often become big ones, and it may be easier to intervene at lower levels while the incident is still manageable.

The change in the reporting procedures has given law enforcement groups, justice statistical organizations, and sociologists a wealth of new domestic violence data to interpret and discuss.

We believe it's time to turn our great statistical machines onto the problem of workplace violence. By making significant changes in the way workplace violence cases are documented, categorized, and reported statistically, it may be possible to devote more time and energy to investigate, arrest, and prosecute the instigators.

Right now, the documentation and statistical reporting procedures for workplace violence cases are a jumbled mix of federal statistics, state-specific numbers, and city or county raw data that creates confusion about who is doing what to whom, where, when, or why. As cartoon hero Pogo so aptly put it, "We have seen the enemy and it is us."

A quote from *The Lipman Report* confirms this:

> According to statistics compiled by a criminologist at a noted northeastern university, the number of employees who kill their bosses has doubled in the past 10 years. While these statistics alert us to the seriousness of occupational violent crime, they only tell a small part of the story because they reflect only the *deaths* resulting from such crimes. A national count of injuries resulting from occupational violent crime is not available.[2]

We call for standardized workplace violence reporting requirements that include uniform documentation procedures at the state and local levels and in conjunction with the appropriate federal agencies. Currently, there is no one federal clearinghouse for this information. The Departments of Labor, Health and Human Services, federal OSHA units, some criminal justice agencies, the Center for Disease Control, and even private sector information-gathering companies offer their own brand of workplace violence statistical material. As we have found during our research for this book, it's hard to interpret it all.

It's time to put everything we know about the topic into a cogent, comprehensive reporting process. This should include who commits crimes at the workplace; how the victims are classified, not just by age, sex, or job type but by rank, job title, duties, and so on; what types of workplace crimes are covered, as in assaults, threats of assaults, intimidation or extortion attempts, vandalism and sabotage; the estimated costs to business of these acts; and finally, homicides.

With more of the right kinds of information at our disposal, it will be easier to formulate national, state, or local level policies to help fight this rising tide of death and violence on the job. Without it, we can only guess what to do next, based on our interpretation of yet another senseless killing in the workplace.

THE FUTURE OF VIOLENCE IN THE WORKPLACE

If by now, after 10 chapters on the subject, you haven't made a workplace violence plan a real part of your thinking, it's time to do so. A look at the organizations who have survived these events indicates many similarities. Large or small, they made changes in their procedures and tossed out the old ways in response to these new traumas.

It has taken the business world a long time to recognize that there is a right way to protect its materials, physical plant, and proprietary information. But people in business are only now coming to a new understanding about the right way to protect employees from each other or from outsiders who seek to do them harm. Based on the last 15 to 20 years of escalating violence in the workplace, it's time for business to take the same steps to protect its workers as it has taken to protect its other assets.

But frankly, the future looks grim. We're going to continue to see increasing levels of workplace violence and workplace homicides. Organizations can lessen the impact of these life-threatening problems only by improving hiring methods; becoming more "psychologically aware" and sophisticated in their preemployment screening; and getting behind some kind of manageable, effective, and fair gun control legislation. Otherwise, the problems of people injuring or killing one another at work will continue to proliferate.

Speaking on a 1993 "Oprah Winfrey Show" devoted to workplace violence stories, James Fox, a well-known Northeastern University professor and author, gave his views on gun control.

> It's easier to get guns, especially shotguns, rifles, and even assault semiautomatics. Our liberal gun laws allow almost anyone, short of a convicted felon or a known psychotic, to go into a gun store and buy what he wants. The availability of guns in the United States—and their resultant use as murder weapons—leads the world. Nowhere else in the world is it possible to walk into a pawnshop, plunk down $100 cash, and walk out with a hunting rifle.

Still others, including New York Senator Daniel Patrick Moynihan, have suggested that since we have a 200-year oversupply of guns and only a 4-year supply of bullets in this country, why not place a moratorium on the sale of bullets? Certain critics have espoused the theory that only cops and soldiers ought to be allowed to possess bullets. This argument, however well-intentioned, is more of a knee-jerk reaction coupled with the intense frustration the gun control issue generates. While it certainly makes sense, any laws attempting to restrict ammunition would surely cause hoarding not seen since the alcohol-free days of Prohibition.

In terms of a workable solution, if you follow our Seven-Step Workplace Violence Prevention model (illustrated in the Preface) from start to end, you will be in a better position to cope with the unthinkable. In the future, we will all be able to look at companies where these traumatic events have occurred and point to what was done right and what was done wrong. Did they prescreen and test their newly hired employees? Did they give their employees outlets for therapy and the opportunity to talk to counselors and therapists? Did management offer programs and educational training for stress control, violence in the workplace, effective supervision, or discipline and termination procedures? Did they use professional security measures? Did they follow up any workplace violence events with counseling and proper recovery time?

And it's not just the corporate world that must take some responsibility to stop the flood of violence in our society. The media "industry" has finally recognized the role it plays in dealing with violence. Our political leaders have started to speak for many of us who say, "No more violence on television! It has a negative impact on our kids, and we're going to do something about it."

While this is important and valuable, it's also clearly misplaced. Just as much energy, if not more, should go into the message that says, "Not just no more violence on TV. How about no more violence in society?"

If business leaders started backing the educational programs that teach our children how to deal with interpersonal situations in nonviolent ways, they will help to raise the next generation of employees who will not be violent. It's time for corporations to invest in not just the infrastructure of its workplace (i.e., more machines, more inventory, or more research and development), but rather in helping to create the next generation of employees who are less prone to use violence as a way to cope with their frustrations.

Whether it's preschool or elementary programs, high school or college classes, this training in nonviolent living skills is an obligation that will fall, by proxy, to the business sector.

As former Xerox chief David Kearns put it in a keynote speech to an audience at an American Society of Training and Development gathering, "We will have to become the educators of last resort. Our labor pool is the only one we have, and it will be up to us to teach these people the life skills they did not get in school."

We would offer one last piece of advice to businesspeople from all companies, no matter the product, the service, or the people they employ:

Don't wait for something bad to happen before you react. Move forward with an intervention plan and act on it before violence in the workplace strikes your company and your employees.

ENDNOTES

[1] Ira Lipman, *The Lipman Report*, September 15, 1992, p. 1. © Guardsmark, Memphis, TN.

[2] Ibid., p. 2.

BIBLIOGRAPHY

Albrecht, Karl, and Steven Albrecht. *The Creative Corporation.* Business One Irwin, Burr Ridge, IL: 1987.

Ayres, Richard M. *Preventing Law Enforcement Stress.* Washington, DC: National Sheriff's Association, 1990.

Bell, Catherine A. "Female Homicides in US Workplaces." *American Journal of Public Health,* June 1991, pp. 729–32.

Bell, Catherine A, et al. "Fatal Occupational Injuries in the US." *Journal of the American Medical Association,* June 13, 1990, pp. 3047–3050.

————. "Homicide in US Workplaces." Washington, DC: US Department of Health and Human Services, September 1992, pp. 1–7.

Boxer, Paul A. "Assessment of Potential Violence in the Paranoid Worker." *Journal of Occupational Medicine,* February 1993, pp. 127–31.

Centers for Disease Control, Morbidity and Mortality Weekly Report. "Occupational Homicides among Women." August 17, 1990, pp. 544–50.

Garland, Ron. *Making Work Fun: Doing Business with a Sense of Humor.* San Diego, CA: Shamrock Press, 1991.

Grote, Richard C, and Eric L. Harvey. *Discipline without Punishment.* New York: McGraw-Hill, 1983.

Hales, Thomas, et al. "Occupational Injuries Due to Violence." *Journal of Occupational Medicine,* June 1988, pp. 483–87.

Jenkins, E Lynn, et al. "Homicide in the Workplace." *AAOHN Journal,* May 1992, pp. 215–18.

Kinney, Joseph A, and Dennis L Johnson. "Breaking Point," National Safe Workplace Institute. Chicago, Sept. 1993.

Levin, Jack and James Fox. *Mass Murders,* Plenum Press: New York, 1985.

Mantell, Michael. *Don't Sweat the Small Stuff.* San Luis Obispo, CA: Impact Publishers, 1988.

Molloy, John T. *Dress for Success.* New York: Warner Books, 1975.

McCaghy, Charles H. *Crime in American Society.* New York: Macmillan, 1980.

National Organization for Victim Assistance. *Crisis Response Training Manual.* Washington, DC: 1986.

Schermerhorn, John R, Jr. *Managing Organizational Behavior.* New York: John Wiley & Sons, 1982.

Seligman, Paul J, et al. "Sexual Assault of Women at Work." *American Journal of Industrial Medicine,* May 1987, pp. 445–50.

Sprouse, Martin. *Sabotaging the American Workplace.* San Francisco, CA: Pressure Drop Press, 1992.

Thomas, Janice L., "A Response to Occupational Violent Crime," *Journal of Safety Research*, Vol. 23, No. 2, pp. 55–62.

————. Occupational Violent Crime: Research on an Emerging Issue. *Professional Safety*, June 1992, pp. 27–31.

Zimmerman, Mark. *The Interview Guide for Evaluating DSM III-R Psychiatric Disorders and the Mental Health Status Examination.* Philadelphia, PA: Psych Press, 1992.

Index

TICKING BOMBS: VIOLENCE IN THE WORKPLACE is also available as a two-part training video series from corVision Media, Inc., 1359 Barclay Boulevard, Buffalo Grove, IL 60089.

The epidemic of workplace violence costs lives. The secondary affects on organizations can also be devastating—destroying credibility and substituting fear for productivity. The first line of defense is *prevention*.

In this new two part video series, designed for supervisors and managers, Dr. Michael Mantell presents his step-by-step model for workplace violence prevention. It includes a systems approach to the problem from interviewing prospective employees to termination. Also covered is a crisis-management approach to violent incidents.

For further information, please contact corVision at 1-800-537-3130.

Other books of interest to you from Irwin Professional Publishing . . .

MILITANT MANAGERS
HOW TO SPOT . . .
HOW TO WORK WITH . . .
HOW TO MANAGE . . .
YOUR HIGHLY AGGRESSIVE BOSS
Carol Elbing and Alvar Elbing

Based on the authors' 10-year study, this book offers step-by-step solutions for those who must cope with aggressive, temperamental managers. Includes case studies of costly management problems and how they were (or weren't) resolved. (240 pages)
ISBN: 1-55623-737-5

STRAIGHT ANSWERS TO PEOPLE PROBLEMS
Fred E. Jandt
Briefcase Books Series

This quick, practical guidebook provides managers with answers to the myriad day-to-day questions and issues they must face in the workplace. Covers employee morale, office gossip, alcoholism, AIDS, stress management, interviewing, meeting preparation, speechmaking, and more. (175 pages)
ISBN: 1-55623-849-5

THE LIVING ORGANIZATION
TRANSFORMING TEAMS INTO WORKPLACE COMMUNITIES
John Nirenberg
Copublished with Pfeiffer & Company

Guides managers to the next step after teams . . . to workplace communities. Nirenberg presents a blueprint for organizations making this transition and includes ways to reenergize a disenchanted work force. (300 pages)
ISBN: 1-55623-943-2

Available at fine bookstores and libraries everywhere.